Parties, Polls and Riots

Politics in nineteenth-century Radnorshire

by
Keith Parker

Logaston Press

LOGASTON PRESS
Little Logaston Woonton Almeley
Herefordshire HR3 6QH
logastonpress.co.uk

First published by Logaston Press 2009
Copyright text © John Powell 2009
Copyright illustrations © as acknowledged 2009

ISBN 978 1 906663 23 0

Typeset by Logaston Press
and printed in Great Britain by
Bell & Bain Ltd., Glasgow

Parties, Polls and Riots

In memory of my mother,
Maisie Kate Parker

Contents

Acknowledgements

In writing this book I have incurred a great many obligations, not least to the historians of both the past and present from whose scholarship I have gained many insights, although responsibility for the conclusions reached, and for any errors in fact or interpretation remain mine alone. My thanks are also due to the staff of many record offices and libraries who dealt with my many queries with unfailing patience and courtesy. In particular my thanks are due to Mr Lawrence Banks who most kindly allowed me access to his family archives; to Mr D. Roy Ll Adams, whose unpublished MA thesis, 'The Parliamentary Representation of Radnorshire 1536-1832' has proved invaluable for the pre-1832 period; and lastly to the Radnorshire Society, who have allowed me to reproduce an article, 'The Radnorshire Cottagers Controversy', published in *The Transactions of the Radnorshire Society* of 2006, in a slightly extended form, as Chapter 6 of this book.

My thanks are also due to the institutions and individuals who have allowed me to reproduce pictures and photographs as illustrations: the Judges Lodgings, Presteigne (pp.5, 21, 45, 54, 60, 61, 64 top, 68, 81, 85, 90, 95, 101, 141, 153 and 159), Powys Archives (p.151), the Radnorshire Museum, Llandrindod Wells (p.154), the late Mrs Cherry Leversedge (pp.12, 33, 51 and 96), Sir John Venables Llewelyn (pp.105), Mr Jonathan Coltman Rogers (p.64 bottom), Mr Roger Bright (pp.107 and 116), National Museums and Galleries of Wales (p.17) and Mr Walter de Winton (pp.27 and 38).

I am also indebted to Andy Johnson of Logaston Press who nudged me into providing greater detail and precision in the text and also 'eased' my sometimes over-formal and academic written style. Lastly, and by no means least, I must thank my wife Joan, who acted as my photographer and has shown, as ever, great patience and forbearance in tolerating my preoccupation with matters historical.

Map of Radnorshire

Introduction

This study explores three aspects of political life in Radnorshire during the 'long' nineteenth century, from the mid-1790s until 1914: the gentry-dominated politics of the first two-thirds of the century; the development of party politics after 1868; and finally the politics of popular protest. The three aspects are by no means mutually exclusive since party politics were not an entirely new phenomenon in 1869, while the gentry continued to exercise considerable influence upon Radnorshire politics in the last third of the century and popular protest had some impact upon politics in the county for much of the period.

In the absence of resident peers, formal politics in the county were monopolised by the leading gentry in the first two-thirds of the century, with parliamentary elections in the Radnorshire county and the Radnor Boroughs constituencies very much the preserve of the Wilkins and Walsh families and of the Price and Lewis families respectively. These families exercised considerable electoral influence since they could 'command' the votes of their own tenants and those of their kinsmen and allies, as well as the votes of local tradesmen and shopkeepers who depended upon the custom of the local 'big house'. Nor were local lawyers, doctors, clergy, bankers and land surveyors immune from pressure since they often depended upon the patronage of the leading gentry and their allies. Since voting took place in public prior to the introduction of the secret ballot in 1872, with the voter stating his choice to the returning officer and a crowd of spectators, few had the courage to vote against their patron and risk their livelihood.

The widening of the franchise as a result of the Reform Acts of 1832 and 1867 does not seem to have curbed the electoral influence of the gentry significantly. Thus a few weeks before the poll in the Boroughs election of 1869, Richard Green Price was able to predict precisely the number of votes the Conservative candidate would receive in Knighton. Nor did the introduction of the secret ballot in 1872 bring to an end the gentry's electoral influence. Most of the gentry made no secret of their political allegiance and in a largely deferential society where local loyalties counted for much, many electors felt obliged to follow the example set by the local squire. Thus in 1900 Powlett Milbank, the retiring Conservative Member for Radnorshire, thought it worth-while to assemble his tenants and dependants at Norton School to urge them to vote for the Conservative candidate, Charles Venables Llewelyn.

Indeed, many feared that the ballot was not secret and that those with influence could find out how an individual had voted. Such fears must have been fuelled by reports in the press, some of them very detailed, as to how the votes had been cast at particular polling stations in the Boroughs elections of 1880 and 1885. At the 1886 county election it was reported that the parties had agreed that the ballot box from each polling station should be counted separately and the assertion was followed by a description of how the two candidates had fared at the various polling stations. From time to time cynics suggested that some of the gentry encouraged a disbelief in the secrecy of the ballot in order to retain some vestiges of their influence. Even in the 1900s the Liberal *Radnor Express* believed that it was necessary to reassure its readers as to the secrecy of the ballot.

Prior to 1869, electors rarely had an opportunity to cast their votes in either of the Radnorshire constituencies. Thus in county elections between 1796 and 1868 only three of the 22 elections, those of 1802, 1835 and 1841, were contested, while in the same period only two of 24 elections in the Radnor Boroughs constituency, in 1812 and 1820, were the electors troubled. In the other elections, in both Radnorshire constituencies, a candidate drawn from the gentry, proposed and seconded by other Radnorshire gentry and enjoying at least tacitly the support of the county elite, was returned unopposed. This aversion to electoral contests stemmed in the main from the unwillingness of the gentry to risk the emergence of bitter divisions in their ranks and the fragmentation of polite society in the county. Yet the lack of contested elec-tions is not an entirely reliable indicator of political ambition on the part of the Radnorshire gentry; an unopposed return was often preceded by a period of intrigue on the part of one or two ambitious Radnorshire gentlemen before they concluded that their chances were too slim to warrant them proceeding to a canvass or a poll.

For the great majority of Radnorshire men, nineteenth-century politics was largely a spectator sport since they did not possess a vote until 1867 in the Boroughs constituency and until 1885 in the Radnorshire countryside. However even an uncontested election brought a break from the monotony of everyday life for the people of either Presteigne or New Radnor where the sole candidate was nominated and duly provided celebratory meals. Contested elections, on the other hand, could generate great excitement with election meetings, sometimes rowdy, held throughout the county or in each of the contributory boroughs coupled with the possibility of 'treating' in the form of free food and drink at the local inn, until such practices were banned. Excitement reached fever pitch at the declaration of the poll, with the successful candidate 'chaired' around the town, while the celebration of victory or the drowning of sorrows could end in an unedifying brawl.

During the first two-thirds of the nineteenth century, although party labels such as Whig, Tory, Liberal and Conservative were applied to parliamentary candidates, they were all expected to be independent in outlook and capable of attracting support from a broad local consensus of opinion. Indeed, a declared narrow party allegiance would have been considered highly divisive, threatening the unity of county society. However, during the last third or so of the century party politics increasingly came to dominate not only parliamentary elections in Radnorshire, but also elections for the county council and district councils. The process began with Richard Green Price resigning the Radnor Boroughs seat in 1869 to make way for Lord Hartington, who was to become leader of the Liberal Party in the Commons in 1875, the first time that narrow party considerations dictated the course of politics in Radnorshire.

From 1869 onwards, every parliamentary election in Radnorshire, apart from the Boroughs elections of 1880 and 1884, was contested. This growing dominance of party allegiance in Radnorshire politics stemmed from two broad factors. In the first place the widening of the franchise as a result of the 1867 and 1884 Reform Acts meant that whereas formerly the gentry and their satellites had tended to share a common interest and outlook, the voters' interests and outlooks now varied widely. The political party represented a means of uniting a range of vested interests and personal priorities behind one convenient label and a common political programme. Secondly, during the last quarter of the century a number of highly contentious issues came to the fore, notably the disestablishment of the Welsh Church and Irish Home Rule. Opinions became polarised since such issues could not be settled by compromise. Party divisions deepened and the political temperature rose sharply, particularly among the less inhibited new voters, and political meetings and demonstrations became more rowdy.

After 1885 the perceived need to defend the Church and the Union saw the old Liberal gentry's families of Radnorshire move into the Conservative fold. By 1890 S.C. Evans Williams of Bryntirion was virtually the only representative of the old Radnorshire gentry loyal to the Gladstonian Liberals, while Charles Coltman Rogers remained in glorious isolation as a Liberal Unionist. Increasingly Radnorshire divided on class and sectarian line, not only in parliamentary elections but also in the sphere of local government, particularly after 1900.

For most of the nineteenth century the gentry dominated not only local politics, but also local government which was in their hands in their capacity as magistrates sitting in Quarter Sessions, appointed to this office by the Crown on the recommendation of the lord lieutenant of the county. Thus most of the population had no voice in local government and lacked the means through which their grievances might be remedied. For the most part the gentry took a paternalistic approach to the local community, but almost inevitably, if interests clashed, those of the gentry took priority.

In such a situation an obvious means of drawing attention to a grievance was through a popular demonstration, often with at least a hint of violence. Such popular protests occurred against the enclosure of some commons, in connection with the Radnorshire Cottagers, the Rebecca Riots of the early 1840s, ostensibly against turnpike tolls, and the later salmon fishing Rebecca Riots of the 1850s to the 1880s and beyond. These demonstrations were surprisingly effective, in part because they attracted a measure of support, or at least sympathy, from the local professional and commercial classes. As a result the local gentry families, usually no more than two or three in any parish and anxious not to lose face, could not afford to alienate the community in which they lived and so were often prepared to temporise with the demonstrators. In any event, the forces of law and order were thin on the ground, even in the closing decades of the century. Thus Thomas Frankland Lewis of Harpton was careful not to alienate the Radnorshire Cottagers in the mid-1830s and, in 1843-44, to address the grievances of the Rebecca Rioters in the report of the Commission of Inquiry into South Wales, on which he served as chairman. Action against those involved in the disturbances met with passive resistance. Controversial prosecutions at petty sessions sometimes failed because witnesses were reluctant to testify. Even juries at the Assizes proved vulnerable to popular pressure and in February 1903 juries brought in verdicts of 'Not Guilty' in four cases of assaults on water bailiffs in spite of overwhelming evidence to the contrary and the judge's clear directions.

1 The Radnor Boroughs Seat, 1799-1868

Prior to the Reform Act of 1832 the right to vote was vested in the freemen or burgesses of the borough of New Radnor and of the boroughs of Cefnllys, Knighton, Knucklas and Rhayader, the contributory boroughs, so called because in the sixteenth century they shared in the franchise in return for contributing to the expenses incurred by the MP in attending the House of Commons. In 1690 it was alleged that Painscastle and Presteigne had originally shared in the franchise but had been disenfranchised on refusing to contribute to the expenses.

In New Radnor the freemen were elected by the Common Council, sometimes termed the 'Twenty-Five' or the Capital Burgesses — a self-perpetuating oligarchy which, on the death of a member, elected his successor — and in the contributory boroughs by the 14-strong jury at the court leet of the manor, presided over by the steward. The borough of Cefnllys was in private hands and had been owned since 1776 by the Walsh family. The three other contributory boroughs were possessions of the Crown and were administered on its behalf by the Steward of Cantref Maelienydd. At the outset of our period the stewardship was held by the Harley family in the person of the fifth earl of Oxford, but in 1823 he was replaced by the Kington solicitors Richard Banks and James Davies. By the mid-1830s Richard Banks was acting alone and on his death in 1871 he was succeeded by a relative by marriage, Frederick Tidd Pratt. The freemen of New Radnor were chosen from the ranks of those residents in the borough deemed to be 'fit and proper persons', in practice resident male householders of some local standing and not in receipt of poor relief, though if a freeman ceased to be resident he still retained the franchise. In the contributory boroughs residence was not a pre-condition and non-residents were elected as freemen in the same manner as residents. In Knighton the oldest son of a freeman became a freeman by right on the death of his father by the payment of a shilling to the court.

The size of the Boroughs electorate in the eighteenth century varied considerably and depended upon the vigour with which the seat was contested and the number of freemen resident or non-resident, created in the contributory boroughs. Faced with the possibility of a contested election in 1774, no fewer than 426 freemen were sworn in at Rhayader, while in June 1790 David Murray, a kinsman by marriage of the earl of Oxford, owed his defeat of Edward Lewis of Downton by 609 votes to 313, to the creation of additional freemen in Knucklas. However it seems that few freemen were created during the remainder of the life of the unreformed House of Commons, since the fifth earl of Oxford, who succeeded his cousin to the earldom and the stewardship later in 1790, created no freemen in his three out-boroughs prior to his replacement in 1823, by which time Knighton had only seven freemen. His successors, Banks and Davies, by 1832 had sworn in as freemen only 'a handful of the most reputable inhabitants of Rhayader' and three or four in Knighton. However, in Cefnllys by 1820 the Walsh family had built up an electorate of 190 freemen, only 16 of whom were resident.[1]

	Electorate		Electorate
1832	529	1857	447
1835	517	1859	407
1837	551	1867	443
1841	500	1869	841
1847	462	1874	968
1852	484	1880	948

Figure 1: The Radnor Boroughs Electorate
(F.W.S. Craig, British Parliamentary Election Results, 1832-1885*)*

The 1832 Reform Act added the borough of Presteigne to the constituency and gave the vote to occupiers of houses rated at £10 a year. Resident freemen in the boroughs retained their vote for life but non-resident freemen, whom, it was alleged, had outnumbered resident voters by five to one, were disenfranchised. In all there were 529 voters on the Boroughs electoral roll of 1832, of whom 276 were resident freemen and 253 were £10 householders.[2] The relatively small number of 'ten pounders' stemmed from the fact that property values and hence rentals were markedly lower in Radnorshire than elsewhere in England and Wales.

Thereafter, until the 1867 Reform Act, the number of voters tended to fall, not so much due to out-migration, but as a result of the death of freemen, who by 1852 numbered 109. Surprisingly, the constituency was dominated by the New Radnor borough which extended far beyond the confines of New Radnor parish. Thus the 1869 electoral roll showed 300 voters in New Radnor, 190 in Knighton, 187 in Presteigne, 139 in Rhayader, 22 in Knucklas and 3 in Cefnllys.[3] The 1867 Act had halted the fall in number on the electoral roll by enfranchising all male householders and lodgers paying £10 a year in rent, thus increasing the number of voters by 90%. Even so the electorate remained small, never reaching a thousand, and the seat remained virtually the pocket borough of the Lewis family of Harpton and the Price family of Knighton and Norton Manor, who were able jointly to bestow the seat upon the Marquis of Hartington in 1869 to suit the interests of the Liberal Party.

1799-1847	Richard Price	Tory
1847-55	Sir Thomas Frankland Lewis	Conservative
1855-63	Sir George Cornewall Lewis	Liberal
1863-69	Richard Green Price	Liberal
1869-80	Lord Hartington	Liberal
1880-84	Stephen C. Evans Williams	Liberal
1884-86	Charles Coltman Rogers	Liberal

Figure 2: Members of Parliament for Radnor Boroughs

Richard Price, 1799-1847

Born in 1773, the son of Richard Price of Knighton, he was of a family which had played a leading role in the county since at least the sixteenth century. He was educated at University College, Oxford, where he matriculated in 1790 and graduated in 1794. In keeping with his family's lineage and status, he served as sheriff of Radnorshire in 1794 and again briefly between February and March 1799. He served as lieutenant colonel commanding the Radnorshire Volunteers between 1803 and 1808 and then as colonel of the Radnorshire Local Militia. Initially he lived at Knighton, but in 1838 moved to his newly built Norton Manor on the estate his family had acquired in 1766.[4]

Plate 1: Richard Price

First elected for the Radnor Boroughs in 1799 with the backing of Alderman Harley, the uncle of the earl of Oxford, 'Member' Price as he was known, fought only two elections, in 1812 and 1820. He was returned unopposed on no fewer than 12 occasions, though in 1802 and 1807 there were plans, which came to nothing, for Thomas Frankland Lewis to contest the seat. Thus in an ingenuous letter of October 1801 Frankland Lewis admitted to Price that he had entertained hopes of the Boroughs seat 'from a sort of hereditary principle', but had been thwarted by the refusal of Walter Wilkins, the county Member, to back him. Lewis concluded by saying that

Plate 2: The Chandos, Knighton, the home of Richard Price until c.*1838.*
Part of the mansion was demolished in the later nineteenth century

of all people I would soonest see myself sitting for the Borough of
Radnor. But believe me, if I cannot, I would rather see you there than
any other man breathing.

Even so Lewis's uncle, Col. William Frankland, was, in 1807, intriguing to
win support for Lewis to replace Price.[5]

In both 1812 and 1820 Price's opponent was Percival Lewis of Downton
Castle, New Radnor, the son of Edward Lewis, MP for Radnor Boroughs
between 1761 and 1790, a London merchant whom Chase Price, MP for
Leominster in 1781 and uncle of our Richard Price, had brought in to oust the
Lewis family of Harpton from the Boroughs seat.

Percival Lewis, 1751-1821, was educated at Westminster School, graduated from Glasgow University in 1776 and was admitted to St John's College
Cambridge but left without a further degree. A student of Lincoln's Inn he
was called to the Bar in 1780 and inherited the Downton estate on the death
of his father in 1791. He was appointed to the Radnorshire Bench in 1792 and
served as sheriff of the county briefly in 1796 and then for a full term in 1797.
Lewis, who spent most of his time on his Hampshire estate, first challenged
him in the election of 1807, but declined the poll and Price was returned
unopposed.[6]

A notice in the *Hereford Journal* of 15 January 1812 to the effect that:

> A new and neat market hall[7] has opened at Knighton, Radnorshire, for the reception of all kinds of grain for sale, which was built by the direction and at the expense of Percival Lewis, Esq., the lessee of the tolls of the market at Knighton

may have been an audacious bid on the part of Percival Lewis to gain support in Price's own backyard prior to another contest. When the election came in the autumn of 1812, Lewis seems to have believed that he had an understanding that Thomas Frankland Lewis would support him against Price and protested strongly when he canvassed on behalf of Price. Lewis's address published in the *Hereford Times* of 5 October, besides giving an insight into the seamier side of electioneering, suggests that he saw himself as a champion of liberty and of the small proprietors and tenant farmers:

> I shall never endeavour to influence or bias [*sic*] you in the free exercise of your elective franchise. You shall never be frightened by me with the menaced loss of your tenancy, or rights of fuel, exercised time out of mind, or throwing open any inclosures which may have been imprudently made by you ...

Six enclosures were under way in the county between 1810 and 1812 and four or five others had been proposed, many of them in or adjacent to one or other of the boroughs, and the prospect of losing valuable rights of common and any encroachments made on commons within the last 20 years must have loomed large in the eyes of many voters. In the same address Lewis also suggested that Price and his allies, in addition to intimidating the electors, were using bribery and corruption in their campaign against him. This allegation may have been made for no other reason than providing grounds for a petition to the House of Commons should Price win the poll. In the event, having polled 48 votes to Price's 154, Lewis gave up.

In 1818 Richard Price was returned unopposed for the Radnorshire Boroughs, but in the general election of 1820, occasioned by the death of George III, he was challenged once more by Percival Lewis, who since 1818 had been residing more or less permanently at Downton, having sold his Hampshire residence. He fared little better than in 1812, receiving 59 votes to Price's 207. Again there were complaints that many illegal voters had been polled for Price and that legal voters who wished to vote for Lewis were rejected, but again Lewis failed to petition the Commons to set aside the election.

For the remainder of his parliamentary career Price was returned unopposed until his resignation in 1847, though from the mid-1830s onwards there was a certain amount of plotting on the part of local rivals. Shortly before the election of January 1835 rumours were circulating that 'a gentleman of liberal principles' was to contest the Boroughs seat. However his rivals preferred to wait for his death or retirement before showing their hand and were content to lobby for support discreetly until then. Amongst his potential successors were Peter Rickards Mynors of Evancoyd, his son Robert Baskerville Mynors, J. Percy Severn of Penybont Hall, and John A. Whittaker of Newcastle Court, while local gossip suggested that Thomas Frankland Lewis of Harpton, Edward Rogers of Stanage and Sir John Walsham of Knill Court also had ambitions to succeed Price.

By the time of his resignation in 1847, Price was the Father of the House of Commons.[8] He took little part in the business of the House, being content in general to support the government, though now and again asserting his independence. In practice he was a thoroughgoing Tory, though he professed to be of independent views. After the end of the French Wars in 1815, he generally supported Lord Liverpool's increasingly repressive administration and only broke with the Duke of Wellington over the granting of Catholic Emancipation in 1829. Not surprisingly he was a consistent opponent of Parliamentary reform.[9]

Even so, he seems to have cultivated a bi-partisan stance within the Boroughs constituency and enjoyed the support of Whigs such as Hugh Powell Evans of Noyadd, and of moderate Conservatives such as Thomas Frankland Lewis. Thus in January 1835, he was nominated by Hugh Powell Evans and seconded by the Tory P.R. Mynors who 'animadverted on the conduct of the Whigs in office', leaving Frankland Lewis to restore harmony by a non-controversial speech.[10]

Price's long tenure of the Boroughs seat stemmed in the main from the status and prestige of the Price family and their extensive estates in the county. These amounted to 8,875 acres (3,592 ha) in 1873 and were located in the Knighton, Norton, Presteigne, Llangunllo and Bleddfa areas. He was also lord of the manors of Bleddfa, South Ruallt (acquired in 1828) and Norton (acquired c.1830). He also owned some 19% of urban Knighton in terms of rateable value in the 1840s. In New Radnor Price could, after 1807, count upon the support of Thomas Frankland Lewis, and in Rhayader he had the backing of Hugh Powell Evans and Thomas Lewis Lloyd.[11]

He also had the support of the Walsh family who controlled Cefnllys borough, though relations with Sir John Walsh were initially frosty as a result of the latter's failure to appoint Richard Green, Price's nephew, as his land-agent in 1826, in succession to Price's brother, Charles Humphreys Price.[12] In Rhayader Richard Price was able to count upon the support of Whigs such as Hugh Powell Evans and the Prickard family, and of Tories such as David Oliver and Thomas Lewis Lloyd.

His local powerbase was such that, although the political temperature in Radnorshire was high in the 1830s as a result of enthusiastic support for Parliamentary reform in Presteigne and widespread sympathy for the Radnorshire Cottagers threatened with the loss of their holdings, there was little incentive for anyone to mount a challenge to Price, for his influence was personal rather than politically inspired. Richard Price's long occupation of the Boroughs seat was also probably aided by the incumbency factor, the general belief that his tenure of the seat was the norm and thus should not be disputed except under exceptional circumstances.

Sir Thomas Frankland Lewis, 1847-55

Born in 1780, the second son of John Lewis of Harpton Court, Frankland Lewis was educated at Eton and Christ Church, Oxford, leaving after matriculation in 1798 in order to administer the family estate which he inherited the previous year. Sheriff in 1805 and subsequently JP and DL of Radnorshire, he had also served as lieutenant colonel in the Radnorshire Volunteers between 1803 and 1808 and in the Radnorshire Local Militia from 1808 to 1816.

With his ambitions to represent a Radnorshire constituency thwarted by the long tenures of Richard Price and Walter Wilkins I in the county seat, he served as MP for Beaumaris between 1812 and 1826 and for Ennis from 1826 to 1828, before succeeding Wilkins in the Radnorshire seat in 1828. After proving his worth on several Parliamentary

Plate 3: Sir Thomas Frankland Lewis

committees and commissions he became successively Joint Secretary to the Treasury in 1827, Vice President of the Board of Trade and a privy councillor in 1828, and Treasurer to the Navy in 1830.

A moderate Tory, he surprised the political world in 1834 by accepting the post of chairman of the Poor Law Commission from the Whig government, an appointment which necessitated his resignation as an MP. He served on the Commission until 1839 when he made way in order to facilitate the appointment of his son, George Cornewall Lewis, as a Poor Law Commissioner. With a reputation as an efficient administrator and as a 'safe pair of hands' he was an obvious choice in 1843 to chair the commission of inquiry into the Rebecca Riots in South Wales, a task for which he received his baronetcy in 1846.[13]

Plate 4: Harpton Court, the Lewis family home

Though still mistrusted by some in the Conservative hierarchy in London thanks to the acceptance of office at the hands of the Whigs, Frankland Lewis decided in mid-April 1846, before Price had announced his retirement, to make a bid for the Boroughs seat and wrote to his son George Cornewall Lewis:

> I am in for it, and I write to all persons who have standing and impor-
> tant interests to say that I shall come to the post (God granting health
> and strength) at the next election.[14]

Almost immediately Lewis was faced with a rival, for the *Hereford Journal* of 22 April announced that J.A. Whittaker 'had complied with a requisition to become a candidate for Radnor Boroughs on the retirement of Mr Richard Price' — so long as he had a reasonable chance of success. For the first time in more than a quarter of a century there was a possibility of a contest.

John Abraham Whittaker (1802-69) was the son of John Whittaker (1774-1843) and Mary, second of the three daughters, the 'Three Graces', of Francis Garbett of Knill. The Whittakers hailed from Essex and settled in the Welsh Marches when the older brother, Abraham Whittaker, sheriff of Herefordshire in 1796, married the heiress to the Lyston estate in Llanwarne. His brother, John Whittaker senior, was a major in the Royal Radnor Militia in 1798 and was described as 'of Cascob' in 1809 when he was appointed sheriff of Radnorshire. Subsequently he purchased Newcastle Court and built up a substantial estate in Cascob, Newcastle, Ednol and Llanfihangel Nant-melan.[15]

J.A. Whittaker was a soldier, serving in the 28th Regiment of Foot and subsequently in the 6th Dragoon Guards. In the autumn of 1843, when the Rebecca Riots broke out in Rhayader, he favoured taking a firm line and was 'as fiery and energetic against the Rebeccaites, as the others are timid', according to Sir John Walsh, the lord lieutenant of the county. Over the next few years Whittaker played an active part in the public life of the New Radnor

Plate 5: Newcastle Court, the home of John Abraham Whittaker, and from 1868 until 1881 the home of the first Lord Ormathwaite and his son, A.J. Walsh

district. In 1844 he strongly criticised the financial settlement imposed upon the creditors of the Radnorshire turnpike trusts after the Rebecca Riots which left some of them out of pocket, while in 1845 he extracted a public apology from Dean Mereweather, the rector of New Radnor, for describing his parishioners as 'smockfrocks and hobnails and insolent persons'. He chaired the meeting at New Radnor to promote the proposed railway line from New Radnor to Aberystwyth and took the lead in securing plans and raising subscriptions for the restoration of Llanfihangel Nant-melan parish church.[16]

In an address to the Boroughs electors of 14 April 1846 Whittaker announced his reformist credentials, advocating constitutional reform, an expansion of education, the rapid introduction of Free Trade, and political reform in Ireland while safeguarding the primacy of the Established Irish Protestant Church. He also attacked the erosion of local self-government by a creeping centralisation in the form of 'commissioners invested with arbitrary and unconstitutional powers', a clear reference to the New Poor Law, unpopular with ratepayers and magistrates alike. He also advocated a thoroughgoing reform of the Established Church in Radnorshire to ensure that the tithes of Radnorshire parishes did not end up in the hands of lay leaseholders or non-resident rectors, but were instead used to increase the stipends of resident clergy, to build much needed houses for them and to provide a modest quantity of glebe land for each parish. Finally he wished to repeal the Act of 1844 which had swept away the Welsh turnpike trusts without compensating the Radnorshire Trusts' creditors as fully as they had hoped.[17]

Much of this was an implicit attack upon the Lewis family, for both Frankland Lewis and his son had served as Poor Law commissioners, while Frankland Lewis had chaired the royal commission which had recommended the replacement of the Welsh turnpike trusts by county road boards. Again, the proposals for the reform of the Radnorshire Church almost certainly had their origins in his resentment at the Lewis family's lease of the Old Radnor tithes from the dean and chapter of Worcester Cathedral, during which virtually nothing of the income had been spent on the parish church or the chapel of ease at Kinnerton. This issue was to provoke a bitter confrontation between Lewis and Whittaker at a vestry meeting early in September 1846.

By mid-August 1846, however, Whittaker, in severe financial difficulties and in indifferent health, was having second thoughts and maintaining that he did not intend to go to the poll unless Russell's Whig ministry gained greater popular support. After a partial canvass Whittaker withdrew his candidacy at the beginning of September. With Price announcing his retirement, the way now seemed clear for Lewis, but the political situation was confused for Peel's repeal of the Corn Laws, which had offered British farmers some protection from foreign grain producers, had split the Conservative party.

Lewis's backing for Peel, the Conservative prime minister, his cautious support for Free Trade and his sympathetic stance towards the grievances of the Rebecca rioters in Rhayader made him vulnerable to a challenge from a Tory Protectionist, while his failure to back the Reform Act of 1832 and his fierce defence of his family's lease of the Old Radnor tithes had not endeared him to the more radical of the local Liberals. His moderate stance may have brought him the support of the local Whigs, but it also confused some of the electorate. Thus in the *Hereford Times* of 16 January 1847, 'A Voter of the Radnor Boroughs' advised voters to support the 'reformer' Whittaker, if he could be induced to stand, rather than the 'Tory' Frankland Lewis. The Protectionist *Silurian*, published in Brecon, interpreted Lewis's stance more accurately, commenting in February 1847 that in Presteigne, 'Russells', supporters of the Liberal, Lord John Russell, and 'Peels', supporters of Free Trade, were in great demand, but that Protectionists were at a very low discount, adding:

> We are surprised and sorry to see the intelligent inhabitants of the county town of Presteigne evincing such a disposition to be taken in.

The *Silurian* thus clearly recognised that Lewis's Tory credentials were in doubt and that he was essentially a Free Trader.

In the end it was the status, local influence and the connections of the Harpton family and their allies, such as the Prices, translated into simple arithmetic, rather than political and party considerations, which mattered. Two letters from Frankland Lewis to his son Cornewall Lewis illustrate this well.[18] On 15 April 1846 Frankland Lewis wrote:

> Whittaker's friends are sanguine, but their chance of success depends mainly upon what Hugh Powell Evans will do with his powerful influ-

ence in Rhayader where there are 50-60 old burgesses resident within seven miles of the borough and 35 ten pounders. I believe Whittaker is personally unpopular in Rhayader on account of the part he took about the Rebecca riots — he it was chiefly who filled the town with London police and soldiers.

Knighton [has] 63 ten pound voters and about 20 burgesses, nearly all I think under the influence of Richard Price. Presteigne has 90 ten pounders of whom I may secure 20 or 30. What surprises me is the amount of Sir John Walsh's influence — Cefnllys is his — it has only 3 ten pounders but has 23 burgesses, all living on his estates in the neighbourhood. He has besides about 10 others in the borough of Radnor ...

There are about 510 old burgesses in Radnor of whom about 130 will be with me. There are about 110 ten pounders of whom Whittaker will hardly poll more than 30 ...

You will see that if I am returned (as I probably must be) it will be by the support of Richard Price, Sir John Walsh, Mynors, Sir William Cockburn, who influences the Downton vote (about 10) ....

In another letter of 9 October, Frankland Lewis dealt with Knucklas borough and with the gentry of the Knighton district:

Richard Price, Mr Rogers and Mr Green (the solicitor) came to my aid at Knighton — they act cordially together and when united nothing can make any way against them. There are 65 ten pounders and 10 remaining burgesses and about 15 ten pounders and burgesses at Knucklas a decayed borough — 90 votes ... They are determined to act together at Knighton and not to admit to discord. ...

In view of the electoral strength of Frankland Lewis which these letters demonstrate, it is not surprising that Whittaker withdrew, and that on 31 July 1847, Sir Thomas Frankland Lewis was returned unopposed, with the Protectionist Robert Mynors proposing him, an ally Robert Lewis Lloyd, as seconder, and another Protectionist, Sir John Walsh, in attendance. The Boroughs seat was basically a Lewis/Price pocket borough and the Conservative *Hereford Journal* of 21 April 1852 freely admitted that in 1847:

The respect entertained for Mr Price induced the constituency to sanction the election of the candidate nominated by Mr Price.

If Frankland Lewis's motive in standing for the Boroughs seat was to keep it warm for his son, his backing for the repeal of the Corn Laws brought him unpopularity and isolated him from many of the Radnorshire establishment and most of the local farming community, since they felt that repeal threatened their interests. As Lady Lewis told Sir John Walsh in November

1849, her husband was so harassed by the bad spirit of the people of the vale of Radnor that it had affected his health. The county meeting in favour of Protection at Presteigne in January 1850 had been dominated by old allies of the Lewis family such as Richard Price, Sir John Walsh and the Revd Dr Richard Venables, all firmly opposed to Free Trade, and the *Hereford Journal* of 21 April 1852 could assert that there was probably

> no constituency which feels more indignant at the unfair treatment which the landed interest has experienced from the fatal policy of 1846 than the Radnor boroughs.

Moreover, instead of agreeing to differ with the Conservative Opposition on this one issue of Free Trade, Frankland Lewis was consistently acting with the Whig ministry on all aspects of policy. He had also offended the voters of Presteigne by using his influence to assist in the establishment of a county court at Knighton which diverted business away from the county town.[19]

By July 1851 a former curate of New Radnor was canvassing Presteigne in favour of Robert Mynors and with dissatisfaction with Frankland Lewis becoming general, Richard Price withdrew his backing. In April 1852 the Radnorshire Conservatives decided to oppose Frankland Lewis at the next election, with no fewer than five possible candidates, including Edward Rogers of Stanage, Percy Severn of Penybont Hall and Robert Mynors under consideration. In face of such opposition Frankland Lewis initially decided to retire in favour of Rogers, though he did not make his decision public.[20]

However the timid Rogers took fright and refused to come forward, and in order to 'prevent any adverse interest being formed and consolidated' to the detriment of his son's chances of succeeding him, Frankland Lewis had no option but to stand again. With the Radnorshire Conservatives thrown into disarray by Rogers' refusal to stand, Frankland Lewis was returned unopposed on 9 July 1852, thanks to the electoral influence of the Lewis family and the unwillingness of the local establishment to force the issue, and with his support for Free Trade unqualified. Thus in his electoral address he asserted that while he would never cease to regret 'the sudden and abrupt termination of the Corn Laws', once the step had been taken, it was irrevocable. As the price of agricultural products began to recover, Protectionist arguments began to lose impact and the threat to Frankland Lewis's tenure of the seat began to fade. As he wrote to his son the Revd Gilbert Lewis in October 1854:

> Yesterday I attended the agricultural meeting at Knighton — how oddly things change. Three years ago the farmers looked very blank at me — yesterday all was mild and cordial greeting.[21]

Sir George Cornewall Lewis, 1855-63

His unopposed return as MP for
Radnor Boroughs on 8 February
1855 following the unexpected death
of his father on 18 January, was by no
means the foregone conclusion that it
might seem initially.

Born in 1806, the oldest son of Sir
Thomas Frankland Lewis, Cornewall
Lewis was educated at Eton and Christ
Church, Oxford, gaining a First in
Classics and a Second in Mathematics.
He entered the Middle Temple and
was called to the bar in 1831, though
he soon abandoned a legal career
on the grounds of ill health. During
the 1830s he served on a number of
government commissions and in 1839
succeeded his father as a Poor Law
Commissioner. Between 1847 and
1852 he represented Herefordshire
in the Commons, sitting as a Liberal,
and holding a number of junior

Plate 6: Sir George Cornewall Lewis

posts in a series of coalition governments. Defeated at Hereford and then at
Peterborough in 1852, he spent the next few years amongst 'the great and
the good', serving as a trustee of the British Museum and as a member of
the Ecclesiastical Commission, though much of his time was taken up with
editing the *Edinburgh Review*.[22]

It was by no means certain that Cornewall Lewis would stand for the
Boroughs seat, for he was a gifted scholar and a prolific author for whom a
literary life held great attractions. According to his brother Gilbert, after his
defeat at Hereford in 1852 Cornewall Lewis 'had become indisposed to return
to an active political life'. Again, he 'disliked electioneering in any form',
while his finances were such that he could not afford to fight a contested
election, and at first there was a real possibility of a contest. George Stovin
Venables, the second son of Archdeacon Venables, was thinking of standing,
while Richard Banks of Kington, Percy Severn, Robert Mynors, Richard
Price, Richard Green and William Stephens of Presteigne were also possible
candidates, according to the Revd Lister Venables.[23]

Cornewall Lewis was finally persuaded to stand by his wife Lady Theresa
and his brother the Revd Gilbert Frankland Lewis. At a public meeting at
Rhayader on Saturday 27 January 1855, care was taken to avoid a partisan

approach and to stress the personal qualities and the public achievements of Cornewall Lewis rather than his Liberal principles. Lewis took the same line in his election address, declaring his adherence to Liberal principles, but insisting that he would not contest the seat on party lines.[24]

Cornewall Lewis and his agent Richard Banks canvassed Knighton, Presteigne and Rhayader thoroughly, taking care to call on men of influence of both political persuasions; Richard Price of Norton Manor, Sir Harford James Jones Brydges of Boultibrooke (the second baronet), J.C. Severn of Penybont Hall and, in the Rhayader area, David Oliver and Thomas Lewis Lloyd. Price, an old school Tory and a Protectionist, had to be handled carefully for his electoral influence in the constituency possibly exceeded that of Harpton Court. Richard Green, Price's eventual heir, could not even guarantee the neutrality of the Price interest and could offer Cornewall Lewis no more than his individual vote. In Presteigne, however, the backing of the Conservative James Beavan was secured, while in Rhayader the support of the High Sheriff, John Jones, proved invaluable. Banks also wrote to the Revd J. Thomas, asking him to use any influence he had in Cefnllys in favour of Lewis.[25]

After the election Cornewall Lewis tended to gloss over his campaign, writing to his friend W.R. Greg that his return 'was accomplished without difficulty' and that he 'had not even to make preparations for a contest'. This complacency, if not arrogance, was to characterise his approach to the by-election of March 1855 necessitated by his appointment as Chancellor of the Exchequer, since at that time appointment to a ministerial post required electoral approval. Encouraged by letters of support from Henry Lingen of Penlanole, Robert Mynors, Thomas Lewis Lloyd and Sir John Walsh and by his brother Gilbert's assurance that:

> The Radnor people will never think of you coming down. The seat is perfectly safe,

Cornewall Lewis wrote to his agent Richard Banks that he was too busy to come down for the election. Banks insisted that he should do so in order to avoid offending the electors, and James Davies, Banks's business partner travelled to London to see Lewis and drive home the point. Accordingly, Cornewall Lewis spent the weekend at Harpton Court, issued an election address pledging his adherence to 'principles of social improvement and progressive reform' and was duly returned unopposed on Monday 5 March 1855.[26]

Lewis was again returned unopposed in the general election of 28 March 1857. With no other candidate in sight he thought it advisable to spend two days canvassing in Presteigne and Knighton, for form's sake at least. In the general election of 1859 he was once again returned unopposed on 30 April.

Again he went through the motions of campaigning, canvassing Knighton, Presteigne and Rhayader, recruiting Richard Green (Green Price from 1861) and the solicitor Jonathan Green to assist him and publishing an address. His appointment as Home Secretary necessitated a by-election scheduled for 27 June and Cornewall Lewis, regarding this as a formality, asked his election agent Banks if he thought it desirable for him to be present. Banks replied that it was advisable for Lewis to attend in order to avoid the taunt that he treated the seat as a pocket borough. Cornewall Lewis duly obliged and was once more returned unopposed.[27]

Cornewall Lewis's election campaigns were not conducted on party lines, though he made no secret of his own political allegiance. His election addresses were general in character and his canvassing was directed at gaining the support of as many as possible of the local establishment, irrespective of their political stance. Election days at New Radnor were celebratory rather than political occasions. The carriages of Cornewall Lewis and his friends were escorted from Harpton Court by supporters and tenants on horseback, the procession usually led by a band; in April 1859 by the band of the Royal Radnor Rifles. Flags in the Lewis colours of yellow and green were flown from Bailey Glas, the hill overlooking the borough, and from the Eagle and the Radnorshire Arms, two of New Radnor's inns, while the Town Hall was decorated with wreaths of laurel and slogans backing Lewis such as 'We are all proud of him' and 'Sir George Cornewall Lewis, the poor man's friend'. Inside the Town Hall, once the legal formalities had been completed and the returning officer had declared Lewis as elected, the speeches tended

Plate 7: New Radnor Town Hall

to be short, genial and non-controversial. Only once, in April 1859, was this convention breached when Richard Green make a highly partisan speech, 'radical in tone and containing some disparaging remarks', which Sir John Walsh took to be directed at him.[28]

Cornewall Lewis's unambiguous support of Free Trade brought him the support of many of the tradesmen, craftsmen and most of the professional classes in the boroughs of Knighton, Presteigne and Rhayader for whom Free Trade was an article of faith, while the improving fortunes of agriculture meant that many farmers and leading landowners such as the Prickards and the Lewis Lloyds renewed their traditional loyalties to Harpton Court. Other more apolitical voters may have been more impressed by the high offices of state held by Lewis than by his other qualities.

Even so Cornewall Lewis was respected rather than popular in the constituency at large, for although he had the esteem of the Radnorshire elite, Sir John Walsh, for example, finding him an admirable travelling companion, his rather cold and detached manner probably appeared intimidating to many of the farmers, craftsmen and tradesmen who made up the greater part of the Boroughs electorate. As his brother Gilbert noted, Cornewall Lewis was not used to talking with the farmers and country people, and his understanding of them was far less happy than had been the case with his father. His physical short-sightedness may well have reinforced the impression of aloofness.[29]

The decisive factor behind the unchallenged Lewis tenure of the Boroughs seat was the close alliance between the two dominant families of the constituency, the Lewises and the Prices. During the time of Frankland Lewis and Richard Price there had always been a certain tension between the two who differed sharply in their views; Richard Price a traditional Tory and Protectionist and the moderate Conservative Frankland Lewis, a cautious Free Trader. By 1855 Price was in his eighties and the Price family interests were increasingly in the hands of his nephew Richard Green who, in the 1840s and early 1850s, had shifted gradually from Conservatism to Liberalism and Free Trade. From 1855 onwards he had increasingly identified himself with Cornewall Lewis and placed the Price interest at the disposal of Harpton Court. Green clearly had ambitions to succeed to the Boroughs seat and as early as 1857 was urging Cornewall Lewis to challenge Sir John Walsh for the county seat, maintaining that 'the borough can ... be easily managed by a good Liberal'.[30]

One of the leading statesmen of his age, widely respected by both sides of the House of Commons and generally regarded as a future prime minister, Cornewall Lewis died suddenly on 13 April 1863 at Harpton Court at the age of 56. Though his health was by no means robust, his death came as a great surprise and Richard Green Price's opportunity to represent the Boroughs in the Commons came earlier than he might have expected.

Richard Green Price, 1863-69

Born in 1803, the second son of George Green and his wife Margaret, the sister of Richard Price of Norton Manor, Richard Green served his articles in Worcester and with another solicitor, Thomas Peters, set up a flourishing legal partnership in Knighton, moving into banking in 1836 when he became a partner in the Kington, Knighton and Radnorshire Bank. Over the next few decades he greatly influenced the development of Knighton, playing an important part on the Local Board of Health, set up in 1853 to improve the water supply and sanitation of the town, and other measures of urban renewal. He was also instrumental in the formation of the Temeside Agricultural Society, the Knighton Farmers' Club and the Knighton Company

Plate 8: Richard Green Price

of the Radnorshire Volunteers. He also helped to create Knighton's modern townscape, for he took the lead in building the Farmers' Club, the Assembly Room, the Sheep Market and later the Norton Arms Hotel and several adjacent shops. His promotion of the Knighton and Central Wales railway lines not only helped to reaffirm Knighton's status as the leading market town of the county and to develop Llandrindod Wells, but also served to raise his profile in the county as a whole.

On the death of Richard Price in 1861 he inherited the Norton Manor estate, assuming the additional surname of Price by royal licence. He probably found the transition from a well connected professional man to a member of the county elite relatively easy since he had moved in establishment circles for some time as his uncle's man of business and latterly, during the 1850s, as county treasurer. He was also an experienced local politician, having acted as the political agent first for Frankland Lewis, then Sir John Walsh (in the county seat) and later for Sir George Cornewall Lewis.

Following the death of Cornewall Lewis, Green Price was thus well placed to succeed him in the Boroughs seat. However he did not have a completely free run for Lewis's close friend Sir Edmund Head, a Privy Councillor and a former Governor of Canada, had some ambitions in that direction and had the backing of some of the local Liberal leaders. However Head was assured by F.L. Bodenham, Lewis's former adviser, that 'if Green Price wished to be in Parliament, his influence will be too strong for any other candidate to contend against' and took no further steps in the matter.[31]

With no rival in the field and following requisitions from electors in Knighton and Knucklas asking him to come forward, Green Price declared his candidature. However party politics were beginning to intrude, even in out of the way Radnorshire and he announced that if elected, he would support Lord Palmerston's government and vote as a Liberal Conservative, a designation which brought a mixed reaction from the *Hereford Times*. In the 'second sheet' of the issue of 25 April the newspaper commented:

> Before men appointed a pilot they might reasonably ask how he meant to steer when the wind came.

It went on to pour cold water on Green Price's candidacy:

> The political reputation of the constituency which returned Sir Cornewall Lewis is not likely to be sustained by choosing a successor on merely local grounds.

However, the *Hereford Times* quickly revised its views and in its 'first sheet' of the same issue, typeset a day or so later, gave Green Price its backing, declaring that he was

> not more Conservative than his esteemed and lamented predecessor, in fact he is a Liberal.

The *volte face* probably stemmed from the arrival of further requisitions from the electors of Presteigne and Rhayader which showed that Green Price had the backing of the majority of the electors in the constituency.

The *Hereford Journal* was more generous, noting that while Green Price's views did not coincide exactly with its Conservative stance, he was at least free from the taint of radicalism, was not a nominee of the government and would thus enter the Commons 'unfettered and unpledged'. With New Radnor thronged with his supporters wearing rosettes of red and blue, the colours of Liberal Conservatism, Green Price was returned unopposed on 23 April 1863.[32]

Green Price was again returned unopposed in the general election of 1865. With no hint of a possible rival, the election passed off quietly, the most dramatic incident coming when the large band of horsemen escorting the carriages of the Green Price party from Norton Manor drew up in a large half circle outside the Town Hall at New Radnor to receive Green Price with cheers. Inside the hall Green Price was proposed by the Revd Sir Gilbert Frankland Lewis and seconded by his future son-in-law, Thomas Baskerville Mynors. The occasion was notable, according to Sir John Walsh, for clear statements of their political stances by Frankland Lewis and Green Price as a Whig and an 'advanced Liberal' respectively. Frankland Lewis also expressed his satisfaction that Green Price had disassociated himself from 'that nondescript class of politician known as Liberal Conservatives'.[33] Green Price had thus moved one stage further on his journey from his Tory views of the 1830s to his more radical stance of the 1880s and now, as a dedicated Liberal, was convinced of the need for thoroughgoing reform.

At first sight the general election of the autumn 1868 seems to have been cast in the same mould as all the Borough elections since 1820, as on 17 November Green Price was again returned unopposed. However, as a result of the Reform Act of 1867, which gave the vote to male householders and £10 lodgers, the Boroughs electorate had increased by 90% and the new voters were an unknown quantity. Moreover there was, for a time, the possibility of a contested election, which galvanised the Green Price camp into a vigorous campaign.

Green Price's potential rival was George Augustus Haig, 1820-1906, the son of an Irish distiller who had first worked in the brewing industry and then sold Scottish and Irish spirits before becoming a wine merchant in London in 1850. In 1858 he purchased more than 2,500 acres (1,012 ha) in Llanbadarn Fynydd, Llananno and St Harmon and built Pen Ithon Hall. Able if eccentric, he strongly opposed Gladstone's proposal to disestablish and disendow the Irish Church. An Irish Protestant, he believed that such a measure would be to the advantage of the Catholic Church in Ireland, while disestablishment might have important constitutional implications for the Church of England. Haig's address to the 'Protestant Electors' issued at the end of August suggested that he hoped to create an alliance of Conservatives, Low Churchmen and nonconformists strong enough to unseat Green Price who had wholeheartedly identified himself with Gladstone and the disestablishment of the Irish Church.[34]

The campaign on both sides was sometimes highly personal. Thus the *Hereford Times* of 29 August hinted that Green Price's High Church views inclined him to support the Irish Catholic Church rather than the Established Church in Ireland which was Evangelical in tone. On the other hand, a letter in the *Hereford Times* of 12 September described Haig's address as 'a meddling and uncalled for interference of a perfect stranger'. Haig's intervention and the presence on the electoral register of many new voters meant that Green

Price held meetings in each of the boroughs and canvassed them thoroughly. Not all his meetings passed off peaceably; that at Presteigne was attended by 'some newly enfranchised voters' and there were 'a few outbursts of feeling and some interruptions'.[35]

Green Price also felt compelled to make a clear statement of his view on the religious issue. He explained that his firm Protestant principles would guide him in his support of Gladstone and that 'the Established Church and the Nonconformists would find him a zealous opponent of the Roman Catholics'. His choice of two Anglican clerics, the Revd Sir Gilbert Frankland Lewis and the Revd T.C. Prickard as his proposer and seconder respectively at his nomination may also have been designed to reinforce his religious credentials. However Haig's campaign, essentially single issue, was far too narrowly based to have a wide general appeal, while his attack on Green Price's religious stance seemed to be unfounded. After an unfavourable canvass, Haig wrote to Green Price on 22 October 1868 to inform him that he was withdrawing from the contest. He attributed his failure to attract support to an understanding between Green Price and Walsh, the county MP, not to encourage opposition to each other in their respective constituencies. He alleged that in several boroughs, particularly in Presteigne and Knighton, most Conservative voters were pledged to support Green Price. With Haig withdrawing, Green Price was returned unopposed at New Radnor on 17 November.[36]

Nationally the political landscape was changing since party divisions were hardening as Whigs, Radicals and Free Traders were coalescing into the Liberal Party, while Protectionists, Tories and those intent on extending the British Empire were uniting under Disraeli into the Conservative Party. In this situation an ambitious MP could only hope to achieve his objectives by identifying himself wholeheartedly with one of these parties. Green Price was the first of the Radnorshire politicians of the modern age to identify himself completely with a party leader and his programme and his willingness to fight the contest on party lines may well have assisted him in securing the backing of many of the new electors who had gained the vote as a result of the Reform Act of 1867.

2 The County Seat, 1796-1868

In the nineteenth century the Radnorshire parliamentary seat was virtually the preserve of two of the major landowning families in the county: the Wilkins (de Winton) family of Maesllwch, who held the seat from 1796 until 1828 and again from 1835 until 1840; and the Walsh family, who held it from 1840 until 1880 and again from 1885 until 1892. Although the county electorate was much larger than that of the Boroughs, it was still small enough, until 1885, to enable a major county family, together with its allies and an efficient electoral organisation, to exercise sufficient control to secure the election of its nominee.

1796-1828	Walter Wilkins	Whig
1828-34	Thomas Frankland Lewis	Conservative
1835-40	Walter Wilkins (de Winton)	Liberal
1840-68	Sir John Walsh	Conservative
1868-80	Hon Arthur Walsh	Conservative
1880-85	Sir Richard Green Price	Liberal
1885-92	Hon Arthur J.H. Walsh	Conservative
1892-95	Francis Edwards	Liberal
1895-1900	(Sir) Powlett Milbank	Conservative
1900-10	(Sir) Francis Edwards	Liberal
1910	C.L. Dillwyn Venables Llewelyn	Conservative
1910-18	Sir Francis Edwards	Liberal

Figure 3: Members of Parliament for Radnorshire 1796-1918

Prior to 1832 only 40 shilling freeholders (owners of land worth £2 a year in rentable value) had the vote, the election being held sometimes at New Radnor or, more usually, in Presteigne. The 1832 Reform Act added to the electorate £10 copyholders (small farmers who held their land on a very long lease), £10 leaseholders of not less than 60 years, £50 leaseholders of not less than 20 years and £50 tenants at will (those terminable at short notice).

Plate 9: J.M. Ince's engraving of Broad Street, c.1830. The votes were counted and the poll declared in the county elections in the old Shire Hall (centre background) and, after 1830, in the present Shire Hall (left foreground)

Polling stations were set up in each of the county's six Hundreds, at Clyro, Knighton, Painscastle, Penybont, Presteigne and Rhayader. The Reform Act of 1832 did not increase the electorate significantly for whereas 935 had voted in the 1802 election, only 1,046 voters were registered in 1832 and by 1835 the electorate had increased to no more than 1,076, two-thirds of whom were 40 shilling freeholders and a further 28% were tenants at will.[1]

1780	886	1865	1,587
1802	935	1868	2,016
1832	1,046	1874	2,431
1835	1,074	1880	2,434
1837	1,944	1885	4,539
1841	2,067	1892	4,535
1847	1,943	1895	4,838
1852	1,802	1900	5,219
1857	1,662	1906	5,466
1859	1,656	1910	5,971

Figure 4. The Radnorshire Electorate

The marked increase in the electorate between 1835 and 1837 stemmed from the efforts of Walter Wilkins III and the Whigs to maximise the registration of their supporters, a strategy not immediately imitated by Walsh and the Conservatives. The decline in the electorate after 1841 reflects not only the decline in the population of the Radnorshire countryside as a result of migration to the industrial areas of south Wales and the Midlands, but also the lack of contested elections which reduced the incentive for local politicians to embark upon a registration drive.

The 1867 Reform Act added to the electorate £12 householders, £5 copyholders and £5 leaseholders of not less than 60 years and increased the electorate by 27%. It also provided for an increase in the number of polling stations in the county from six to eighteen. Although over the next decade or so the population of the county fell, the number of electors increased markedly as sharp divisions between the parties, coupled with contested elections restored the incentive for the parties to ensure that prospective supporters were on the electoral register.

Walter Wilkins I, 1796-1828

The Wilkins family, important in legal and banking circles in Brecon, extended their influence into Radnorshire when Walter Wilkins, 1742-1828, acquired the extensive Maesllwch estate from Sir Humphrey Howorth in 1772, by foreclosing on a mortgage he held on the estate and making an additional cash payment. The estate, which amounted to 4,956 acres (2,006 ha) in 1873, took in most of the Radnorshire hundreds of Colwyn and Painscastle (see Figure 5) and brought him great electoral influence in the south-western area of the county.

Educated at Christchurch College, Brecon; Winchester and Reeve's Academy, London, Wilkins had entered the service of the East India Company on the nomination of his mother's kinsman, Lord Camden, becoming a writer (a clerk or a merchant's assistant) in Bengal in 1758. He had a successful career in India, becoming senior merchant and governor of Chittagong and a member of the East India Council. He amassed a

Plate 10: Walter Wilkins I

huge fortune through private trading and returned to England in 1772. Wilkins served as High Sheriff of Radnorshire in 1775 and, according to Roy Adams in his thesis 'The Parliamentary History of Radnorshire, 1536-1832', was already harbouring parliamentary ambitions for the county seat, having thought of standing against Chase Price in 1774 and against Thomas Johnes senior in 1777. He stood unsuccessfully against Thomas Johnes junior in 1780 and although defeated, he had made his intentions clear and when Johnes withdrew from the seat in 1796, Wilkins was returned unopposed.[2] He held the Radnorshire seat until his death in 1828,

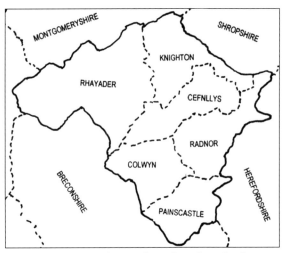

Figure 5: The Radnorshire hundreds

facing only one contested election, in 1802, being returned unopposed in 1806, 1807, 1812, 1818, 1820 and 1826.

His opponent in 1802 was John Macnamara of Chilton Park in Wiltshire and of Llangoed Castle, Breconshire. After an anonymous notice had circulated through the county in January asking the freeholders not to engage their vote for the next election as 'a gentleman whose property connects with the county' was likely to stand, Macnamara announced his candidacy in June, only to withdraw it a few days later. However on the first day of the poll, 15 July, Macnamara decided to stand after all, and when the poll ended on 19 July, he had polled 57 votes to Wilkins' 577.

In the *Hereford Journal* of 29 July 1802, Macnamara sought to explain himself, claiming that he had stood because the privileges of the freeholders and the rights of the county of Radnor had been 'outraged by intemperate, unconstitutional and Asiatic coercion and despotism'. He claimed that Wilkins had 'resorted to the most gross exertion of undue influence and every species of illegality unparalleled in the annals of electioneering, even in the most corrupt borough' and explained his own low poll in terms of his prevailing upon many freeholders not to vote for him because he did not wish 'to subject them to implacable malignity' at the hands of Wilkins and his supporters. He also claimed that the sheriff had allowed large numbers of unqualified electors to vote for Wilkins. Such allegations formed the grounds of his unsuccessful petition to the House of Commons to set aside the election result.

Macnamara's intervention in Radnorshire politics is not easy to explain, for he did not own a sufficiently large estate in the county to make him part of its establishment and was thus much more of an 'outsider' than Wilkins. He may have been seeking to exploit resentment on the part of some members of the Radnorshire elite at Wilkins' wealth, particularly as it originated in trade. 'Nabobs', such as Wilkins and Sir Harford Jones Brydges, who had made fortunes in India, were far from popular with the long established county families and Macnamara's reference to 'Asiatic ... despotism' and his intrigues with Thomas Frankland Lewis and Percival Lewis of Downton in the run up to the election give some credence to this view. However, Macnamara's intervention, far from undermining Wilkins' position, had the effect of strengthening Wilkins' support in the county, according to Thomas Frankland Lewis, who took Macnamara to task in a letter of 30 October:

> You have harassed Wilkins so that people here have learnt to pity a man they could not admire.[3]

It has been thought that Wilkins' tenure of the seat was never completely secure and that a challenge was always possible. However the evidence for this assertion is no more than one undated letter by a Montgomeryshire correspondent to the effect that Wilkins was always looking over his shoulder and

> as Member for Radnorshire he is under the necessity of paying much more court to his constituents than the voters on this side of the hill are accustomed to receive from their representatives ... at present Wilkins' wealth gives him an ascendancy but notwithstanding there is no one who can so well support the expense of an contest as himself, still it is an event which he looks for every election.[3]

Wilkins may well have faced the possibility of a challenge during the first sixteen years of his tenure of the seat. In addition to the challenge of Macnamara in 1802, a letter from the latter to Frankland Lewis in 1812 suggests that Percival Lewis at least thought he had some understanding with Frankland Lewis with regard to the two Radnorshire seats at some time in the past, possibly 1807. In 1812 Frankland Lewis, having decided that Wilkins had no real backing in the county beyond that provided by his wealth, briefly considered standing against him, having secured promises of support from Hugh Powell Evans of Noyadd, who dominated Rhayader Hundred, and Edward Rogers of Stanage. In the end Lewis was swayed by Richard Price, the Member for Radnor Boroughs who counselled patience, arguing that in view of Wilkins' age, Lewis would do better to wait until his retirement or death.[5]

However, after 1812 there is no evidence to suggest that Wilkins' tenure of the seat was under threat, probably because Frankland Lewis had, in 1812 staked his claim, having an understanding with Hugh Powell Evans of Noyadd, Edward Rogers of Stanage and Richard Price that he would be cordially supported whenever another opportunity offers itself — Wilkins is nearly 72 and it can hardly be that he can expect to be returned again.

As Frankland Lewis announced in his election address in 1828:

I now come forward to redeem a pledge I have more than once publicly given, that I would offer myself as a candidate for the honour of your suffrage whenever that event [the death of Wilkins] shall occur.

He had made his intentions widely known and with his influential backers may have frightened off potential rivals and thus had unwittingly strengthened Wilkins' position.[6]

Even so, Wilkins' influence was limited, partly because he was never able to win over important elements in the Radnorshire establishment, who envied his wealth and, as Tories, had little sympathy with his reformist stance. Broadly Whig in sympathy, Wilkins' platform was his residence in the county and his independence which led him to be critical of virtually every ministry. In practice however he was a reformer who consistently voted in favour of 'moderate' parliamentary reform, Catholic Emancipation, the promotion of popular education, reform of the penal code and against repressive measures such as the repressive Six Acts of 1819.

Even though his direct electoral influence did not extend beyond the Hundreds of Colwyn and Painscastle, Wilkins held the seat for thirty-two years without a serious challenge. Frankland Lewis was convinced that this was attributable, in the main, to his great wealth, for Wilkins was prepared to spend lavishly at election time and in the absence of strict regulation of election expenses there was a fine, almost non-existent line between legitimate expenses and the illegal 'treating' alleged by Macnamara in 1802. Even uncontested elections could involve considerable expenditure: thus the *Hereford Journal* of 1 July 1818 reported that:

dinners were provided at every public house [in Presteigne]; and the Nobility, Gentlemen etc of that place and vicinity partook of a most sumptuous entertainment at the Radnorshire Arms ... And last not least, the prisoners in the county gaol return their grateful thanks for a very plentiful dinner and good ale ...

Wilkins' wealth also enabled him to gain support amongst the magistracy and the ratepayers by lending the county large sums at low rates of interest to assist with extraordinary expenditure. Thus in 1798 he loaned the county £700 after the storms of 1797 had destroyed many of the county's bridges and £2,000 in 1820-21 in order to build a new county gaol.[7]

His wealth also enabled him to transform even uncontested elections into carefully orchestrated public demonstrations of widespread popular support which may have deterred potential rivals. Thus following his unopposed return in 1818 the *Hereford Times* of 1 July described the traditional chairing ceremony:

> a very superb and handsome chair was in readiness to receive him, tastefully ornamented with pink and blue silk, and a purple and gold canopy, in which he was carried, preceded by elegant flags, with the mottos 'Long may he live', 'No Corn Bill' and a grand triumphal arch with the inscription 'The intrepid champion of our Constitutional Bulwarks, Wilkins' was also erected, under which the procession passed.

Proceedings in 1820 were equally lavish according to the *Hereford Times* of 29 March:

> The chairing took place immediately after the election, and was conducted with great magnificence. The flags and banners were particularly elegant, the band of music full and effective, and the procession of freeholders equally numerous and respectable. The whole thing passed off without the slightest accident, not with-standing the streets were crowded to excess. The windows of the houses were filled not only with the ladies of Presteigne, but by almost every lady of distinction in the county wearing bonnet knots of the member's colours, azure and pink and waving their handkerchiefs to the passing procession. Every house of entertainment was open for the good cheer of the freeholders and all comers. The poor prisoners were not forgotten, being regaled with roast beef, plum pudding and plenty of good ale.

There was, moreover, a general reluctance to force a contest which would have threatened the delicate balance of interests and obligations underpinning polite society in the county. Thus on several occasions Wilkins' nomination as member for the county was seconded by one of his political opponents: Richard Price, the Member for the Boroughs and a 'firm unbending Tory'. For his part Wilkins always took care to look for consensus. In his address of 1802 he simply undertook to oppose any measure which encroached upon 'the just liberties of the people', while in his address of 1818 he boasted that in 20 years in the Commons he had

> never given any vote in favour of measures that tended to protract the miseries of war, to increase the public burden or to abridge the rights and liberties of my fellow countrymen, or to deprive those who have complained of being plundered and oppressed of the means of justification and redress.

Again, in his election address of 1820, he made it clear that he stood as an independent, without ties to any party or faction, although he personally favoured moderate parliamentary reform and opposed the repressive Six Acts.[8]

Thomas Frankland Lewis 1828-34

Within a few days of Wilkins' death in London on 17 March 1828, Frankland Lewis announced his intention to contest the by-election and had begun a canvass. At first it did not seem that he would get a clear run for in the *Hereford Journal* of 2 April the Revd Walter Wilkins, the nephew of the late Member, Middleton Evans of Llwynbarried and Frederick Jones of Brecon asked the freeholders 'not to be hurried into promises by an early canvass', but to wait for a county meeting. Another notice signed by Whigs, many of them Presteigne residents, asked the sheriff to hold such a meeting, preferably on 5 April, but the sheriff opted instead for 8 April, the day before that fixed for the election. In the same issue of the *Journal* Frankland Lewis announced that his canvass had been favourable to him, though it had not met with universal support. Thus it seemed likely that, with both the Lewis and Wilkins factions mobilising their supporters, Radnorshire faced its first contested election for more than twenty-five years.

At the county meeting the Revd Walter Wilkins announced that he had hoped that Walter Wilkins II, the son of the late Member, would contest the seat, but that he had declined on grounds of ill health. He went on to commend Frankland Lewis for his sensitivity in not canvassing in the vicinity of Maesllwch Castle and the surrounding area until after the funeral of the late Walter Wilkins. The atmosphere of consensus was shattered by Sir Harford Jones Brydges who accused the sheriff, David Thomas of Wellfield, of electioneering by holding the county meeting in Presteigne on a day which clashed with the sitting of Great Sessions at Brecon, which meant that many of the gentry of south-west Radnorshire, mainly in the Wilkins camp, were unable to attend.

He then launched a highly personal attack on Frankland Lewis, casting doubt on his ability to act independently as a check on the government by virtue of his post as Vice President of the Board of Trade. On behalf of his tenants in the parish of Old Radnor, he complained of the high tithes paid in the parish to Frankland Lewis, to whom the tithes had been leased by the dean and chapter of Worcester Cathedral. Finally he criticised Frankland Lewis for ensuring that only his tenants and allies were appointed as magistrates in the borough of New Radnor. Once he had finished his speech Jones Brydges left the hall without waiting to hear Frankland Lewis's reply.

Frankland Lewis denied that his ministerial post meant that he could not act independently if necessary, pointed out that since Jones Brydges possessed only two farms in Old Radnor, his two tenants could not claim to be representative of the parish and explained that since magistrates in New Radnor could only be chosen from the Capital Burgesses, who had to be resident in the Borough, Jones Brydges and some other landowners were ineligible.

On 9 April Frankland Lewis was returned unopposed, nominated by Richard Price and seconded by the Whig, Hugh Powell Evans. The bi-partisan mood of the occasion was maintained by the crowd attending the chairing and the large attendance at the dinner held in a marquee at the Radnorshire Arms where, in a graceful speech the Revd Walter Wilkins declared that by his conduct Frankland Lewis had won the county and deserved to keep it.[9]

Sir Harford Jones Brydges, (1769-1847), however, was not reconciled, and remained deeply hostile towards Frankland Lewis. Descended from the Jones family of Trewern, who had played an important role in Radnorshire affairs in the sixteenth century and the first half of the seventeenth, he had restored family fortunes as a result of his service with the East India Company between 1783 and 1811, serving as Resident in Baghdad 1799-1807 and then as British envoy to the Court of Persia. In 1812 he purchased the Boultibrooke estate which amounted to 3,090 acres (1,250 ha) in 1873. He served as sheriff of Radnorshire in 1816 and subsequently as chairman of the Bench, in which office he was responsible for the plan to build a new county gaol and shire hall. In politics he was a convinced Whig and the accession of William IV and the formation of a Whig government in 1830 gave him an opportunity to champion the cause of reform of Parliament and by doing so, build up his influence in the county.

Frankland Lewis was returned unopposed on four further occasions; in March 1830 on his appointment as Treasurer of the Navy, in August 1830, May

Plate 11: Boultibrooke, c.1930, the home of Sir Harford Jones Brydges

1831 and December 1832. However, thanks to Sir Harford Jones Brydges' personal antipathy towards Frankland Lewis the proceedings could be far from uneventful. The election of March 1830 passed off quietly since Jones Brydges was not present as he was preoccupied in mobilising opposition to a recommendation of the commission of inquiry into the judicial system that the Welsh courts of Great Sessions should be abolished and the assize system extended to cover Wales. Under this scheme Presteigne would lose its two annual sittings of Great Sessions and Radnorshire would be placed under the jurisdiction of Hereford assizes. This arrangement would be inconvenient for much of Radnorshire and Presteigne would lose materially and in terms of prestige and status.

The *Hereford Times* of 10 February contained a notice from Jones Brydges notifying the Radnorshire freeholders of the recommendation and advising them to press for a county meeting to discuss the situation. A petition signed by 55 freeholders from the Presteigne district was dispatched to the sheriff who agreed that a meeting should be held at the Shire Hall on 9 March. At the meeting which was dominated by Jones Brydges and Dr Jenkins of The Grove and his connections, a petition opposing the recommendation was carried with only two dissenting votes.[10]

The death of George IV in June 1830 necessitated a general election, scheduled in Radnorshire for 9 August. In an address to the electors Frankland Lewis was able to assure them that he 'had used every exertion to give effect to the wishes of the county' with regard to the Welsh Judicature Bill and had secured an amendment ensuring that the assizes were to be held at Presteigne twice annually, and was duly returned unopposed. Once more the consensus of the meeting was shattered by a personal attack on Frankland Lewis by Jones Brydges, who maintained that since Lewis was an office holder he could not follow an independent line in the Commons and then went on to criticise the abolition of the old Welsh judicial system. In the course of his speech Jones Brydges also made an oblique reference to the need for Parliamentary reform, saying that people should be reminded that it was their duty to procure an honest and independent House of Commons by exercising their franchise freely and not selling their votes. Again he left the meeting without waiting to hear replies to his speech, despite the Revd Dr Richard Venables' request that he should remain.[11]

The resignation of Wellington and the formation of a Whig government had encouraged hopes of an early reform of Parliament, but the rejection the first Reform Bill by a Commons committee in March 1831 resulted in widespread disappointment. The *Hereford Journal* of 23 March reported a meeting to promote a petition in favour of Parliamentary reform in Presteigne in which Harford Jones Brydges had taken the lead. The proposed inclusion of Presteigne in the Boroughs constituency was welcomed, but since in the Radnor

Boroughs seat non-resident freemen outnumbered resident freemen by five to one, the tradesmen of towns such as Knighton and Presteigne would have little electoral influence. The petition from the 'Inhabitants and Householders of Presteigne', backing reform and the exclusion of non-resident freemen from the franchise, was presented in the Commons by Frankland Lewis on 22 March.[12]

In the meantime Harford Jones Brydges and his Presteigne supporters, along with the Revd Walter Wilkins, asked the sheriff to call a county meeting to express support for the Reform Bill. The meeting was held on 5 April and was attended by Frankland Lewis and Richard Price, both of whom had voted against the Bill on the Second Reading. Price was unsympathetic to any reform but Frankland Lewis was not opposed in principle, having voted for the Bill on the First Reading, though he believed that the Commons needed more information before any decisions could be taken as to which borough constituencies should be abolished.

Frankland Lewis and Price tried to amend the original petition so that it did little more than condemn the nomination of borough members by individuals, the use of bribery and corruption, violence and intimidation and seek to reduce the expense of elections. However the meeting rejected their amendment and opted for the terms of the original petition which was to be presented in the Commons by Frankland Lewis and in the Lords by Earl Grey. At the end of the meeting 25 of those present adjourned to the Radnorshire Arms where it was decided to set up a Grey Coat Club, to meet annually at Presteigne on 1 August, the ostensible object of which seems to have been to encourage the production of Radnorshire grey cloth. In practice it soon became a Whig electoral organisation.[13]

Following the dissolution of Parliament in mid-April 1831 the two factions, the supporters of Frankland Lewis and the advocates of reform, sprang into action. The *Hereford Journal* of 27 April contained a notice of support for Frankland Lewis signed by 113 Radnorshire freeholders including most of the Radnorshire establishment such as Richard Price, Edward Rogers of Stanage, John Whittaker, Hugh Powell Evans, Richard Banks of Kington and James Davies, the Radnorshire clerk of the peace. The same issue also included a letter from 'Alfred' which attacked Frankland Lewis, alleging that while he had done nothing for the county, Lewis had secured for himself a place and 'all he could catch in the political scramble', the writer going on to advise freeholders not to engage their vote since 'an honest man who will support the long wished for Reform in Parliament' was going to offer himself for election. Most guessed that 'Alfred' was Jones Brydges, but the identity of the 'honest man' remains uncertain. It may have been Jones Brydges himself, but it seems more likely to have been Edward Romilly, the third son of Sir Samuel Romilly, who was certainly taking soundings in the county as to his chances of success.

However in the *Hereford Journal* of 4 May, Romilly, while admitting that he had come into the county to support any candidate pledging to support the Reform Bill, and if necessary to stand himself, announced that he would not come forward as a candidate since many who had supported Reform at the Presteigne meeting of 5 April were now backing Frankland Lewis and that he himself had come too late into the field to have any real chance of success. The same issue of the *Journal* also contained Frankland Lewis's address which repeated his objections to the Reform Bill as it stood while pledging his support for 'any definite, intelligible, well arranged measure for reforming our representative system' which did not reduce the number of English MPs by 60 as the current Bill envisaged.

At the election on 5 May, Frankland Lewis was returned unopposed, nominated by Richard Price and seconded by Hugh Powell Evans. In the speeches which followed, the Whig William Davies of Cabalfa asked why Frankland Lewis had not presented the petition in favour of Parliamentary reform to the Commons, while the Revd Dr Richard Venables warned that the envisaged reduction in the number of English MPs and increase in the number of Irish members would greatly increase Catholic political influence. Frankland Lewis portrayed Jones Brydges as a disappointed man who had hoped for a peerage and a pension on his return form Persia and maintained that as 'Alfred' Jones Brydges had been backing Romilly, who was not a Radnorshire freeholder, a charge subsequently denied by William Davies, Romilly's uncle. With regard to the county petition in favour of Reform, although it had been left at Harpton on the day after the meeting, it had not come into his hands until the 20 April. On the following day he had took it into the House, but owing to the pressure of business there had not been an opportunity to present it until 22 April, when Parliament was dissolved.[14]

Once the election was over the political temperature in the county seems to have fallen sharply for there appears to have been little appetite for controversy. Thus, following a pamphlet war between Jones Brydges and Frankland Lewis, instigated by the former, in a letter published in the *Hereford Journal* of 1 June a 'Radnorshire Freeholder' designated Jones Brydges 'The Radnorshire Agitator' and took him to task for

> his determination not to let the few embers of discontent which remained after the last Radnorshire election expire.

However in mid-October Harford Jones Brydges renewed his campaign for Parliamentary reform and in the *Hereford Journal* of 26 October there appeared a requisition to the sheriff signed by 41 electors asking him to call a county meeting to draft an address to William IV in favour of Parliamentary reform. With the exception of the Revd Walter Wilkins of Maesllwch, Jones

Brydges, Revd James Beebee, rector of Presteigne, and Cecil Parsons, a wealthy Presteigne lawyer, the signatories were, in the main, Presteigne tradesmen. The sheriff, Thomas Duppa of Llanshay, Knighton, duly convened a meeting at the Shire Hall on 1 November.

The meeting found Joncs Brydges at his most pompous for he rounded upon Duppa for addressing his notice to the 'freeholders' rather than to the 'freeholders and inhabitants' and for omitting the name of one of the petitioners, Dr Jenkins. He then made a personal attack on Frankland Lewis before proposing that the address, which seems to have been drawn up by him, should be adopted. His motion was seconded by the Revd Walter Wilkins of Maesllwch and supported by Sir John Walsham and William Davies of Cabalfa. It was agreed that the address should be presented to William IV by Jones Brydges and a deputation of gentlemen.[15]

Jones Brydges' championship of reform was clearly popular in Presteigne for in the *Hereford Times* of 28 November there appeared a notice thanking him

> for the prompt attention he had on so many occasions paid to the wishes and interests of the town and the able and unflinching support he has given to the cause of Reform.

The notice was signed by Thomas Beaumont, the bailiff of Presteigne and 162 townsmen.

The passing of the Reform Act in June 1832 was celebrated in Presteigne by the Reform Festival held on 11 August 1832. Proceedings began with the ringing of church bells and then a procession was held though the streets led by carts containing 12 sheep which were to be slaughtered and distributed to the poor, 300 loaves of bread and barrels of cider. The procession was headed by a band and banners carrying legends such as 'Be watchful of our rights' and 'The freeholders of the County of Radnor return their thanks to Earl Grey for his faithful service to Parliament'. Proceedings concluded with a dinner at the Radnorshire Arms where the company dined off a haunch of venison provided by Jones Brydges and 'an excellent dessert from the gardens of Boultibrooke.' Sadly Sir Harford was unable to attend for his wife, Lady Sarah, had recently died.[16]

The return, unopposed, of Richard Price and Frankland Lewis, both opponents of the Reform Act, in December 1832, raises questions as to the extent of support for the cause in the county at large. One can understand the enthusiasm in Presteigne since, as a result of the 1832 Act, the town became a contributory borough, but elsewhere there would seem to have been little enthusiasm for the measure, apart from Whig gentry such as Sir John Walsham, the Wilkins family and William Davies of Cabalfa. However it seems clear that political considerations and allegiances counted for less than personal factors and family connections and patronage when it came to choosing a Member for the county or for the Boroughs.

Walter Wilkins III, 1835-40

In August 1834 the Whig government offered the Conservative Frankland Lewis the chairmanship of the newly formed Poor Law Commission which was to administer the reformed Poor Law, a post which he had no hesitation in accepting. The appointment was not as surprising at it might appear initially. Frankland Lewis had expertise in Poor Law matters for he had written the Report of the Select Committee on the Poor Law in 1817, and in a number of minor government appointments from 1822 onwards he had proved himself to be a competent administrator. Politically he was acceptable since he was not an inflexible Tory but a moderate Conservative.

The appointment required Lewis to resign his seat in Parliament and this gave Walter Wilkins III, the son of Walter Wilkins II (d.1830) and the grandson of Walter Wilkins, the former Radnorshire MP, the opportunity to challenge for what the Radnorshire Whigs had come to regard as the Wilkins family seat. The first hint that he would contest the seat came in the *Hereford Journal* of 20 August in the report of Lewis's resignation. Wilkins lost no time in making his first canvass and, in his electoral address of 23 August, identified himself closely with his grandfather who, during his long tenure of the seat

Plate 12: Walter Wilkins III

had never sought either honour or emolument for himself or his family, preferring your approbation, and the consciousness of having honestly discharged his duty to you.[17]

Wilkins, born in 1809, had matriculated at New College, Oxford, and inherited the Maesllwch estate on the death of his father in 1830. On his return to Radnorshire he became a magistrate and in 1833 was appointed sheriff. His abiding passion was for field sports, particularly hunting, and by 1834 he was master of the fashionable Pytchley Hunt in Leicestershire, a position which he resigned to contest the Radnorshire seat, though he kept a pack at Maesllwch in order to indulge his passion. In his diary Sir John Walsh, his opponent in 1835, rather priggishly characterised Wilkins as ill-educated and a hard riding and hard drinking Tony Lumpkin, too fond of low company for his own good, although later in his 'Retrospective' he acknowledged that Wilkins was 'neither a fool nor a blackguard' and 'had something of the gentleman about him'.[18]

In the meantime Richard Price, the leading Radnorshire Tory, approached Edward Rogers of Stanage to stand against Wilkins in the Conservative interest. Rogers had parliamentary experience, having been one of Bishops Castle's two MPs from 1820 until the seat was abolished in 1832, but alarmed by the speed with which Wilkins had begun his campaign, Rogers at first prevaricated and then, much to Price's fury, decided to withdraw as he felt that 'his nerves and health were not equal to such a contest'. His tardiness made it difficult for any other local Conservative to come forward as many voters, thinking that Wilkins would probably be returned unopposed, had pledged their vote to him. The Radnorshire Conservatives were therefore reduced to promising that they would bring forward a candidate but without the ability to say who it would be.[19]

It was at this point that Sir John Walsh threw his cap into the ring. Born in 1798, he was the son of Sir John Benn Walsh, who had been created a baronet in 1804. He matriculated at Christ Church, Oxford, in 1816, though he did not graduate. He inherited two fortunes made in India, for in 1819, when he came of age, he inherited his grandfather John Walsh's extensive estates in Radnorshire, Ireland and Cumberland, while on his father's death in 1825, he inherited a fortune of more than £100,000 and the family seat of Warfield Park in Berkshire. Since 1830 he had been MP for the borough of Sudbury in Suffolk, but wanted a county seat which he felt carried greater status and would be more secure once it had been won.[20]

Walsh had paid an exploratory visit to Radnorshire at the end of August 1834 and had written to the leading Radnorshire Conservative gentry to see if they would support him. On receiving favourable replies he decided to visit the county again, setting out towards the end of November, armed with a letter of credit for £12,000 drawn on the Kington Bank. His first visit was to James Davies, a partner in the bank and brother-in-law of Frankland Lewis,

> a tall grave-looking, middle-aged man, with a cool, self possessed and businesslike manner, and a great composure in his demeanour.

Davies explained that a new complication had arisen: Sir Robert Peel was in the process of forming a Conservative administration, the Whig government having fallen, and Frankland Lewis though he might be offered a post in Peel's cabinet, which would necessitate his contesting the election for the seat from which he had so recently resigned.

Davies's advice was to visit the Radnorshire gentry, sounding them out and conducting a secret canvass, the result of which would only be made known if Frankland Lewis decided to remain as chairman of the Poor Law Commission. This Walsh did and was favourably received, though many made it clear that their support was conditional on Lewis deciding not to contest the seat, while Richard Price tried to impose a new condition on him, that Walsh should acquire a seat in the county which would become his normal residence.[21]

On his return to London Walsh decided to out-manoeuvre Lewis by exposing his tactics to the Conservative leadership, calculating that Lewis was not as indispensable to Peel as he thought and that Lewis's acceptance of office from the hands of the Whigs had placed him in *mauvais odeur* with the leadership. Walsh's interviews with the Conservative hierarchy in London confirmed his suspicions, the duke of Wellington observing:

> No doubt Mr Frankland Lewis is a very able man and could be of great assistance to Robert Peel in Parliament too ... But as far as opinion goes, it is since Mr F. Lewis has himself chosen his present office he had better remain where he is.

Having resigned his Sudbury seat, Walsh hurried back to Radnorshire, and after explaining what had transpired in London to James Davies, gained his backing. Next day he began canvassing the length and breadth of the county with Richard Green, his election agent, and David James, the Presteigne solicitor and Walsh's man of business in Radnorshire.[22]

Wilkins and his supporters were also busy. In the upper Teme valley and at Llanbister and Llanbadarn Fynydd where backing for the Radnorshire Cottagers, threatened with the loss of the encroachments, was strong, the Presteigne Radicals Cecil Parsons and Robert Lewis, together with Thomas Morgan of Glasbury were active. Thus at Llanbister Morgan was urging his listeners in the name of God come forward and support Mr Wilkins who will set you free from the claws of the Crown.

At Rhayader, Wilkins, accompanied by Sir Harford Jones Brydges and Sir John Walsham, received a rousing welcome. About half a mile from the town they were met by 'the whole population', the horses taken from between the shafts and the coach pulled into town by Wilkins' supporters, preceded by a band. A similar demonstration occurred when Wilkins visited Builth.[23]

Both sides also conducted campaigns in print. In his rather bland electoral address Wilkins advocated economy, the reduction of taxes, abolition of places — paid government appointments involving little or no work — pensions and sinecures, reform of the Church the maintenance of peace at home and abroad and the continuation of civil liberties under the constitution of King, Lords and Commons. His supporters also filled the correspondence columns of the Whig *Hereford Times* week after week with praise of Wilkins and criticism of the outsider Walsh. Walsh's addresses were more overtly political in tone, for in addition to backing Peel's Tamworth Manifesto advocating moderate Conservatism, he stood on a platform of protection, the repeal or partial repeal of the malt tax, freedom of conscience and full civil liberties for dissenters and their exemption from church rates.[24]

Not surprisingly, since it was the first contested election in the constituency for more than 30 years, a large number of anonymous election pamphlets or squibs were published, most of them negative in tone. A number of them have survived, notably in the Banks Archives. One in favour of Wilkins includes the lines:

> Come let us unite with heart and by hand
> To support — not a stranger — but a man of our land

A five verse song in support of Walsh to be sung to the tune of 'Yankee Doodle' lampooned Wilkins' youth and political inexperience:

> My Mummy's lap I've not left long,
> For I am but four and twenty

In another squib or pamphlet, 'Viator' poured scorn on Wilkins' claim that if elected he would persuade the House of Commons to protect the encroachments of the Radnorshire Cottagers, and pointed out that in their manors the Wilkins family insisted upon their manorial rights being observed to the letter and gave encroachers short shrift.[25]

No expense seems to have been spared by either side. When canvassing, dinners were held by Walsh for supporters, not only in the towns of Knighton,

Presteigne and Rhayader, but also in hamlets such as Llanbister and Llanbadarn Fynydd, while more humble supporters were treated to at least a glass of cider or beer. Green seems to have spent Walsh's money rather too freely, for in his diary Walsh grumbled that in addition to a dinner at the Chandos Arms in Knighton, Green had arranged for eight other public houses in the town to be thrown open 'where everybody feasted, whether voters or not', without consulting him. The following day Walsh noted another 'great and unnecessarily expensive' treat at New Radnor. In all Walsh reckoned that he had spent £4,000 on his campaign and Wilkins at least as much, judging by his bill from the Radnorshire Arms, Presteigne, which shows that expenditure in that house alone for the last eight days of the election campaign amounted to £466.[26]

By the close of 1834 both candidates were optimistic. Wilkins had completed a second canvass and announced that the result was 'most honourable to you (the electorate) and most gratifying to us'. In Rhayader Hundred he could rely upon the support of the highly influential Hugh Powell Evans, who objected strongly to the influence exercised in Radnorshire by 'outsiders' such as Richard Banks and James Davies of Kington. Thomas Thomas of Pencerrig and David Thomas of Wellfield also supported Wilkins, while honour dictated that those such as Hugh Vaughan of Llwynmadoc, who had promised Wilkins their vote, should keep their word, in spite of the fact that they now favoured Walsh. Wilkins could also rely upon the support of the tenants of the large Maesllwch estate. On the other hand, James Davies had calculated that with 540 votes out of the 1,074 registered promised to Walsh and with about a hundred voters either dead, neutral or disqualified, Walsh should have a majority of rather more than a hundred.[27]

The Whig *Hereford Times* of 3 January 1835 considered that Wilkins was the decided favourite but by the following week was hedging its bets and predicting that the election day 'would be the severest ever contested in the county'. Certainly the proceedings on nomination day, 13 January, were rowdier than had been the case for decades. The nomination of Walsh by Frankland Lewis was accompanied by groans and shouts of 'No Tories' and when Wilkins was nominated by Hugh Powell Evans, he could scarcely be heard for cheering. For the Liberals, Jones Brydges made an inflammatory speech and the Revd Dr Richard Venables replied in kind on behalf of the Conservatives. Polling took place 16-17 January and the result was declared on Monday, 19 January, Wilkins winning by 27 votes, with 483 votes against Walsh's 456.

An analysis of the voting pattern by electoral districts gives some insight into voting behaviour. In the first place it demonstrates the extent to which landlords could command the votes of their tenants, particularly £50 tenants at will. Thus the Maesllwch estate lay mainly in the Painscastle electoral

Electoral district	Wilkins	Walsh
Colwyn	57	35
Knighton	88	157
Painscastle	123	22
Penybont	43	74
Presteigne	60	33
Radnor	35	88
Rhayader	77	47

Figure 6. Voting pattern by electoral district, 1835
(Source: Hereford Times, *24 January, 1835)*

district and to a lesser extent in the Colwyn district, two of the four electoral districts in which Wilkins obtained the majority of votes cast, some of them out of the great respect which the voters had for his grandfather. His majority of the votes cast in the Rhayader area reflected the electoral influence of Hugh Powell Evans, the 'ould squire', now being eroded by the growing influence of David Oliver and the Lewis Lloyd family. His strong showing in the Rhayader and Presteigne districts may also have been a result of the activity of the Grey Coat Club, whose most influential members were Jones Brydges and Hugh Powell Evans. This was certainly the view of the *Hereford Times* which congratulated the Club on its part in Wilkins' success. Wilkins' reasonable showing in the Knighton district, despite the large Walsh estates in the northern half of the district probably, was probably a result of Whig and Radical agitation in the locality on behalf of the Radnorshire Cottagers.

The *Hereford Times* had no doubt that Walsh's surprisingly good showing, despite his late entry into the electoral race, was the result of Tory landlords commanding the votes of the very vulnerable £50 tenants at will, those who lacked any security of tenure since they were yearly tenants who could be given notice by the landlord by the beginning of the new farming year, usually Lady Day, 25 March. It is worth noting that Walsh's estates lay mainly in the area covered by the Knighton, Penybont and Radnor electoral districts, the three districts in which he obtained a majority of the votes. Walsh's tenants and dependents were no doubt motivated by the same mixture of deference, loyalty and fear as Wilkins' tenants in the Painscastle and Colwyn districts. For his part Walsh attributed his failure to his late entry into the contest, the greater skill of Wilkins' agents, their readiness to resort to bribery and his own failure to win over nonconformists in any significant numbers.[28]

While Wilkins was chaired around the streets of Presteigne and his health drunk in all the inns of the county town at his expense, the real celebration was at Glasbury where Wilkins and his leading supporters dined in style. The church bells were rung, a large bonfire was lit and the population of the surrounding area joined in the celebrations. According to the *Hereford Times* of 28 January, a crowd of more than two thousand consumed an ox, four sheep, 1,200 loaves and six hogsheads of cider in celebrating Wilkins' victory.

The death of William IV in June 1837 necessitated a general election for which Wilkins was well prepared. The Grey Coat Club was still meeting regularly, while the Radical elements in the county, particularly in Presteigne, were still campaigning vigorously on behalf of the Radnorshire Cottagers, and both groups could be counted upon to back Wilkins. Again, he and his lawyers had been watching the county electoral register carefully and using the revision courts, which ruled on eligibility to vote, to ensure that as many Wilkins supporters as possible were registered to vote and contesting the registration of any voter thought to favour the Conservatives. The number of voters on the county electoral register had increased by more than 80% between 1835 and 1837 and the great majority of these new voters were thought to be supporters of Wilkins. Walsh had been nursing the seat to the extent of visiting Radnorshire regularly and being present on all important occasions such as the assizes, quarter sessions and local race meetings, but he had taken care not to commit himself to contesting the seat come what may, for he felt that Frankland Lewis, Price and 'the attornies' (sic), Banks and Davies, were using him. Significantly, the one Conservative electoral organisation set up in 1835, the Knighton Conservative Association, was allowed to lapse. Finally, after some soul searching, Walsh decided in 1837 not to contest Radnorshire, instead standing unsuccessfully at Poole.[29]

Attempts to persuade Henry Thomas of Llwynmadoc, Breconshire, or Edward Rogers of Stanage to stand as the Conservative candidate failed. However Kenyon J. Parker, a London barrister, came forward in the Conservative interest, promising to support reforms 'consistent with the stability of the constitution' and offering the electors of Radnorshire 'an opportunity for emancipating themselves from the dominance of the Whigs'. 'The great unknown', as he was termed by Jones Brydges, paid one short visit to Radnorshire, but failed to stay the course and on 31 July Wilkins was returned unopposed and the usual celebrations ensued, with the Presteigne inns thrown open for the electors and six hogsheads of cider provided for the poor.[30]

However, within a few months the balance of power within the constituency began to shift, giving local Conservatives hopes that they might regain the seat. In September 1837 Wilkins fell seriously ill at Aberystwyth and never completely regained full health, a situation which created a degree of uncertainty. Thus with doubts over his health continuing, in the *Hereford Times* of 28 November 1838, Wilkins was forced to deny the rumour that he was retiring, insisting that he would carry on as long as he had the confidence of the voters. Wilkins' position was also weakened by divisions in the ranks of the Grey Coat Club which may have surfaced at the celebrations of Victoria's coronation in Presteigne in 1837, for while Jones Brydges chaired a celebration dinner at the Castle Inn, his fellow Club member A.H. Wall presided at a rival dinner at the Radnorshire Arms, attended by other members such as the Presteigne attorney, King Stephens. The standing of the Club also suffered when it was alleged that, in order to disguise the poor attendance at the Club dinner at the Castle Inn on 24 May 1838, Jones Brydges had enrolled his head gardener, his working bailiff and his coachman as members and had paid for them to attend.[31]

Sir John Walsh, 1840-68

Plate 13: Sir John Walsh, later the first Baron Ormathwaite, in his dress uniform as Lord Lieutenant of Radnorshire

After failing to secure the Poole seat in 1837, Walsh regained his Sudbury seat in 1838, though he still had designs on Radnorshire. Initially his chances seemed slim for his refusal to contest the seat in 1837 had alienated Richard Price who was now backing Edward Rogers, while Frankland Lewis cherished hopes that the Radnorshire seat would launch his son Cornewall Lewis on a parliamentary career.[32]

Gradually things moved in favour of Walsh, for Price's enthusiasm for Rogers waned, while in 1839 Frankland Lewis was preparing the way for Cornewall Lewis to succeed him as a Poor Law commissioner. Moreover he still retained the support of other senior local Conservatives such as J.C. Severn and his son Percy of Penybont Hall, John Whittaker and P.R. Mynors of Evancoyd, while Walsh's donation of £100 to the Conservative association for watching the register, set up in the autumn of 1837, showed that he was serious in his ambition.[33] By the end of 1839 Richard Price, Frankland Lewis, Edward Rogers and the Revd Dr Richard Venables had also come round.

Walsh was also quietly seeking to erode public confidence in Wilkins, for he could not afford to campaign too aggressively against a sick man since this would have alienated public opinion. The methods employed were revealed by a Whig correspondent who complained bitterly in the *Hereford Times* of 19 January 1839 that while Wilkins was dismissed in the local press by his opponents as 'a good fellow' only 'fit to follow the hounds', Walsh was regarded as a *non pareil*, an author and a man of real ability. Even so the letter writer preferred Wilkins, 'a tried man who does not pretend to flash and dazzle with eloquence'.

Towards the end of November 1839 the Revd Dr Richard Venables informed Walsh that Wilkins, who had now taken the name of de Winton, the family's original name, by royal licence, had deteriorated to the extent that 'he could go off any day' according to his apothecary. A few days later Walsh commissioned the Hay solicitor Pemberton to inform him immediately if de Winton was to die suddenly or if his life was despaired of. De Winton died in the early morning of 28 May 1840 and Walsh, in London, was informed the following day. He immediately resigned his Sudbury seat and secured the support of Frankland Lewis. Writs for elections in Radnorshire and Sudbury were moved that evening and Walsh set out for Presteigne, arriving at 11 am on 30 May. He immediately canvassed the town, assisted by David James, his agent, his brother Edward Lee James and Dr Jenkins of the Grove, who had switched his allegiance, and was favourably received in the town 'which was before so hostile a quarter'. The ground had been prepared for him as his address, printed in London, had been circulated in the town the previous day.[34]

The Whigs appear to have been taken off guard by the speed with which Walsh had reacted to de Winton's death. Thus the *Hereford Times* of 30 May commented:

> There seems to be a pervading apathy throughout the county, but we hope it will be raised in time that Radnorshire men will do their duty.

Given that de Winton's deteriorating health was common knowledge and that in the Grey Coat Club the Whigs had a basic electoral organisation, it is difficult to understand why the Whigs had no contingency plan. There was, however, a growing coldness between Whig club members such as Jones Brydges, H.P. Evans, Walsham and their Radical allies such as the Parsons brothers, probably as a result of the Whig government's failure to act on behalf of the Radnorshire Cottagers.

The *Hereford Times* of 30 May had speculated that a Liberal candidate would be in the field, and placards were issued calling upon electors to reserve their votes. However Jones Brydges' attempt to persuade first Thomas Prickard and then Thomas Evans of Llwynbarried to stand came to nothing.

General Sir Love Jones Parry, who had represented the county of Caernarfon in the Commons between 1835 and 1837, arrived in Presteigne on 2 June to explore the possibility of standing in the Liberal interest, but after a brief canvass decided to withdraw.

Walsh's canvass, however, was going well, with many pledges of support, while some potential opponents were adopting a stance of neutrality. This was certainly the case with the old Whig, Hugh Powell Evans, who commented:

> Do you think, Sir John, that if we had intended starting, we should have sat with our hands before us, allowing you to canvass the county first.[35]

On nomination day, 10 June, the houses of Walsh's supporters in Presteigne were decorated with blue flags and streamers, laurel and oak boughs, while 'the windows of the different houses exhibited an array of lovely women decorated with blue favours'.

Walsh was returned unopposed and chaired through the streets of the town in 'an elegant car' covered in blue satin and decorated with blue ribbons. The 'good and the great' of the county dined at the Radnorshire Arms, while humbler supporters were also provided for as meal tickets were distributed for all the Presteigne inns except the Oxford Arms, which refused to co-operate. Cider was also distributed in the course of the evening to all and sundry, with the inevitable resulting 'scenes of drunkenness of a revolting description' according to the sour report in the Whig *Hereford Times* of 13 June, together with several 'pugilistic encounters'. The Conservative *Hereford Journal*, flushed with victory, took a more relaxed view:

> The whole proceedings were conducted with the utmost good feeling if we except a fight or two among the humbler classes, who seem to regard an exhibition of this kind as indispensable on such an occasion.

The general election of July 1841 was a result of a defeat for the Whig government in the Commons on a motion of no confidence in its plans to repeal the Corn Laws. Within a few days it became clear that Walsh would face opposition for he noted in his diary that the Radicals Guy Parsons and T.L. Townsend were active, while Hugh Powell Evans and his brother-in-law Prickard were thought to be conspiring. In mid-June Lord Harley, the heir to the earl of Oxford, issued his electoral address, stressing the Liberal sentiments and traditions of his family and his support for civil and religious liberty, but emphasising his disagreement with the government's proposal to repeal the Corn Laws which, by imposing a duty on imported grain, gave British farmers a measure of protection against foreign competition.[36]

Harley had some grounds for optimism, for the revising barristers had allowed the Radnorshire Cottagers, to be included on the electoral register, and the great majority of those could be expected to back him rather than Walsh who, although he had not condemned them publicly, had not taken a neutral stance. The Grey Coat Club, said by the Radical J.P. Glen in the *Hereford Times* to be 'dead or dying of inanity', had been replaced by a Liberal Association, chaired by A.H. Wall, in which energetic Radicals such as Glen, Townsend and the Parsons brothers were prominent.[37]

Though Walsh privately regarded Harley as a 'second edition' of Walter Wilkins III and a 'stupid, ignorant booby', he took him seriously and canvassed thoroughly, declaring that he stood for Conservative principles in Church and State and the maintenance and support of British agriculture, that is, he opposed the amendment of the Corn Laws. In an electoral address published in the *Hereford Times* of 30 June he pointed out the contradiction in Harley's stance, that if he was elected, by supporting the Whig government he was backing a modification of the Corn Laws, a policy of which he disapproved.

Yet Harley's candidacy was complicating Walsh's relations with some of his supporters, for Richard Price declined to propose Walsh because 'he owed so much in early life to the Oxford family', though eventually, with bad grace, he agreed to second Walsh's nomination. P.R. Mynors declined to take a prominent role in Walsh's campaign as the earl of Oxford was backing the campaign of his brother T.B.M. Baskerville of Clyro Court, who was standing in the Liberal interest in Herefordshire.[38]

Electoral district	Harley	Walsh
Colwyn	54	111
Knighton	93	330
New Radnor	28	136
Painscastle	104	72
Penybont	63	134
Presteigne	42	80
Rhayader	120	102

Figure 7. Voting pattern by district, 1841

Voting took place over 9-10 July and at the end of the first day it was clear that Walsh would win decisively for he led by 871 votes to 429. From the figures given in the *Hereford Times* of 14 July it is possible to analyse the voting pattern by electoral districts. Thus Figure 7 shows that Walsh dominated the poll in those electoral districts in which his estates lay and where Lewis of Harpton and Price influence was considerable, while Harley polled well in the Painscastle district, where de Winton influence remained strong, and Rhayader, where Hugh Powell Evans and the Prickards still exerted much influence. Surprisingly Harley polled badly in the Presteigne district, traditionally a Whig/Radical stronghold, possibly as a result of some Whigs, alienated by the Radicals' aggressive championship of the Radnorshire Cottagers, switching their support to Walsh. With the total adjusted to include non-resident votes, Walsh polled 1,102 votes and Harley 522.

The Liberals seem to have been taken aback by the scale of their defeat and a Presteigne Conservative gleefully commented in the *Hereford Times* of 14 July, 'All the Whig party in our town look fifty years older than they did last Friday!' Harley attributed his defeat to the failure of the Radnorshire Cottagers to back him in sufficient numbers, thanks to the influence exercised by Richard Banks in his capacity as steward of the Crown manors. He alleged that Banks and his ally Morris Sayce canvassed trespassers on the commons in the Crown manors in Walsh's interest and had attended polling stations to intimidate known trespassers into voting for Walsh. The implication was that those with encroachments on such commons who did not vote for Walsh would shortly find their encroachments thrown open, with their fences pulled down.

The Commissioners for Woods and Forests who supervised the administration of Crown lands had instructed Banks to be impartial and on receipt of Harley's complaint asked Banks to explain himself. He maintained that he had attended only one polling station, that at New Radnor, in order to cast his vote and asked that Harley should either substantiate his charges or withdraw them. Harley replied that on nomination day Banks had been at the Shire Hall in Presteigne, 'amongst the warmest cheering Walsh' and that Guy Parsons had seen him at Penybont polling station on the first day of the poll with James Davies, while a supporter of Walsh had stated that Banks had also attended Rhayader polling station on that date. Harley also had evidence that Banks and Davies had also been at Penybont polling station on the second day of the poll and that both of them had attended Walsh's central committee room at Llandegley, facts confirmed by Walsh's diary. The commissioners, however, do not appear to have taken any action against Banks. The diary also suggests that some of the Presteigne Radicals were thought to be considering an appeal to the House of Commons to set aside the election, though in the end they took no action.[39]

The 1841 election cost Walsh about £4,000, but it was money well spent since he was unchallenged for the remainder of his time in the Commons, being returned unopposed in 1847, 1852, 1857, 1859 and 1865. Even so, initially he was not as secure as one might assume, for his appointment as Lord Lieutenant of Radnorshire soured his relations with Frankland Lewis, Richard Price and Edward Rogers for a time, while the repeal of the Corn Laws in 1846 had raised the political temperature as Walsh's stance on this question provoked opposition in both Whig and high Tory circles in Radnorshire. Walsh had written to Sir Robert Peel, the Prime Minister who had introduced the repeal of the Corn Laws, declining to support the measure, had spoken against it on the second reading and in his election address made it clear that he could not support repeal. On the other hand he abstained in the division which led to the fall of Peel's government and was by no means an arch-Protectionist for he maintained a low profile at the Protectionist meeting held at Presteigne at the end of January 1850 and steered clear of attaching himself to Derby and Disraeli, the Conservative Protectionist leaders. In the circumstances it is not surprising to find that in 1847 some Conservatives such as Richard Price and the Severns of Penybont Hall were hostile and that the Radical A.H. Wall was said to be plotting, while in 1851 there was a rumour that a Peelite would contest the next county election.[40] Walsh's moderate stance had thus offended every shade of political opinion in the county.

By the mid-1850s rising agricultural prices had taken the heat out of the Repeal issue and although Richard Green, Walsh's former agent, had defected to the Whigs along with others, mainly in the Rhayader area, there was no talk of opposition. The elections of 1857 and 1865 were particularly quiet, for the former was described in the *Hereford Times* of 4 April as 'a most uninteresting affair' while the *Hereford Journal* of 22 July said of the 1865 election:

> Within half an hour there was scarcely an outward and visible sign that a county election had taken place.

However the lack of incident and the lack of crowds probably resulted as much from the legislation against 'treating' as from the fall in the political temperature and local apathy.

The size of Walsh's majority in 1841 may have deterred potential rivals in the short run, but his retention of the county seat from 1840 until 1868 when he was raised to the peerage as Baron Ormathwaite can be attributed to a number of factors. The dislike of contested elections by the establishment may have contributed, along with the popular belief that there was a tacit understanding between the two sitting members in order to avoid a contest in either constituency. Alternatively the lack of contested elections in either constituency until 1869 may have been the result of a conscious decision on the part of the county elite to ensure that both Conservatives and Liberals in Radnorshire were represented in the Commons. This was certainly the belief of many in the county, as H.M. Jones, the Presteigne postmaster recalled in 1875:

> Radnorshire had been peculiarly noted for what we might term the carrying on of a particularly even balance of power: for a great many years it had sent 'one in and one out' to the House of Commons.[41]

The steady extension of the Walsh estate in the county from about 6,000 acres (2,428 ha) in 1833 to nearly 12,500 acres (5,059 ha) in 1873 may also have been a factor, for it greatly increased the number of votes he could command. Walsh also exercised considerable powers of patronage in the county as a result of his appointment as Lord Lieutenant in 1842, an appointment which gave him control over commissions and promotions in the county militia and the volunteer corps, and the dominant influence in the appointment of justices of the peace in the county.[42]

More significantly he took great care to nurse the constituency and showed considerable skill in doing so. He kept a close eye on the electoral register to ensure that potential supporters were included and unqualified voters thought to be hostile to him weeded out. He also gained good will by his regular attendance at quarter sessions and other official occasions and at major social functions in the county such as the Radnorshire Agricultural Society show or Knighton races, and by his generous donations to church restoration appeals and other causes in the county. Given that he never acquired a seat in the county, instead renting successively Downton, Knill Court, Newcastle Court and Eywood near Titley, the prominent role he played in county society is surprising.

He was also assiduous in his canvassing, paying attention to opponents and the uncommitted as well as his supporters, and not only visiting the seats of the gentry, but also meeting the rank and file electors by attending farmers' ordinaries on fair days and race days. Throughout his political career he saw himself as independent in his views rather than a narrow party man at the beck and call of the Conservative hierarchy of the Carlton Club, the oldest Conservative club. As he wrote in his diary in 1854:

> While I remained strongly attached to Conservative politics, I wished to preserve an independent position as regarded party.[43]

Plate 14: Knill Court, the Radnorshire home of Sir John Walsh from 1839 until 1866

Such a stance broadened his electoral appeal and brought him a measure of support from some Whigs in the county, notably the two sons of the Revd Dr Venables, the Revd Richard Lister Venables and George Stovin Venables, since for much of Walsh's political career the political parties were in a state of flux after the bitter controversy over the Repeal of the Corn Laws and there was little love lost between Whig and Radical elements in the Liberal Party. However by the 1860s the line dividing Conservative and Liberal became much clearer and the room for manoeuvre on the part of the more independent MPs was greatly reduced. Thus Walsh found himself brought more tightly within the orbit of the Conservative party organisation controlled by the Carlton Club. Significantly, his two requests of 1858 and 1859 to Lord Derby to be raised to the peerage were couched in party political terms. In March 1858 he saw his request as being part of a plan to strengthen the Conservative party in the House of Lords, while in January 1859, with the possibility of a dissolution of the House in the air, he suggested that should he be raised to the peerage, he could ensure the return of his son Arthur as the Member for Radnorshire, thus maintaining Conservative strength in the Commons.[44]

3 The Radnor Boroughs Seat, 1869-85

When in the run up to the 1868 Boroughs election Richard Green Price identified himself unreservedly with Gladstone and Liberal policies, he was committing himself to party politics to an extent not seen previously in nineteenth-century Radnorshire constituencies. Party politics made a further advance in the county when, in January 1869, Green Price announced that he was resigning his seat in favour of Lord Hartington, a move designed to further the interests of the Liberal party rather than those of the constituency. The scheme was welcomed by the Liberal leadership since Hartington was to be Postmaster General in Gladstone's government, with a seat in the Cabinet, but had been defeated in the general election of November 1868.

When informed of the scheme by Green Price in December 1868, Gilbert Frankland Lewis had objected strongly since he wished to see the seat held by a Radnorshire man rather than an outsider and had hoped to see his son, Herbert Lewis, ultimately succeed Green Price. However when the Earl of Clarendon, Gladstone's Foreign Secretary, intervened on behalf of Hartington, Gilbert Frankland Lewis agreed, provided that the local Liberals were fully consulted, so that the scheme did not appear to be a naked exercise of Lewis/Green Price electoral power and that at the next general election Hartington would seek a seat elsewhere. Frankland Lewis remained dubious of the scheme since he feared that local resentment might lead to a contested election and the erosion of Lewis/Green Price electoral influence, but the family connection with Clarendon carried the day — his brother Cornewall Lewis had married Clarendon's sister Therese — and he reluctantly gave way.[1]

The Marquis of Hartington, 1869-80

Spencer Compton Cavendish assumed the courtesy title of the Marquis of Hartington in 1858 when his father became the Duke of Devonshire. Hartington was a Liberal grandee, sitting in the Commons for North East Lancashire, who served in the War Office in 1863. He had no connection with Radnorshire until January 1869 when Green Price proposed resigning in Hartington's favour.

Plate 15: *The Marquis of Hartington*

During the last week of January Green Price brought Hartington to introduce him to the Boroughs. Conscious of the need to gain the approval of the electorate Green Price organised a public meeting in each of the contributory boroughs, chaired by a reliable supporter, such as Isaac Rutter in Knighton, Cecil Parsons in Presteigne and Thomas Prickard in Rhayader, the understanding being that if the local Liberals did not approve, Hartington would give way and Green Price would seek re-election. At each meeting, after Green Price had explained his action, a resolution in favour was proposed by an eminent local supporter — Dr Covernton at Knighton, Dr Richardson at Rhayader and Captain Corbett at Presteigne — and carried by an overwhelming majority. Such meetings, clearly packed, were clearly designed to give the arrangement the appearance of popular backing.[2]

The introduction of a complete stranger, no matter how distinguished, provoked some resentment, for the arrangement was clearly in the interests of the Liberal party rather than the constituency. The Conservative *Hereford Journal* of 23 January suggested that in return for arranging Hartington's return for the Boroughs, he would rent Norton Manor at a rent high enough to compensate Green Price for giving up the seat. According to the *Journal*, Hartington would quit the Boroughs seat at the end of the Parliament and then 'Norton Manor would retire in favour of Harpton Court', suggesting that the Lewises of Harpton were colluding with Green Price. The same issue of the *Journal* also contained two letters highly critical of the arrangement: 'Slippery Dick' of Rhayader had no doubts, the electors 'had been bargained for and had been sold', while 'Simon Legree' of Kington, noting that there were 841 voters on the constituency register, advertised:

> 841 Whites for sale. I have driven them for five years, and I can put them on my word as being generally tractable and well trained.

When Richard Green Price received a baronetcy in Gladstone's Dissolution Honours List in 1874 cynics saw this as the reward he received for sacrificing his seat to Lord Hartington.

Despite some reservations on the part of the Hon Arthur Walsh who had succeeded his father as Conservative Member for the county in 1868, Lord Ormathwaite (the previous MP, Sir John Walsh), together with Robert Mynors of Evancoyd and Captain James Beavan, decided to exploit the unease and contest the Boroughs seat in the Conservative interest, selecting G.H. Philips of Abbey Cwm Hir as their candidate. The Abbey Cwm Hir estate, amounting to 6,236 acres (2,524 ha) in 1873, had been purchased in 1837 by Francis Aspinall Philips of Ardwick, Manchester, who had made his fortune in the textile industry. The estate had been vested in his second son, George Henry, born in 1831 and educated at Christ Church, Oxford. In keeping with his status as proprietor of one of the largest estates in the county, after serving as sheriff in 1860, Philips was appointed a JP and deputy lieutenant for Radnorshire.[3]

The reluctance of Arthur Walsh to back a challenge to Hartington may have stemmed from a belief that it would be difficult to mount an effective challenge from scratch in the few weeks available. Alternatively he may have feared that a Conservative intervention in the Boroughs would provoke a Liberal challenge in the county seat. This was certainly the theme in the letter from 'A Radnorshire Subscriber' published in the *Hereford Times* of 30 January 1869, which suggested that the Liberals had twice treated Arthur Walsh with great consideration by not contesting the County seat in the two elections of 1868 and went on to ask of any prospective Conservative voter:

Does he think that if Philips is returned for the Boroughs Walsh would not meet with strong opposition in the county?

Plate 16: Abbey Cwm Hir, the home of G.H. Philips

The uncertainty surrounding Philips' candidacy can be seen in Ormathwaite's diary. On 23 January he noted that Stephens believed that Philips did not have a chance of winning and on 12 February that Mynors was urging Philips not to go to the poll, yet on 18 February that a meeting held at Penybont decided that Philips should go ahead. Given that the election was scheduled for 25 February, these last minute misgivings did not augur well for Philips' chances.[4]

Publicly however the Conservatives campaigned energetically, each of the boroughs were canvassed thoroughly and public meetings held in each one. In his address Philips stressed his advocacy of 'Progressive Conservatism, the Constitution and Freedom of Worship' and his opposition to Irish disestablishment in that as member of the Established Church he upheld 'the Protestant character of the religion of our country'. In the public meetings, however, the central theme was that Hartington was an outsider, foisted on the electorate by the Lewis and (Green) Price families and that Radnor should be represented by a Radnorshire man. Thus Robert Lewis Lloyd, introducing Philips in a meeting in Rhayader, commented:

> If they were willing to accept the first gentleman, be he lord or commoner who was thrust down their throat, then God help them.[5]

The nomination of candidates on 23 February was the liveliest such occasion for decades. Hartington was nominated by the Revd Sir Gilbert Lewis and seconded initially by Cecil Parsons. There were some doubts as to the legality of Parsons' action since he was not qualified to vote in the Boroughs seat, so Captain Corbett formally took his place. Philips was nominated by Captain Beavan of Presteigne, who was barracked after he alleged that the seat had been a pocket borough of the Price and Lewis families for decades. Philips' nomination was seconded by Mr J. Edwards of Broadheath, Presteigne, who was 'greeted with derisive epithets'. After he maintained that the voters wanted a Radnorshire man and that

> The Conservative voters had no idea of being transferred from pillar to post at the behest of a few individuals

(referring to the Liberals' selection of Hartington) he was constantly interrupted and could be heard only with difficulty. When Hartington made his speech accepting the nomination, he too was barracked, being interrupted by cries of 'Bought and sold'.[6]

At the election on 25 February, Hartington scored a decisive victory, receiving 546 votes against Philips 176, in a turnout of 86%. A breakdown of the vote shows that, in spite of the marked increase in the electorate, the great landowners could still 'command' the votes of their dependents, either through pressure or as a result of deference. It would, after all, take considerable moral courage to stand up in public and vote against one's landlord's wishes and interests. Thus in the Price/Lewis strongholds Hartington received 162 out of 172 votes cast in Knighton, 197 out of 255 votes in New Radnor and 120 of 150 votes cast in Presteigne. At Rhayader, his home district, Philips did less well than might have been expected, gaining 67 out of 120 votes cast, as the major landowners in the borough were divided in their loyalties.[7]

At the declaration of the poll Hartington's speech was interrupted by at least one shout of 'Who sold the Boroughs?' and this charge was to haunt Richard Green Price for the

Plate 17: Revd Gilbert Frankland Lewis, by Rannie Swinton, 1843

rest of his political life. Thus when contesting the county seat in 1874 and 1880 he was taunted at the hustings with

> There was an MP came from Norton,
> His stay in the House was a short 'un,
> For as I am told,
> Radnor Boroughs he sold,
> And the Marquis of Hartington bought 'em.[8]

Given the very hot contest for the county seat five years later in 1874, when both Green Price and Haig sought to oust Arthur Walsh, the Boroughs election of that year went off very quietly, despite the prediction of the *Globe* that the Liberal intervention in the county constituency would provoke Conservative retaliation in the Boroughs seat. Hartington simply ignored Gilbert Frankland Lewis's reminder that the understanding was for Hartington to retire from the Boroughs seat at the end of the Parliament since

> With your personal and political connexions, at a general election you
> will have no difficulty in finding a seat with a more important constitu-
> ency and where you have legitimate influence,

offering only to consult with Green Price. Since his brother-in-law, the Whig grandee the earl of Clarendon had died in 1870, Gilbert Frankland Lewis had no means of exerting pressure upon the Liberal leadership and had no option but to accept Hartington's candidacy.[9] Possibly because they were preoccupied in keeping the county seat, possibly because they were in awe of Hartington's status, and possibly because they did not wish to alienate some of their supporters such as the Venables brothers, who had Whiggish sympathies, the Conservatives did not sanction an official candidate initially.

Even so, Hartington did not get a free run, for he was opposed by Captain George William Cockburn of the 42nd Highlanders, the Black Watch, and a veteran of the Indian Mutiny. He was a son of Sir William Cockburn of Downton and resented the imposition of Hartington on the Boroughs by the Price/Lewis establishment, but gained little support, even though he was kindly received at meetings at Knighton, Presteigne and Rhayader, thanks to his engaging, if somewhat eccentric manner, which led him to represent himself as 'a thoroughbred Welsh pony' running gamely against 'an English racehorse', Lord Hartington.[10]

Hartington on the other hand attracted widespread and enthusiastic support, particularly from the Knighton townspeople, who seem to have adopted him as one of their own. Even so he made little attempt to nurse the constituency, preferring to visit the Boroughs occasionally for social events. When he arrived at Knighton railway station on 29 January 1874 to begin his campaign, he was greeted by a huge crowd; supporters took the horses from between the shafts of the carriage sent to collect him and drew it to his hotel, the Norton Arms, through cheering crowds. However the occasion was marred by a tragedy, for as the coach came down the slope from the railway bridge, it ran over the 7-year-old son of a railway carpenter, Robert Morris, who subsequently died of his injuries. Unaware of the accident, Hartington took the opportunity to address the crowd from the steps of his hotel.[11]

At the election, on 6 February, the first to be held by secret ballot, Cockburn, standing as a Conservative, gained 162 votes to Hartington's 612. He blamed his defeat on the pressure exerted in the Boroughs by the agent of the Harpton estate and the failure of the tenant farmers to understand that the ballot was indeed secret.[12]

By mid-1879, with a general election becoming increasingly likely, Hartington, since 1875 the leader of the Liberals in the Commons, began to consider contesting his old constituency of North East Lancashire in order to break the Conservative monopoly of the Lancashire seats. In the end it was decided that he should also contest the Radnor Boroughs as insurance, but the Boroughs Liberals were to have a candidate ready to fight the by-election should Hartington win both seats.[13]

For the most part the local Liberal establishment supported this solution, although the Revd Sir Gilbert Frankland Lewis had some reservations concerning Hartington's candidacy. The minority view amongst the Liberals was reflected in the letter of 'An Elector in the Vale of Radnor' in the *Hereford Times* of 23 September 1879:

> Electors will prefer one who lives amongst us, who is bound to us by the ties of property and one who spends his money amongst us.

He went on to blame the Price/Lewis monopoly of power in the Boroughs constituency for the imposition of an outsider on the constituency, reflecting the view of the Conservative *Hereford Journal* of 23 August which likened the Boroughs electorate to a shuttlecock 'for the Harpton Court and Norton Manor battledores'.

In the end the local Liberals and Conservatives agreed that Hartington should be given a free run and be returned unopposed. However on nomination day, the maverick Captain Cockburn decided to intervene. He found a proposer and a seconder amongst those drinking in the Eagle Inn, but when he tried to pay his deposit of £75 by cheque, the Bailiff of New Radnor and returning officer, R.B. Mynors, refused to accept it. Cockburn then sent some children to houses in New Radnor in an attempt to find the necessary cash and when they failed to return, he set out to raise it himself. When, after two hours, Cockburn had failed to re-appear, Mynors declared Hartington returned unopposed.[14]

His success was greeted with delight in Knighton and a torchlight procession, led by the Leintwardine band, with banners inscribed 'The Marquis of Hartington and Sir Richard Green Price for ever' and 'Welcome to Mr S.C. Evans Williams', the reserve candidate in the event of a by-election, who was cheered through the streets.[15] As Hartington was indeed also returned for North East Lancashire, and opted to sit for that constituency, a by-election was necessary.

Stephen Charles Evans Williams, 1880-84

The possibility that Hartington would win the North East Lancashire seat had been anticipated by both parties and the Liberals had been seeking a suitable candidate since mid-1879. Amongst those mentioned as possible candidates were Sir Henry James, a kinsman of the Rogers family of Stanage and a future attorney general, and Isaac Rutter, the wool stapler and bailiff of Knighton who, as a Primitive Methodist, could be expected to appeal to nonconformists. The local Whig element favoured George Stovin Venables, a barrister and parliamentary counsel, the second son of the Revd Dr Richard Venables

Plate 18: Stephen Charles Evans Williams

of Llysdinam. He would have gained the support of the Revd Sir Gilbert Frankland Lewis, the Revd T.C. Prickard, the leader of the Liberals in the Boroughs constituency, and Charles Coltman Rogers of Stanage Park, but was concerned at Gladstone's drift towards more radical policies and was unwilling to take part in any selection process. Such a process was deemed necessary by the local leadership in order to prevent a split between the Whig and Radical wings of the local party. Accordingly it was decided that ten representatives of each of the boroughs in the constituency should meet at the end of October 1879 to select a candidate by majority vote.[16]

This system of selection was favoured by Joseph Chamberlain and the Birmingham Liberals, and although such a 'Brummagem' caucus was far from popular in the Radnor Boroughs, it was a means of maintaining party unity and selecting the candidate with the widest support. This proved to be Stephen Charles Evans Williams of Bryntirion, a descendant of David Williams of 'The Red Shop' in Rhayader, whose grandmother, Abigail was a sister of Hugh Powell Evans of Noyadd. A substantial land owner, educated at Westminster School and Christ Church, Oxford and Lincoln's Inn, Evans Williams was a close ally of Sir Richard Green Price and like him had steadily become more radical over the years. A requisition asking him to stand had been circulating in August 1879 and he had issued an address backing electoral reform, the removal of restrictions on the transfer and cultivation of land, reform of the Game Laws and of local taxation and increased local self-government. Though he was a loyal Churchman, he was prepared to advocate disestablishment of the Anglican Church, though he believed that the time was not yet ripe for this.[17]

His Conservative opponent was Cecil Alfred Tufton Otway, a captain in the 2nd Life Guards, born in 1845, who took up residence at The Grove, Presteigne in 1874 and moved to Newcastle Court in 1881. His family were no strangers to the county since his maternal grandfather, General Sir William Loftus Otway CB, had purchased the Grange of Cwmdeuddwr from the Duke of Newcastle in 1844 and had lived at Cwm Elan during his stays in the county. Once in residence at The Grove, Captain Otway maintained a high profile in the south-east of the county, despite his seemingly indifferent health.

A four–in-hand coaching enthusiast, in the summer of 1875 he ran a coach between Kington and Llandrindod Wells and in the following year, between Presteigne and Rhayader. In the autumn of 1879 he played a leading role in setting up a football team in Presteigne and in raising funds for its cricketers. His gifts of money and coal to the poor of Knighton and Presteigne at Christmas in 1878 and 1879 led to accusations that he was nursing the Boroughs seat, a charge given some validity

Plate 19: Captain Cecil Otway

by W.O. Banks' introduction of Otway to a Conservative meeting in Knighton: 'This is the gentleman who gives coal to the poor'.[18]

Otway claimed to be a moderate Conservative and a champion of the Church. He opposed disestablishment and the widening of the county franchise, advocated measures to relieve the distress of agriculture and commerce and favoured the continuation of Sunday opening of public houses.[19] His relative youth, his open, easy manner, together with his obvious interest in sport brought him much popularity amongst the younger voters, as did Mrs Otway's breaking with convention and addressing some of her husband's political meetings. The young, well-connected and glamorous cavalry officer was very popular with most people in the county, although Sir Richard Green Price sought to undermine his campaign by suggesting that Otway had not lived in Radnorshire long enough to justify his contesting the Boroughs seat.

By contrast Evans Williams seemed rather pedestrian and thoroughly provincial to many outside the Rhayader area where his qualities were better known. He does not seem to have been well regarded by some in the Radnorshire establishment, not even by such Whigs as the Venables brothers of Llysdinam or the Lewis family of Harpton Court. His willingness to compete for the support of the rank and file party members in the caucus system of selection and his enthusiasm for the more radical elements of Gladstone's programme such as the widening of the franchise and the introduction of compulsory education, seemed to some to show that he was essentially a politician, ready to put the interests of his party before those of the Boroughs. The *Hereford Journal* had no doubt that Evans Williams was no more than a creature of Sir Richard Green Price who, by standing for the county seat and backing Evans Williams for the Boroughs, was 'riding two horses'. Later the newspaper cast doubts upon Evans Williams' standing:

> The descent from Sir George Cornewall and the Marquis of Hartington to Mr Evans Williams is certainly very great.[20]

Orchestrated by the Liberal party agent, Hugh Vaughan Thomas, and the Conservative agents Williams Stephens of Presteigne and E.H. Cheese of Hay-on-Wye, both sides campaigned vigorously. Both held meetings in each of the boroughs and some of these were seriously disrupted by organised groups of opponents. This was particularly so in Knighton and Presteigne where feelings ran high and virtually all the houses in both towns showed either Conservative or Liberal colours. In Presteigne a Liberal meeting in the Assembly Rooms, invaded by 20 or 30 youths and young men, almost ended in a pitched battle. At Knucklas a man was killed when he was struck on the head by a stone thrown from the crowd.[21]

It was perhaps a sign of a new political age that on nomination day the county establishment took a back seat, for Otway was proposed by Captain James Beavan, the son of a Presteigne blacksmith and still not completely accepted by the county elite, seconded by John Bostock Rogers, a farmer of Knighton, while Evans Williams was proposed by Isaac Rutter of Knighton and seconded by the Presteigne builder, John Davies. Voting took place on 14 May and initially it was believed that Otway had won, for at close of the poll at 4 pm it was reported that at Presteigne Otway had received two-thirds of the votes cast, at New Radnor a 'large majority' of the votes, while at Knighton the polling was equal. It was thought that only at Rhayader had Evans Williams secured a majority of the votes. It was thus with some relief that the Liberals greeted the final result, in which Evans Williams polled 458 votes to Otway's 390, with a turnout of 89.7%. The majority of 68 was much less than the Liberals had been expecting, while Otway's defeat was explained by the *Hereford Journal* in terms of 'broken promises and deceit' and 'superhuman efforts on the part of Norton Manor' and was regarded as a moral victory by the Conservatives.[22]

At Rhayader Evans Williams was greeted by cheering crowds who dragged his carriage to the town hall where he thanked his supporters. At Presteigne, however, Otway received a more rapturous welcome. The band of the 1st Radnorshire Volunteers met the Otways on their return from New Radnor a little way from the town and supporters drew the Otway carriage to the Radnorshire Arms. Otway, having a heavy cold, was unable to speak, but his younger brother Jocelyn and Captain Beavan addressed the crowd. Rejoicings continued the following day when, preceded by the Volunteers' band, Otway's coach was 'pulled through the length and breadth of the town' by supporters while others followed with flags and banners. Otway's 'cardinal flag' also hung from many of the houses — instead of the usual Conservative blue, Otway had used red as his election colour, to signify the red coat of the British soldier.

During the week after the election both Evans Williams and Otway received enthusiastic welcomes from their supporters at Knighton where feelings were still running high. Prior to leaving for London to take up his seat in the Commons Evans addressed a huge crowd from the balcony of his hotel, the Swan, and the following morning supporters pulled his carriage from the Swan to the railway station. The next day when Otway arrived in Knighton by train, his carriage was drawn to his hotel by his supporters in a large procession headed by a German travelling band which happened to be in the town at the time.[23]

Charles Coltman Rogers, 1884-85

Although Otway had been ill since the beginning of 1883 and was advised to avoid a damp climate, in June 1884, while convalescing at Brighton, he accepted an invitation to contest the Boroughs seat at the next election. However he died at Brighton in August and thus the Conservatives were left without a candidate when Evans Williams resigned the seat unexpectedly at the beginning of October. The obvious local candidate was Sir Herbert Lewis of Harpton Court, but he declined to stand. Captain Otway's younger brother Jocelyn was willing to contest the seat for the Conservatives, but he was abroad until 28 October and since nomination was scheduled for 30 October, his candidacy was impracticable. Reluctantly the local Conservative leadership had to face the prospect of a Liberal walkover.[24]

Evans Williams' resignation astonished the local Liberals, one of whom described the news as 'a thunderbolt'. As Williams gave no public explanation for his action any discussion of his reasons must be at best conjectural. He may have felt duty bound to resign as the seat was certainly scheduled for abolition in the redistribution of seats which would accompany the extension of the franchise as a result of the Third Reform Bill then on its way through the Commons. During the 1880 election campaign the Conservatives had argued that a vote for Evans Williams was a vote for the abolition of the Boroughs seat, an argument he countered by vowing not to vote for any measure which entailed its abolition. In the autumn of 1884 Williams was thus faced with the prospect of failing to support his party or going back on his word.[25] However, the long periods of time he spent at European spas in the later 1880s and after he left the county in 1895 suggests that his resignation may have stemmed from health problems, though there is no reference to his health in the local Press.[25]

One potential successor to Evans Williams was Charles Coltman Rogers of Stanage. He was in Scotland at the time of the resignation, but even so the Knighton Liberals began a campaign on his behalf, a move which caused annoyance in some of the other contributory boroughs, particularly in Presteigne. The son of the Revd John Rogers, born in 1854 and educated at Eton and Brasenose College, Oxford, Charles Coltman Rogers served as a magistrate in Herefordshire and

Plate 20: Charles Coltman Rogers

Shropshire and as a magistrate and deputy lieutenant in Radnorshire, where he was appointed sheriff in 1882.

A rumour briefly circulated that the prominent south Wales Liberal, Arthur Thomas, the future Lord Pontypridd would in fact be the Liberal candidate.[26]

Plate 21: Stanage Park by J.M. Ince, the home of Edward Rogers and Charles Coltman Rogers

Another possible candidate was the Revd T.C. Prickard, a substantial land-owner in the Rhayader area and a kinsman to Evans Williams, but he ruled himself out of the running almost immediately. Instead, after Rogers had met a Liberal delegation and consented to stand, Prickard had accompanied him on visits to each of the boroughs and had taken the chair at Rhayader where Rogers was formally adopted as the Liberal candidate. In the eyes of some, however, he was still the second choice, for at the Rhayader meeting, according to the *Hereford Journal*, there was general disappointment that Prickard had declined selection, while some believed that Rogers' politics were not 'strong enough', in other words that his views were too Whiggish.[27]

In his election address Rogers stood on a platform of general support of the Liberal cause and Gladstone's administration and in particular in support of the Reform Bill, and the alteration, if necessary of the constitution of the House of Lords to achieve this. He backed the other elements of the Liberal programme, notably reform of the system of local government and local control of the liquor trade. He addressed at least one public meeting in each of the boroughs over the next fortnight or so, possibly to show that he was taking the election seriously though he was fully aware that the Boroughs seat would be abolished within a year or so.

At New Radnor on 30 October Rogers was returned unopposed. Again the Liberal establishment figures kept a low profile for he was proposed and seconded by Thomas Duggan of Evenjobb and John Stephens of Womaston respectively representing the farming interest, and proposed and seconded by Isaac Rutter of Knighton and John Davies of Presteigne, representing the commercial interests of the constituency. (Multiple nominations had evolved as a means of demonstrating the breadth of a candidate's electoral support.) The following evening Rogers took his seat in the Commons, supported by his cousin, Sir Henry James, the Attorney General, and Sir Richard Green Price. His stay at Westminster was short, for the Radnor Boroughs seat ceased to exist at the dissolution of Parliament in November 1885, being merged with the county constituency.[28]

With its tiny electorate the Radnor Boroughs seat could never claim to be typical, for it was little more than a pocket borough at the disposal of the Lewis family of Harpton Court and the Prices of Norton Manor. Indeed that the seat survived the redistribution of seats of 1832 and 1867 suggests that the two families were not lacking in influence in the right quarters. Even so they and their allies were compelled to recognise that the establishment could not ride roughshod over the interests and aspirations of the electorate, and party politics began to make headway, initially as a way in which the establishment could control the new voters after the 1867 Act by marshalling them behind the programme and organisation of a political party. Sir Richard Green Price was perhaps the first of the local politicians to recognise this.

By the 1880s, however, party politics in the Boroughs had progressed further, for although Liberal candidates were still very much from the county establishment, their selection was largely in the hands of the rank and file members of the six borough committees of the party. Perhaps symptomatic of this shift in power was that the formal nomination of the Liberal candidates was entrusted not to establishment figures, but to men representing the farming and commercial interests of the constituency.

4 The County Seat, 1868-92

The development of party politics in the constituency tends to be obscured by the dominance of the Walsh family for more than half a century apart from a brief interruption of five years. In this situation the local Conservatives had little incentive to develop a permanent and county wide party organisation since they could rely on the Walshes to fund the watching of the electoral register and the barristers to watch over the party's interests at the annual revision courts. Nor for at least the first 30 years or so of Walsh dominance was there any incentive for the Liberals in the constituency to organise, given the *de facto* arrangement whereby in return for not disturbing the Lewis / Price control of the Boroughs seat, the Walshes had a free hand in the county constituency.

As a result of the Second Reform Act of 1867 the Radnorshire electorate increased by more than 50% by the mid-1870s, increasing the pressure upon local parties to organise effectively. The Third Reform Act of 1884 increased the pressure still further by adding to the electorate all male householders and £10 lodgers and transferring the Boroughs' voters to the county electoral register after the abolition of that constituency, thus increasing the electorate from 2,434 in 1880 to 4,539 (which still included a number of non resident voters, estimated at some 300 in the 1900s), an increase of more than 85%. The increase in the electorate in the closing decades of the period was largely the result of the rapid growth of Llandrindod Wells, though the sharp rise in the political temperature may also have contributed, since it ensured that neither party neglected the registration process. However it should not be assumed that all adult males had the vote after 1884, for a minority of adult males remained disenfranchised until the 1918 Act which gave the vote to all adult males and to women aged over 30. Thus the number of male voters registered in Radnorshire in 1918 was 6,736, an increase of nearly 13% on the 1910 figure of 5,971, despite the heavy mortality of the 1914-18 War and the dislocation which the war produced.[1]

Arthur Walsh, 1868-80

*Plate 22: Arthur Walsh,
second Baron Ormathwaite*

When Sir John Walsh was raised to the peerage in March 1868 as Baron Ormathwaite of Ormathwaite, taking his title from the paternal estate in Cumberland, it was widely anticipated that he would be succeeded as the Member for Radnorshire by his son. Arthur Walsh had been born in 1827 and had followed a military career, serving as a captain in the 1st Life Guards. In 1858 he had married Lady Katherine Somerset, a daughter of the duke of Beaufort. In preparation for serving as the Member for Radnorshire, Walsh had been one of the MPs for Leominster since August 1865 when he topped the poll on a moderate Conservative platform of religious toleration, a strict economy in public affairs, but one that nevertheless ensured the safety of the Kingdom and maritime supremacy, the maintenance of the constitution in Church and State and a willingness to consider moderate parliamentary reform.[2]

With the Ormathwaite peerage announced, William Stephens, the Presteigne solicitor who served as Ormathwaite's agent and the Conservative party agent, suggested delaying the announcement of Walsh's candidacy for the Radnorshire seat until after the Assizes on 25 March and Quarter Sessions on 2 April. The grounds for doing so were two-fold: an early announcement would give potential rivals such as the Liberal Green Price and Frankland Lewis an opportunity to work up an opposition; while a delay would give Ormathwaite an opportunity to lobby the magistrates in Arthur Walsh's interest.[3]

However Ormathwaite's diary indicates that private soundings had been taken long before those dates, for on 19 March the Revd Richard Lister Venables had written declining to propose Walsh, while on the following day Richard Banks and his sons, along with Cecil Parsons, promised their support. Ormathwaite was relieved to have the support of the Banks family, for if they had declined the Revd Sir Gilbert Frankland Lewis might have backed a move by Green Price and his allies. After the assizes Thomas Lewis Lloyd, Henry Lingen of Penlanole and Edward Middleton Evans pledged their support.[4]

Walsh's electoral address was published in the *Hereford Times* of 11 April and made great play of his father's long tenure of the county seat. Walsh went on to portray himself as a moderate Conservative who backed a 'temperate and judicious foreign policy' and pledged himself to support the government while reserving the right to take an independent line if necessary, thus evading the charge of being a party politician.

Ormathwaite and Stephens may have seen nomination day as an opportunity to demonstrate such great support for Walsh as to intimidate potential rivals and opponents into lying low for some years to come. Thus the *Hereford Times* of 25 April published a notice to the effect that the friends of Walsh were to meet at Dolley Bridge on Tuesday 28 April, to escort him to the Shire Hall at Presteigne. Another notice announced that a special train would leave Builth Road Station 'to convey parties desirous of attending the Hon Arthur Walsh's election at Presteigne on 28 April', while carriages would be made available at Knighton Station to convey parties to Presteigne.

Walsh's escort on nomination day was probably the largest witnessed at an election in Presteigne, for in addition to the Walsh family coaches, it comprised 250 horsemen and 60 coaches, gigs and omnibuses containing Walsh's tenants and his many supporters from the upper Teme valley. The procession was so long that the tail was still at the approaches to the town when the Walsh coaches were drawing up at the Shire Hall. For the nomination proceedings the Shire Hall was packed with Walsh's supporters wearing dark blue favours (ribbons and rosettes) and he was duly returned unopposed, proposed by Walter de Winton and seconded by R.B. Mynors. After Walsh had been chaired, the crowds dispersed to 'ordinaries' (the standard meal provided) at the Radnorshire Arms, the Duke's Arms and the Bull Inn, as legislation in 1854 had banned 'treating' and celebratory dinners.[5]

If Stephens and Ormathwaite had intended to overawe potential opponents by a show of strength, their scheme seems to have worked, for in the general election of November 1868, Walsh was returned unopposed without undue exertion. At the beginning of October Walsh issued an electoral address, written at a shooting lodge near Fort William in Scotland while indulging his passion for shooting, backing religious toleration and resistance to any attack on 'those Protestant institutions bequeathed us'. He believed that the issue of parliamentary reform had been laid to rest by the Reform Act of 1867 and that the immediate need was to check the growth of local taxation which was a 'grievous burden' on land owners and farmers. He appeared to have made little or no attempt actually to canvass or campaign in the constituency.

On nomination day, 19 November, surrounded by friends and supporters, he was proposed by R.B. Mynors and seconded by Edward Middleton Evans in a speech described as 'an exhaustive dissertation upon political matters' and returned unopposed. In his acceptance speech Walsh strongly denied the

Plate 23: George Augustus Haig

contention by G.A. Haig, the Conservative candidate in the Boroughs seat, that he and Green Price had colluded to prevent opposition to each other in the two Radnorshire constituencies. However this charge may have gained some credibility by Walsh's failure to campaign energetically and the less than enthusiastic Conservative support which Haig gained in the Boroughs election.[6]

The political temperature in the constituency rose markedly in the early 1870s and the election of February 1874 was certainly the longest the county had ever experienced and one of the most ill-tempered. The campaign began when Haig, now standing as an unofficial Liberal, published the first of his many election addresses in the *Hereford Journal* of 3 May 1873 in which he announced that in view of a rumour that Parliament was to be dissolved in October, he intended to stand on a programme of disestablishing the English, Welsh and Scottish Churches. Since they could not afford to give Haig a start, his rivals Walsh and Green Price were compelled to enter the race on 6 May and 12 May respectively.

The ill feeling stemmed from Green Price's resignation from the Boroughs seat in 1869 in order to 'give' it to Hartington and his bid to win the county seat in order to give the Liberals control of both Radnorshire seats, thus breaching what many thought was a tacit understanding between the parties to divide the spoils. The *Hereford Journal* of 8 November wondered why Green Price was so anxious to be the Member for Radnorshire:

> One would suppose gentlemen who have reached the shady side of seventy to be tolerably free from ambition, or personal ambition at least.

Plate 24: Pen Ithon, the home of George Augustus Haig

Its leading article went on to repeat a suggestion of Haig's that Green Price was hoping to get his son instituted to one of the many livings controlled by the duke of Devonshire and to hint that two of Green Price's sons-in-law had obtained their appointments as a Poor Law Inspector and as a captain in the 77th Regiment respectively through the influence of Lord Hartington. It concluded:

> Radnorshire does not want a septuagenarian with a policy bounded by his family circle.

While these specific charges were quickly refuted by the Green Price camp, a great deal of suspicion remained concerning his dealings with Hartington.

Green Price's bid for the county seat did not have the backing of the Revd Sir Gilbert Frankland Lewis and the other members of the county's Whig establishment, ostensibly on the grounds that if he succeeded the many Conservative gentry of Radnorshire would have no voice in the Commons. The main reason however was that Green Price's candidacy might well provoke the Conservatives into a determined attempt on the Boroughs seat and usher in an age of contested elections which might create deep divisions in Radnorshire society. Moreover a Green Price victory in the county election would give him, already the major force in the Boroughs seat, unparalleled political influence in both Radnorshire constituencies. From the point of view of the Whig gentry it would have been preferable for Green Price to take over the Boroughs seat from Hartington and keep it warm for Sir Gilbert's son, Herbert.[7]

Walsh, standing on the Conservative programme, had no need to elaborate on policy details and in his address of 6 May pointed out that in 1868 Haig, 'lately settled in the county', had stood as a Conservative and had campaigned against the disestablishment of the Irish Church, he was now standing as a Liberal advocating the disestablishment. During the campaign Walsh's supporters lost no time in pointing out that Haig did not have the backing of the Liberal leadership. In a more personal attack 'A Voter', who gave his address as Montreux, wondered if 'a tradesman' could represent Radnorshire, while 'An elector' condemned Haig as a 'Vicar of Bray', ready to ditch his principles in order to further his interests.[8]

For the most part Walsh left campaigning in the hands of a committee chaired by R.B. Mynors and consisting in the main of the county's leading land owners. Initially the list of Walsh's supporters contained 68 names, but by the beginning of June the number had grown to 93. The publication of such a list may have been an attempt to adapt the traditional electoral influence of the landowners to the new age of the secret ballot. Another means of doing so seems to have been for the agent of an estate to send round a book to the tenants with a request that they sign their names in it to pledge their support for Walsh. Given that rumours were circulating that the ballot was not secret and that those with influence could discover how an elector had voted, such methods could preserve the landlords' ability to command the votes of their tenants. Haig realized this and spent time at each of his meetings explaining the voting procedure in detail and assuring his listeners that the ballot was indeed secret.[9]

Green Price, standing on Gladstone's well publicised programme, could afford to ignore policy details and could rely upon Price family influence and the strong Liberal traditions in the county to rally support, even if many of the Whig elite failed to endorse him. He argued that Ormathwaite had destroyed the political consensus in Radnorshire by encouraging Philips to stand for the Boroughs seat in 1869 and claimed that his candidacy for the county seat was not a 'tit for tat' gesture, but because it had been misrepresented in the Commons by the Walsh family for decades. He had hoped that Arthur Walsh would be a Liberal Conservative, but he had voted against the disestablishment in Ireland, the Education and Ballot Acts and against the Burial Bill, thus demonstrating that he was an orthodox Conservative with no Liberal sympathies.[10] Like Haig he identified the nonconformist vote as vital if Walsh was to be defeated and thus much of the campaigning consisted of a sustained competition between the two Liberal candidates for the votes of the nonconformist tenant farmers.

Haig had a lively and original mind and his whole electoral strategy was based on a programme of the disestablishment and disendowment of the Welsh Church, along with the reform of the tenancy, game and salmon laws, all measures which he thought would appeal specifically to this group and which would drain away support, not only from Walsh, but also from Green Price. His agent, Thomas Gough, targeted the Baptists, the largest nonconformist group in the county since, unlike the Primitive Methodists, Independents and Wesleyans, he believed they acted as a political society and were in the main tenant farmers. He believed that Primitive Methodists did not as a rule interfere in politics except as individuals and that Green Price had 'a considerable hold upon them at the bottom of the county', while Walsh had great influence with them in the neighbourhood of Llanddewi Ystradenni. The Wesleyans, on the other hand, were free from political influence 'apart from a sprinkling of Toryism in their hearts', but their numbers were small. Even so, Gough provided Haig with lists of ministers and influential members of all nonconformist denominations in central and eastern Radnorshire.[11]

Haig, an Irish Protestant, believed that as the Irish Church had been disestablished, in the interests of consistency the English, Welsh and Scottish Churches should also be disestablished, and thought there were grounds for expecting the backing of Radnorshire nonconformists. Though they were now able to marry in their own chapels and no longer contributed to the maintenance of the parish church through paying a compulsory church rate, nonconformists were still subject to discrimination. Nonconformist tenant farmers were still liable to pay tithes to support, at least in theory, the Anglican Church, while nonconformist Poor Law guardians did not take kindly to the insistence of the central Poor Law authorities that there was an Anglican monopoly on the appointment of workhouse chaplains. Again, the burial service of a nonconformist in the parish churchyard had to be conducted by an Anglican clergyman in accordance with the prayer book, a situation which could cause great distress when it came to the burial of the child of Baptist parents.

Significantly most of Haig's election meetings throughout the county were held in Baptist chapels, usually with a nonconformist minister in the chair. At such meetings the main target was not Walsh but Green Price who was attacked for his High Church tendencies, his prevarication on the issue of disestablishment and his backing for Church schools as opposed to the non-sectarian Board schools. For his part Green Price and his supporters, including the Revd Kilsby Jones, concentrated upon attacking the ambiguities in Haig's proposals.

Thus with regard to the tithes taken from the hands of absentees and returned to the parishes for the use of resident clergy, both Anglican and nonconformist, Haig was vague as to which clergy would benefit and as to who would participate in making decisions as to how tithe income would be distributed between the clergy in each parish once the Church had been disestablished and disendowed. Similarly he was imprecise initially as to who would have the right to ground game such as rabbits if this was taken from the landlord. Another subject upon which Haig was attacked, notably by the Revd Thomas Dyke, the Primitive Methodist minister at Hay-on-Wye and an ally of Green Price, was upon the Permissive Bill which envisaged each community voting on the granting or renewal of licences to sell alcoholic drinks in that locality.[12] Given his interests in the liquor industry, Haig was against the Bill while the nonconformists, most of them teetotallers, were strongly in favour.

The local press, particularly the *Hereford Times*, was also used by the two Liberal candidates and their supporters, frequently at such a great length as to be the despair of the uncommitted Radnorian or the uninvolved Herefordian. Haig was the worst culprit, often with two or three lengthy letters in a single issue, and some went as far to suggest that he should be charged for any further contributions. The debate between the two factions sometimes reached arcane levels, as when there was a dispute as to how many nonconformist clergy were resident in Radnorshire and the proportion supporting each of the two rivals. The Green Price campaign also had a dark side, for at the outset

Haig was being depicted in gossip as 'the worst landlord in the Principality', a charge which 'A Freeholder' elaborated upon in a letter published in the *Hereford Journal* of 21 June, 1873.

By the autumn of 1873 concerns were growing at the potential split in the Liberal vote and it was suggested that a ballot should be held throughout the county to assess the support for Haig and Green Price respectively and that the one with the least support should withdraw. However it was impossible to identify Liberals with any degree of certainty since there had not been a poll in the seat since 1841. Haig suggested that a poll should be held in the chapels with ministers balloting members, but Green Price had reservations as such a scheme had obvious drawbacks, since not all nonconformists were Liberals and not all Liberals were nonconformists. With neither prepared to give way, Walsh's chances of retaining the seat were greatly enhanced by the split in the Liberal vote. In Knighton and Presteigne there was fury at Haig's insistence on standing and at Knighton, Thomas Gough alleged, men were employed to tear down Haig's posters. The *Hereford Times* eventually came down on the side of Green Price and accused Haig of being a Tory taking 'a leap in the dark to Disestablishment', since he opposed Liberal policy in general and the abolition of income tax in particular.[13]

Most seem to have considered the election a close contest between Walsh and Green Price, with Haig not in the race. According to the *Hereford Journal* of 7 February unfounded rumours were circulating that Green Price had agreed to vote for disestablishment and that Haig had agreed to withdraw. This may have been the inspiration for 'a shamefully mean and disgraceful trick', for on the morning of election day, 11 February, telegrams were sent from Newtown to ten polling stations in central Radnorshire and the Teme valley to the effect that Haig had retired and that his supporters were to vote instead for Green Price. At Felindre news of Haig's alleged retirement was circulated by the Knighton town crier. As might be expected some voters switched their vote to Green Price and when the result was declared the following afternoon, Haig had polled 100 votes, Green Price 832 and Walsh 889. Not surprisingly, given that this was the first election by secret ballot, 88 ballot papers were rejected by the returning officer.[14]

At the declaration Walsh made a short speech which was well received, but when Green Price rose he was received with 'deafening cheers'. He claimed that if Haig had not stood he would have won by 43 votes and went on to deny that he or any of his supporters had had anything to do with the Newtown telegrams. When Haig rose he was greeted with shouts of 'Turncoat' and such a storm of hoots, groans and hisses that he was unable to be heard. He was escorted from the Shire Hall by two policemen, but even so he and his son were pelted with flour bombs as they made their way to the Radnorshire Arms, with Haig, according to R.W. Banks, 'a pitiable object'.[15]

Thomas Gough eventually identified the sender of the telegrams as a journeyman carpenter from Rhayader, though he doubted if he would sign a document acknowledging his guilt since 'It is a very difficult thing to get a Radnorshire man to sign anything'. In the meantime Green Price's claim that he would have won by 43 votes if Haig had not stood was challenged by G.H. Philips of Abbey Cwm Hir, who said that he had been told by several of Haig's voters that if he had not stood they would have voted for Walsh. Nor were the Conservatives completely happy, for Walsh's majority was far smaller than they had expected as a result of broken promises and the complacency of some 200 non-resident voters who thought that his seat was so safe that they had no need to attend the election.[16]

In 1875 Walsh succeed his father as Lord Lieutenant of Radnorshire, but in spite of his enhanced status he had decided as early as mid-1878 not to defend the seat at the next election. The main reason for this decision was probably financial, for with a relatively small annual allowance of £1,000 from his father, a large family and an expensive hobby — shooting game, he had been borrowing since the 1850s. His seat in the Commons added to his financial difficulties as he was expected to give generously to every good cause in the county, notably to each of the many church restoration funds. One of his first efforts at retrenchment was to limit his donations to such funds to those parishes in which the family estates lay. Again, the Conservative gentry of the county expected him to fund the party out of his own pocket and in 1875 and 1878 Walsh refused to fund a registration drive unless they contributed.[17]

This lack of an effective local leadership may have contributed to his disillusionment, for by late June 1878 Walsh was writing to Mynors on the many complaints he had been receiving from the party rank and file of the apathy of the local leaders. There seems to have been internal divisions within the party, with the old leadership, notably Robert Mynors and Percy Severn, at odds with rising new men such as Otway and Cheese, the Hay-on-Wye solicitor. William Stephens, the local Conservative agent, seems to have been unable to deal effectively with these divisions since his authority within the party had been compromised. In September 1874, he had sanctioned the loan of Conservative flags and banners to Joseph Arch for an Agricultural Labourers' Union demonstration at Presteigne, much to the fury of many of the county's farmers, while his wife had helped to serve refreshments at the conclusion of the rally.[18]

Sir Richard Green Price, 1880-85

Once Walsh had made his intention of resigning clear, Stephens came under pressure from the Carlton Club and the Conservative leadership to find a candidate. In June 1878, seemingly without consulting Ormathwaite or Walsh, he called a meeting at Penybont to consider the candidacy at which

Otway and Cheese took prominent parts, though no decisions were reached. The 'Old Guard' were furious and Mynors protested to Walsh that such a meeting disturbed the peace of the county prematurely since no dissolution of the Commons seemed imminent. Walsh tried to calm matters down and wrote to both Otway and Mynors, telling Otway that he, Walsh, would take no part in the choice of his successor, and warning Mynors that a candidate would need to be chosen quickly, otherwise Green Price would have a free hand. Subsequently another meeting was held at Penybont and after both G.H. Philips and Percy Severn had declined to come forward, Mynors was selected in preference to Cheese or Otway.[19]

Green Price, created a baronet in the Dissolution Honours of 1874 and the acknowledged leader of the Liberals in the county, was their obvious candidate. However, his age was against him, his health was far from robust and some suspected that he had 'sold the Boroughs' to Hartington in 1869. Even after his adoption as the official Liberal candidate there were calls for him to stand down. In the *Hereford Times* of 30 August 1879 no fewer than three correspondents called on him to step down in favour of Herbert Lewis, the son of Frankland Lewis, while even in mid-March 1880 spurious circulars were sent to Radnorshire voters, allegedly from 'an advanced Liberal', advising Baptists not to vote for either candidate. The *Hereford Times* of 3 April suggested that the circulars 'smelt strongly of Penithon' (Haig's home) and that Haig was seeking revenge for the telegrams incident of the 1874 Boroughs election.

Robert Baskerville Mynors, 1820-1889, was the oldest son of Peter Rickards Mynors of Treago, Herefordshire and Evancoyd, Radnorshire, and was educated at Eton, Christ Church, Oxford where he was awarded BA in 1841, and the Inner Temple. A JP and DL Radnorshire, he served as sheriff of the county in 1856. He had played an active part in the administration of the county since the 1840s and had been active in the Conservative interest since his youth. He believed that the extended and bad-tempered campaign of 1873-74 should not be repeated and by mid-July had contacted Green Price and explained that he did not wish for any personal antagonism to colour the coming electoral contest. Green Price, anxious not to repeat the rigours of the 1873-74 campaign, agreed with Mynors that no personal declarations should be made, and that no canvassing was to be carried out by either candidate 'until the proper moment arrived near the time of the contest', though of course neither candidate was able to bind his supporters. The 'proper moment' was agreed to be the dissolution of Parliament, scheduled for February 1880. Despite this, Green Price issued an address to the electors in the *Hereford Times* of 25 October 1879 declaring his platform to be 'Peace, retrenchment and reform'.[20]

In line with the agreement, both sides began their campaign at the beginning of March, 1880. Faced with a short campaign Mynors placed great emphasis on local committees, one for each of the electoral districts, headed by a leading local Conservative, almost invariably one of the local squires. The committee was responsible for the campaign in the district, most importantly the canvass of the voters. Each district committee was to appoint two representatives to serve on the central committee which was to co-ordinate the election campaign. The district committees were not large; that for Presteigne for example, chaired by Captain James Beavan, consisted of three tradesmen together with William Stephens as agent and H. Martin Jones, the postmaster, as secretary.[21]

In his election address Mynors advocated a foreign policy of 'defence not dominion', religious liberty for nonconformists, freedom of conscience and a reduction of taxes on agriculture. Green Price could frame his election address in much broader terms, since he was well known to the electors, and it consisted of little more than a description of his political career and his support for the Liberal programme as exemplified by Gladstone and Hartington. With a campaign of little more than a month, the meetings organised by the two agents, both of them Presteigne solicitors, William Stephens acting for Mynors and William Wakelin for Green Price, were necessarily fewer than usual.

Invariably the atmosphere became rather more heated than Mynors would have liked. Thus the *Hereford Journal* of 13 March described Green Price's speech at his opening meeting at Knighton as consisting of 'misstatements, facts garbled, fiction boldly affirmed as facts, with a high seasoning of partisan virulence'. For Green Price, his son Dansey, along with the celebrated Llandrindod nonconformist minister, Kilsby Jones, in addition to speaking at Liberal meetings throughout the county, conducted a spoiling campaign. They interrupted Conservative meetings to ask questions designed to embarrass Mynors on such topics as Sunday closing of public houses and the Burial Bill which would have allowed nonconformist clergy to conduct funeral services in churchyards, measures which Mynors opposed, hoping that his answers would alienate nonconformist voters. The tension which the campaign could generate is perhaps best illustrated by an incident at Knighton on the Saturday prior to the election when a bell-ringing practice began in the parish church just as a Liberal meeting ended at the home of Isaac Rutter. With the bells ringing as the local Liberals streamed out of the meeting, local Conservatives complained to the vicar that the bells were being rung for Sir Richard.[22]

Nomination day showed that in the county constituency, unlike in the Boroughs, the major landowners still held sway, for Mynors was nominated by J.P. Severn and seconded by Edward Meredith of Bailey Noyadd, while Green Price was proposed by C.C. Rogers of Stanage and Thomas Prickard of Dderw and seconded by Herbert Lewis of Harpton Court and Thomas Vaughan of the Skreen. Election day, 6 April, was busy as turnout was high, just short of 80%, but uneventful. When the poll was declared at the Shire Hall Presteigne on the following day Green Price won far more easily than many had expected: 1,137 votes to 800 for Mynors. For the first time for 40 years Radnorshire would not be represented in the Commons by a member of the Walsh family.[23]

A Knighton correspondent in the *Hereford Times* of 8 May suggested that Green Price had been returned 'by a majority of 337 liars' who had promised their vote to Mynors. However, Walsh and Stephens placed much of the responsibility for the Conservative defeat upon Mynors' unorthodox ideas on electioneering. Certainly the short campaign did no harm to Green Price, who was well known, if not always popular, throughout the length and breadth of the county. Mynors on the other hand was not well known outside Conservative circles or beyond the New Radnor-Kington-Presteigne area, and a longer campaign would have enabled him to raise his profile throughout the county at large. Again it seems possible that not all Walsh's personal following transferred their allegiance to Mynors, who was very much the party loyalist, whereas Walsh had cultivated the image of an independent 'of Conservative principles'.

Sir Richard Green Price's second spell in the Commons was not an auspicious one. He was dogged by financial difficulties as a result of the agricultural depression, his heavy and somewhat rash investments in local railways and the need to provide for his large family of five sons and seven daughters: for each of his sons a public school education and a small allowance thereafter until they were settled; and a season in society and a marriage settlement for each of his daughters. His health was also deteriorating, partly as a result of old age; he was 77 in 1880, and had suffered with asthma since the late 1860s. His health problems necessitated long absences from the House and sometimes visits abroad to benefit from a drier climate during the winter. In the spring of 1884 Green Price fell seriously ill and recovered only slowly, spending much of the year convalescing. A critic calculated that between February and August 1884 he had been present in the House for 6 divisions out of a total of 216 and between October 1884 and January 1885 he had been present for 7 divisions out of 289. More unkindly it was suggested that some in the county were wondering

> As to whether Sir Richard was the representative of the County in the House of Commons, or a representative of the House of Commons in Radnorshire.[24]

Even some of a more charitable disposition felt that the county was virtually disenfranchised as a result of his ill-health.

At the end of May 1884 the Radnorshire Liberals held a meeting at the Rock House Hotel, Llandrindod Wells, chaired by the Revd T.C. Prickard, to discuss the representation of the county. Green Price had been notified of the meeting and sent a letter to confirm that he would contest the seat at the next election, providing that his health permitted. This was accepted by the meeting which then discussed possible candidates, should Sir Richard be unable to stand, notably Revd T.C. Prickard, J. Williams Vaughan of the Skreen and Charles Coltman Rogers of Stanage. However, no decision was taken and the matter was left in abeyance until there were more evident signs of a dissolution. The question was obviously exercising Liberals throughout the county for the *Hereford Times* of 7 June, which reported the meeting, contained a letter from 'Greycoat' who, while hoping that Green Price would stand, believed that steps should be taken to select a candidate in case of his retirement or death. 'Greycoat' favoured S.C. Evans Williams, the Boroughs Member, rather than a Whig such as Sir Herbert Lewis of Harpton, J. Williams Vaughan of the Skreen or C.C. Rogers of Stanage.

The thoughts of the Conservatives were also turning to the question of selecting a candidate and at the beginning of June 1884 a meeting of leading local Conservatives, including R.B. Mynors, Sir Herbert Lewis, Captain James Beavan and Edward Middleton Evans was held at the Severn Arms in Penybont to consider the matter, but no decision was taken.

Selection of the candidates progressed slowly. As a result of disagreements between the parties as to the redistribution of parliamentary seats which was to accompany the Third Reform Act of 1884, a general election under the new voting arrangements was not likely before November or December 1885. Under these circumstances neither party felt any need to reach an early decision as to a candidate. However there is also some evidence that the failure of the local Liberal and Conservative parties to select their candidates early was to some extent a reflection of poor leadership and organisational weaknesses. Thus the report of the Liberal meeting at the Rock House Hotel at the end of May 1884 led to a war of words in subsequent issues of the *Hereford Times* in which it was alleged that the meeting represented an attempt by the Knighton Liberal Association to impose their will upon other Liberals in the county.[25]

Meanwhile, in May the second Lord Ormathwaite—the former Radnorshire Member, Arthur Walsh, who had succeeded to the title in 1881 — reported to Mynors that the Conservatives of the upper Teme valley felt abandoned by the Conservative gentry, who were failing to give a lead.[26] In the *Hereford Journal* of 17 January 1885 Mr Powell of Howey Hall called for a public meeting to elect a candidate who would representative of the party as a whole rather than only of a small section of it. The latter remark may well have been aimed at Penry Lloyd, the former chief constable of Radnorshire, now agent of the Maesllwch estate, who seems to have been using the Wyeside Farmers' Association to further his parliamentary ambitions, but who, in the *Hereford Times* of 17 January, had finally declined a requisition from the members of the Association to stand at the next election. In the *Hereford Journal* of 28 January Powell of Howey Hall went on to express doubts as to the efficiency of the local party organisation:

> Our election machinery has become too cumbersome and old fash-
> ioned. If we had a little more vigour at headquarters and a good agent
> ... we should show a different point in future.

In practice however, the local Liberals could not make a firm decision until Green Price decided if he would stand or retire from the seat, while the Conservatives could not make a decision until Lord Ormathwaite made up his mind as to the candidacy of his son, Arthur H.J. Walsh, the popular choice as far as the rank and file Radnorshire Conservatives were concerned. Ormathwaite had doubts as to his son's ability to defeat Richard Green Price and hoped that the latter would retire before he contested the seat. In a letter to Col Duncumb, his son's commanding officer, in August 1884 Ormathwaite expressed the hope that his son would continue his military career, as he doubted that he had the powers of endurance needed for one in parliament.[27]

Arthur H.J. Walsh, 1885-92

In mid May Ormathwaite and other local leaders such as R.B. Mynors decided to form a Radnorshire Conservative Association with the Rhayader solicitor Edward Wood as secretary. At the same meeting at Penybont it was announced that Ormathwaite had received a number of requisitions asking that Arthur H.J. Walsh be asked to contest the county seat. A week or so later, on 22 May Sir Richard Green Price announced his decision to resign at the dissolution and the Liberals selected Charles Coltman Rogers as their candidate.[28]

It now was important that the Conservatives announced a candidate

Plate 25: Arthur H.J. Walsh, third Baron Ormathwaite

quickly. With Green Price out of the picture Ormathwaite had the scenario he had hoped for, though he still had considerable reservations as to his son's chances of success, and on 5 June at a meeting at Penybont Arthur H.J. Walsh accepted the nomination as Conservative candidate for the county. The oldest son of Lord Ormathwaite, he had been born in 1859, educated at Eton, and held a commission in the 1st Life Guards, from which he resigned in February 1886.

With the electorate increased by more than 85% as a result of the Third Reform Act, an effective party organisation was clearly a prerequisite for a successful election campaign. The Conservatives recognised this from the start when Edward Wood, the secretary of the Association, was placed in charge of organisation and of overseeing the monitoring of the electoral register. At a Conservative meeting at Glasbury in early July, the Hay-on-Wye solicitor E.H. Cheese carefully explained the registration process and the latest dates by which electors could register and objections be lodged. He stressed the need for 'strong working committees' to be formed in all the parishes in the Constituency for campaigning purposes.[29]

Great store was placed on canvassing which, much to the indignation of Liberal traditionalists, was often entrusted to the ladies of the local 'big house' and their associates in the nearby Primrose League 'habitations'. (The Primrose League was a Conservative organisation named after Benjamin Disraeli's favourite flower, its constituent parts being referred to as habitations). While the main argument of these 'butterflies of society' was said to be that Walsh 'was such a nice young man', others held that they were demeaning themselves 'by doing the Tory dirty work'. Again, Sundays were often chosen for canvassing since it was much more likely that the voter would be at home, a practice much disapproved of by most nonconformists.[30]

With the experienced Sir Richard Green Price on hand, the Liberals paid great attention to the registration of voters. However in this campaign Rogers insisted that there should be no canvassing since this placed undue pressure upon the voter and could be seen as intimidation if pushed too far and thus against the principles of the secret ballot. While it later emerged that not all were in favour of this stance, Rogers did get the approval of the local Liberal leadership. As Edward Meredith of Bailey Noyadd pointed out in a letter to the *Hereford Times* of 5 December 1885, Rogers instead attended every fair and market in the county that he was able to, and shook hands with every voter he could meet. By the end of October Rogers was already claiming that he had spoken at 24 meetings. Meanwhile his supporters ignored the ban and canvassed regularly.

Both candidates published their electoral addresses fairly late in the campaign. Walsh's, from Eywood and dated 2 November, was couched in general terms and presented him as a Conservative with progressive views, essentially a Liberal Conservative. He favoured widening the base of local taxation by taxing personal wealth as well as property, thus reducing the tax burden on most property owners. He backed the Conservative demand for a royal commission into the depression in trade and agriculture and deplored Gladstone's foreign policy, which he regarded as disastrous.

Rogers' address, dated 18 November, was much more detailed. After a general declaration of support for Gladstone, Rogers declared himself in favour of a drastic reform of the land law, reform of local government with an accompanying inquiry into local taxation, an amendment to the Agricultural Holdings Act in favour of the tenant and Free Trade. His support of disestablishment of the Welsh Church was more qualified, for he believed that recent endowments should not be interfered with and that 'the vested interest of the clergy should be respected', that any tithe income they had should not be touched. On the vexed issue of Irish Home Rule Rogers was equivocal for while he was 'anxious to give freedom to all classes', he wished to maintain 'the integrity of the Empire'.[31]

Rogers used some humour in his speeches, which did not please everyone. One critic maintained that 'farmers and taxpayers do not want grave subjects treated with levity', while another objected to his 'weak vapid jokes'. Perhaps his most effective dart was his comparison of Liberal Conservatives with mixed pickles in that one could not judge exactly what a Liberal Conservative stood for.[32]

The Conservatives found it necessary to match the Liberal programme of meetings throughout the county. Neither party relied exclusively upon its candidate as a speaker. The Conservatives held the advantage in the number of alternative local speakers, being able to call upon Mynors, the Venables brothers and Penry Lloyd, while the Liberals' principal speaker, Sir Richard Green Price, was unable to undertake a heavy programme owing to his age and infirmity. However, his son Dansey Green Price, and Kilsby Jones were in fact more effective speakers and excelled in making telling points at Conservative meetings by their questions and interventions. Both sides made use of eminent outside speakers, Rogers of his kinsman, Sir Henry James, solicitor general in Gladstone's Ministry 1880-85, while the Conservatives called upon Henry Chaplin, the minister of agriculture in Lord Salisbury's Ministry of 1885-86. In contrast to the Boroughs election of 1880, the meetings of both parties passed off quietly, judging from local press reports.

The elections in the north and south Herefordshire seats in late October 1885 — elections were not held on the same date in each constituency as the election writs instructing the returning officer to hold elections were issued over a week or so — had been won by the Liberals. As the *Hereford Journal* of 5 December preferred to put it, 'the radicals and the labourers have had their way', and the Radnorshire Conservatives were therefore pessimistic about their chances. The Radnorshire election was held on 3 December and the count passed off quietly 'there being an absence of that undue excitement which prevailed elsewhere'. There may well have been a suspicion of an upset at the declaration of the poll on 5 December, as most spectators outside the Shire Hall in Presteigne were reported to have been wearing the blue favours of the Conservatives. Their suspicions proved correct, for Walsh polled 1,880 votes to the 1,813 votes cast for Rogers. There certainly appear to have been some leaks from the count since the *Hereford Journal* of 12 December reported that while the majority of Knighton voters had supported Rogers, the farmers had generally voted Conservative and at Presteigne the Conservatives had polled more heavily than on any previous occasion.

At Knighton, where a Liberal victory had been confidently expected, it was reported that there was 'a gloom over the town' and that 'the Liberals for a time seemed paralysed and puzzled'. In the course of the inevitable *post mortem* some correspondents to the *Hereford Times* of 12 and 19 December attributed the Liberal defeat to the territorial influence of the Walsh family and the activities of the Primrose League. Another correspondent suggested that voters had 'voted for the man not the party' and that some non-conformists had voted Conservative.

The Radnorshire seat was the only loss suffered by the Liberals amongst the Welsh county seats and Walsh was one of only two Conservative MPs returned by the Welsh counties. In the main the Liberal defeat stemmed from their failure to canvass, which left the field clear for the Conservatives, a critical error given that such a large proportion of the electorate were new voters and perhaps in need of some direction. There was a degree of complacency, if not arrogance, in the Liberal assumption that they could rely upon the votes of the nonconformists and of the new electors, thanks respectively to their positive stance on the issue of disestablishment and as a reward for giving the small tenant farmer and the farm labourer the vote by the Third Reform Act.

Other factors also contributed to the Liberal defeat. H. Vaughan Vaughan, the Liberal agent, believed that Rogers was a relatively weak candidate compared with Walsh, and had said as much both before the campaign had got underway and after the election. Certainly his attempts to bring a light touch of humour to some of his election speeches had not gone down well in some quarters. Vaughan Vaughan also believed that the Liberal organisation had been weak at local level, with little being done in some electoral districts.[33]

There is also some evidence to suggest that the Whig element of the Liberal party in Radnorshire was beginning to drift towards Conservatism, even before the issue of Irish Home Rule had come to occupy centre stage, as a result of the increasingly radical direction of the Liberal programme, in particular the growing support for disestablishment. Certainly Sir Herbert Lewis, once considered a possible Liberal candidate, was by 1885 in the Conservative fold, as were the Venables brothers, though George Stovin Venables' letters to his brother Richard of the beginning of June 1885 were hardly enthusiastic as far as Conservatism was concerned. Thus in a letter of 1 June George begrudged giving a donation of £10 to the Radnorshire Conservative Association and warned his brother not to accept office in it, the following day suggesting that they should try to give the Association as liberal a tone as possible.[34]

Even so, both had spoken at Walsh's election meetings and Richard Lister Venables proposed Walsh at the nomination proceedings. George Stovin Venables explained his switch to Conservatism as a result of Gladstone's shift towards radical policies: 'I once gave the Liberals votes, I am as I was, you Liberals have left me.'[35] This erosion of Whig support had been noted by 'Crites' in his letter published in the *Hereford Times* of 5 December 1885 in which he observed that Walsh

Plate 26: George Stovin Venables

was always supported on the platform by 'men of standing and influence' whereas at Rogers' meetings, T.C. Prickard was almost invariably in the chair and Rogers was supported by 'paid agents' such as H. Vaughan Vaughan, the Liberal agent, and Kilsby Jones.

Lord Salisbury's government lasted only a few months and, after it had been defeated in the Commons, in February 1886 Gladstone took office again. However his attempt to give Ireland Home Rule was widely opposed, even by a significant number of Liberals, including Lord Hartington and Sir Henry James. As a result the Bill was defeated and a general election resulted in July 1886.

With their organisation recently overhauled and the sitting Member the obvious candidate, the Conservatives had spent time celebrating their victory of December 1885.[36] The Liberals, meanwhile, decided they needed to over-haul their local organisation. A new Radnorshire Liberal Association was to be formed with branches in each polling district. A council consisting of four representatives from each polling district would be set up with an executive committee of nine members. T.C. Prickard was elected president, J. Williams Vaughan vice-president and H. Vaughan Vaughan secretary. It was decided to undertake a canvass at the next election.[37]

As the Irish Home Rule Bill debate continued, a meeting was held at the Assembly Rooms Presteigne on 12 June under the auspices of the Ulster Loyalist Anti-Repeal Union in opposition to Home Rule. The meeting, billed as non-party, was chaired by Sir Harford James Jones Brydges and addressed by an Irish Protestant clergyman and a working man from Belfast. The majority of those attending, which included R.B. Mynors and William Stephens, seem to have been Conservatives, though one notable Presteigne Liberal, John Davies, a former chairman of the Liberal Association who opposed Home Rule, was also present.[38]

The newly formed county Liberal Association finally met on 21 June 1886 to consider recommendations on organisation, to consider the Home Rule crisis and their candidate for the forthcoming election. After Coltman Rogers had expressed reservations over some aspects of the Home Rule plans and Williams Vaughan junior had ruled himself out of contention, the veteran Sir Richard Green Price was selected to contest the county seat. Two days earlier Arthur H.J. Walsh, the sitting MP, had been invited to contest the seat on behalf of the Conservatives. Previous to this, when there had been some concerns over Walsh's health, the Venables brothers had favoured Penry Lloyd, the former Radnorshire chief constable as an alternative.[39]

Green Price's electoral address recognised that the major issue at stake was Ireland and that the choice was between Gladstone's policy of Home Rule and the Conservative policy of coercion. He went on to condemn the county for its failure to remain loyal to Gladstone in 1885 and to remind the Radnorshire working men that they owed their vote to Gladstone. Walsh's address also centred upon Irish Home Rule which he saw as handing over a million and half loyal subjects to the Irish nationalists and £1 million of the taxpayers' money to Irish landlords. He appealed for support from Liberals who opposed Home Rule, reminding electors that Home Rule had been rejected by a majority of the House of Commons, including both Conservatives and Liberals. Walsh also pointed out that the Revd H. Spurgeon, the celebrated and evangelist nonconformist preacher, considered the plan for Home Rule as 'worthy of a mad man'. In conclusion he suggested that Green Price, who had retired upon the grounds of age in 1885, was now even older, at eighty-three, and certainly not wiser![40]

Both sides now began a hectic round of public meetings, and almost inevitably both sides pulled election stunts. The Liberal Association received a letter from the poet Wilfred Scawen Blunt accusing Ormathwaite of evicting his tenants on his estate in County Kerry which was reproduced as a poster. Walsh was able to explain away the evictions to the satisfaction of most, in that after their rents had been reduced by 25%, three tenants in Co Kerry had refused to pay any rent at all and had been evicted. The Conservatives, meanwhile, produced a poster of a letter opposing Irish Home Rule signed by Green Price's son Dansey, next to pictures of Green Price. Dansey had written his letter to a Shrewsbury newspaper before his father had decided to stand.[41]

The growing social gulf between the leadership of the Conservative party and the Liberal leadership was obvious on nomination day for whereas Green

Price was proposed and seconded by two Knighton businessmen, Isaac Rutter and A.H. Wainwright, Walsh was proposed by R.B. Mynors and seconded by Sir Herbert Lewis. Again, while all Green Price's assenters were Knighton businessmen or local farmers, Walsh's included G.H. Philips, Robert Lewis Lloyd, R.W. Banks and General Sladen, all major landowners.

At the declaration of the poll on 9 July Walsh secured 1,910 votes to Green Price's 1,668, thus increasing his majority in little more than six months from 67 to 242. Sir Richard Green Price attributed his defeat to the local Liberals' lack of organisation since the election had come before the planned reorganisation had been completed; the failure on the part of some new voters to understand the issue of Home Rule; and the Conservative success in persuading about 400 of the new voters to abstain. However Green Price ignored the main reason for his defeat, the fact that Home Rule was not popular with some floating voters and some Liberals, including his son Dansey and Charles Coltman Rogers, who chaired some of Green Price's meetings but otherwise had kept a low profile and subsequently declared as a Liberal Unionist. Home Rule may have been an issue which divided another traditionally Whig family for the Revd W.E. Prickard, the brother of the Liberal Association president, T.C. Prickard, had appeared on a Unionist platform backing Walsh at Rhayader. It was rumoured that T.C. Prickard had absented himself during the election campaign because he was reluctant to oppose Sir Richard Green Price in public over Home Rule after having worked with him for a couple of decades. After the defeat of 1886 the local Liberal Association was reorganised yet again and with the Gladstonian Liberals firmly in control and selecting a Gladstonian candidate, Samuel Howard Whitbread, the Revd T.C. Prickard broke with the Liberals, declaring:

> I could take no part in any movement which has for its object the support of Mr Gladstone's Irish policy.[42]

The choice of Whitbread as candidate was a potential cause of division in the ranks of the Radnorshire Liberals. As the *Hereford Times* of 21 July 1888 reported, Ormathwaite gleefully pointed out to the Lower Elvel habitation of the Primrose League at Clyro that the Whitbreads were the most eminent brewing family in England and owned more public houses than any other family in the country, contrasting this with many of Whitbread's supporters who thought that there were too many public houses already. Whitbread was unlikely to be accepted enthusiastically by many Radnorshire nonconformists and they must have been relieved to read in the *Hereford Times* of 23 March 1889 that his offer to resign, on the grounds that he was going on a long journey to Asia and was likely to be away for months, was accepted with alacrity by the county Liberal Association. Nor did Whitbread's successor as prospective Liberal candidate, the Scot, Col. Colquhoun Reade, last long, for selected in June 1889, he resigned in early November the same year on health grounds.

By the late 1880s politics in Radnorshire was beginning to take on many of the characteristics of the modern day. It was becoming party based, with little room in practice for the 'independent Member' so admired in the first half of the nineteenth century, although the term 'party politician' remained far from complimentary. Each party was beginning to develop a clearly defined programme based on the vested interests of its members and the ideals and priorities to which they subscribed and clearly distinguishable from that of its rivals. With the growth of the electorate, the parties increasingly realized the importance of building up a countywide organisation if the support of uncommitted voters was to be secured. Slowly too, the horizons of the local parties began to widen as they looked beyond the county to the electoral picture at regional and national levels. The first sign of this was the increasingly common practice in the 1880s of holding joint meetings with candidates of the same party from neighbouring constituencies. However, despite the best efforts of the local press, the Liberal *Hereford Times* and the Conservative *Hereford Journal*, Radnorshire politics remained for the most part parochial in outlook, with the exception of the big issues of Irish Home Rule and disestablishment of the Welsh Church.

5 A Welsh Dimension

Prior to the 1890s Radnorshire politics were largely English rather than Welsh in character, outlook and personnel, with Welsh issues, beyond those impacting directly upon the county, receiving scant attention. Radnorshire was dominated economically and socially by its thoroughly anglicised southern and eastern fringes and the MPs representing both constituencies were either English, like the Walshes, considered themselves to be English, like the Lewises of Harpton, or were largely English in outlook and upbringing. With the old Whig leadership routed, the new Radnorshire Liberal leadership was not only more radical, but also more Welsh in outlook. Thus in 1888 T.E. Duggan, the president of the Radnorshire Liberal Association, attended a meeting of the South Wales Liberal Federation at Pembroke Dock and, at the prompting of S.C. Williams according to the *Times* of 14 August 1890, the Radnorshire Liberals began to search for a 'genuine Welsh Radical'.

The situation in Radnorshire had begun to change, partly because of a shift in gravity as the more Welsh Radnorshire heartland became more important both socially and economically, partly as a result of the rapid growth of Llandrindod Wells, and began to exercise greater influence in decision-making, not only in politics but in county matters generally. Another important issue of the two decades prior to the outbreak of war in 1914 was the disestablishment and disendowment of the Welsh Church, a matter of deep concern to both churchman and chapel-goer in Radnorshire, which led both groups to view politics from a national rather than a local perspective. Welsh nonconformists thought that now they were in a marked majority in the Principality it was wrong for the minority Anglican Church to continue to be the established or state church, and held the view that whilst its endowments in the form of land and financial investments should remain in the control of the church they should be used for the benefit of the community as a whole. Welsh churchmen, for the most part, wished to maintain the *status quo* and regarded disendowment as nothing less than confiscation of private property.

The final factor was the influence and leadership of Francis Edwards, the dominant figure in Radnorshire politics from 1892 until 1918, although he did not represent the county in the Commons for the whole of that period. It was he who brought Radnorshire into regular contact with the mainstream of Welsh Liberalism and Welsh politics.

Francis Edwards, 1892-95

Plate 27: Francis Edwards

The fourth son of Edward Edwards, an hotelier of Llangollen, Francis Edwards was born in 1853 at Aberdovey and educated at Shrewsbury School and Jesus College, Oxford. After quali-fying as a solicitor he practised for a while in London. In 1880 he married Katherine, a daughter of David Davis of Aberdare, the wealthy owner of Ferndale Collieries. He made his political debut speaking in support of Tom Ellis in the Merioneth election of 1886. A member of *Cymru Fydd* or 'Young Wales', he saw himself very much as a Welsh Liberal rather than a Liberal and was active in the South Wales Liberal Federation, prior to being selected as the Liberal candidate for Radnorshire in 1890. Although a churchman and the nephew of the Revd H.T. Edwards, the dean of Bangor, and of the future first archbishop of Wales, Edwards was a strong champion of the disestab-lishment and disendowment of the Welsh Church. A fluent Welsh speaker, in 1913 he published a translation of Welsh lyrical poetry.[1]

On 12 March 1890 Francis (known as Frank in the 1890s) Edwards, 'a genuine Welsh Radical', was selected as Liberal candidate and initially regarded by many as an incomer and no more than a 'forlorn hope'. Dubbed 'a political adventurer' and 'a Judas who betrayed his Church' (as a churchman who backed disestablishment) by Penry Lloyd, who claimed that he had been approached to be the Liberal candidate, Edwards took care to make it clear that he was prepared for the long haul, for after taking a lease on The Cottage, the old Green Price home in Knighton, he spent a considerable sum on repairs and improvements.[2] Since Sir Richard Green Price's son, the Revd Alfred Green Price, married Edwards' niece Mary Edwards in 1893, it is tempting to see a personal link between the two Radnorshire Liberal MPs, although in fact they never met.

Initially Edwards faced an uphill struggle for he was faced with the formidable Ormathwaite electoral expertise, while the grievances of the tenant farmers of the Radnorshire heartland had been contained by rent rebates and tithe rebates, many of the latter negotiated by one of Walsh's supporters, E. Moseley of Llanddewi Hall, in the late 1880s.[3] Thus the heat had been largely taken out of the tithes issue in the county — a tithe war was then raging in north Wales — even before the responsibility for the payment of tithes had been transferred from the tenant to the landowner in 1891.

Within eighteen months or so Edwards had transformed the situation and by the beginning of October 1891 the *Western Mail*, the 'Tory oracle and the parsons' second prayer book', had grave doubts as to Walsh's chances of retaining the seat:

> Mr Edwards, the Radical candidate, has considerably strengthened his position in the constituency of late. He works hard to gain the confidence and good will of the electors, and is fairly well liked among the gentry and landed proprietors of the county.

Later, the London *Times* also acknowledged his skill in nursing the constituency:

> He has worked unceasingly. He has graced with his autograph the family bible of every voter, and though conventionally a Churchman has 'read a chapter' in every Radnorshire dissenting chapel. He has attended, like a preacher, every Dissenting tea and function, and every fair and market with the regularity of a drover, and has been generous as well as active ...[4]

To add to Conservative concerns, in the closing months of 1891 Arthur Walsh began to hint that he would not seek re-election. Thus at Aberedw in mid-October he asked the electors to support the Conservative candidate 'whoever he might be'. However he did not make a final decision, thus creating a cloud of uncertainty which was not dispersed until 5 January 1892, even though most people expected an election in at most a few months, when a formal announcement was made that Walsh would not contest the seat, 'through private circumstances'.[5]

In a letter to the Revd R.L. Venables of November 1891 Walsh gave some indication of these private circumstances: the strain of personal attendance in the county — particularly as he did not have a residence in Radnorshire, and had to bear all the expense of the seat since Conservative headquarters in London refused to make a grant, while the county Conservative Association was receiving few subscriptions. The increasing financial difficulties of the Walsh family — Baron Ormathwaite was declared bankrupt in 1895 — gave this last factor particular relevance. Moreover Arthur Walsh did not enjoy good health, and in 1891 was unable to fulfil some speaking engagements.[6]

The uncertainty generated by Walsh's failure to reach a decision quickly in the closing months of 1891 was compounded by the failure of the Radnorshire Conservatives to begin to select their new candidate until 21 March 1892. In the intervening months no fewer than nine possible candidates were discussed in the local press, including the former Liberal candidate Charles Coltman Rogers; Robert Lewis Lloyd; Powlett Milbank, the son-in-law of Sir Richard Green Price; Sir Herbert Lewis and Captain J.A. Bradney of Monmouthshire. The choice was finally between Lewis and Bradney, but even then there was confusion. Initially Lewis was selected, thanks to Walsh influence according to some, but he ultimately withdrew on grounds of ill health in favour of Bradney in mid-April. However this was not the end of Conservative difficulties, for in mid-May Edward Wood, the able and efficient Conservative Association secretary, who was also acting as election agent, resigned and was replaced by the Builth solicitor, Alfred Gwynne Vaughan.[7] The Conservatives thus faced the prospect of an election campaign with novices at the helm.

Joseph Alfred Bradney, 1859-1933, of Tal-y-coed, Monmouthshire, was educated at Harrow and Trinity College, Cambridge. He was a JP and DL in Monmouthshire where he had served as sheriff in 1889. He did have a personal link with Radnorshire, in that in 1883 he had married Annie Rosa Sophia, the only daughter and heiress of Edward Jenkins of Nantygroes, Whitton. A captain in the Royal Monmouthshire Engineers Militia since 1882, in the summer 1892 he was promoted to the rank of lieutenant colonel and became officer commanding the 3rd Volunteer Battalion, South Wales Borderers. Once selected as a candidate for Radnorshire he moved his family to The Grove at Whitton, which had been his mother-in-law's home. A Welsh speaker, who was teaching his children the language, he was subsequently to achieve a considerable reputation as a scholar.[8]

With the dissolution of the House expected in June and an election in early July, both sides embarked on a series of meetings across the county, each candidate sometimes speaking at two meetings in a day. Edwards was a gifted orator, but the energetic and enthusiastic Bradney was not such a fluent speaker. On one occasion at Knighton on 30 June, after a long tirade against Irish Home Rule by a Dr Usher, an Irish Baptist minister, the meeting ended in uproar and Bradney was unable to get a hearing.[9]

The prospect of an election was welcomed by the Radical *Brecon and Radnor Express* which noted that:

> For nine successive elections, all of which contests, except one of an unimportant nature, Radnorshire accepted a Walsh as its member with the obedient docility of a spaniel.

The paper hoped there was a chance to show that the Radnorshire seat was not 'as much an appanage of the Walshes as their lands and their chattels'. Initially optimistic about Edwards' chances, the newspaper began to worry later as rumours circulated that some Baptists and Congregationalists were going to vote Conservative, though it took some consolation from the view of the late Dr Thomas of Pontypool who had asserted somewhat extravagantly that:

> A Tory Baptist is as meaningless an expression as a sober drunkard, a chaste adulterer, an honest rogue, a trustworthy lawyer or a wise fool.[10]

Edwards' platform had as its main themes Irish Home Rule and the disestablishment and disendowment of the Welsh Church, but also urged amending the registration laws to reduce the qualifying time, which could take more than two years, for inclusion on the electoral register; carrying into law the Welsh Liquor Traffic Veto, which would enable a two-thirds majority of the ratepayers to introduce a prohibition on the sale of intoxicating liquors in the parish or district; the introduction of district and parish councils; and further reform of the land law in favour of the tenant farmer.

Bradney's address rejected the idea of Irish Home Rule out of hand, made no mention of the disestablishment issue and stressed the achievements of Lord Salisbury's ministry which, since 1886, had provided free education up to the age of 12 and a new system of local government, the county councils, while abroad it had avoided war but maintained the standing of Britain. The *Times* was optimistic:

> The prospects in Radnorshire are in themselves good. The county is Conservative, Ormathwaite decidedly popular and, if he were not, unfortunately a peer, no Radical would contest the seat.[11]

Perhaps the most interesting side issue of the campaign was the attempt of Sir Dansey Green Price to rehabilitate his father's reputation in the eyes of the Unionists and the Conservatives. He maintained that his father had not stood in 1886 because he believed strongly in the justice of Irish Home rule, but only out of loyalty to Gladstone whom he counted as a personal friend. This view was rebutted however by Dansey's half-brother, Whitmore Green Price, one of the few members of the family to remain loyal to the Liberals, at least for a while.[12]

At the election, held on 12 July 1892, Edwards polled 1,973 votes to Bradney's 1,740, increasing the Liberal vote by more than 18% on 1886. The victory was celebrated with great enthusiasm, particularly in Knighton, which had adopted Edwards as its own and had also provided his election agent in the form of the solicitor, C.M. Nixson.

For its part the Conservative *Hereford Journal* took the result philosophically, expressing surprise that Bradney had polled as many votes as he did:

> To expect Mr Bradney, at the eleventh hour, to win a seat which had been carefully nursed by Mr Frank Edwards for years, was altogether out of the question.

The London *Times* laid the responsibility for the loss of Radnorshire squarely on Arthur H.J. Walsh, the son of the second Lord Ormathwaite:

> Mr Walsh, till a few months before the election securely enjoyed his honours and then suddenly announced his retirement. Name after name was then put forward by the Unionists, Mr Walsh apparently having little or nothing to do with them. At last and too late Mr Bradney was chosen, and a right gallant fight he made. Had the late member, before retiring, made sure of a successor and used well his own and his family's great and deserved influence to back him up, the Separatists would not today hold Radnorshire.[13]

The *Brecon and Radnor Express* of 8 October 1896 saw the problem as being a lack of direction at the centre, for the Conservative County Association had not met for nearly a year prior to the election, which had been managed by district committees and Primrose League branches. This would suggest that the long tenure of the county seat by the Walsh family had sapped the initiative of the local Conservatives and made them over-reliant on the Walsh family.

Inevitably the loss of the seat produced bruised feelings on the part of a few local Conservatives and one farmer in the Presteigne area dismissed two labourers for voting for Edwards rather than for Bradney. The Liberals were quick to exploit this, and placed the case in the hands of the Voters' Protection Association who engaged London solicitors and counsel. However nothing came of the affair, although the publicity produced a few donations for the unfortunate labourers, whilst the farmer concerned remained unapologetic:

> If a man will give me his conscience as well as his day's work I will have him, if not, he goes!

Some time later, two domestic servants at one of the 'big houses' near Presteigne who attended a revivalist meeting at the Wesleyan chapel in the town, were told that they would be dismissed if they attended the chapel again.[14]

Powlett Milbank, 1895-1900

After the resignation of Lt Col Bradney as the Conservative candidate in September 1892, Powlett Milbank was selected in his place. He had inherited a fortune estimated at £400,000 or £22,000 a year from his great uncle, the second duke of Cleveland. Both his father, Sir Frederick Milbank, and his father-in-law, Sir Richard Green Price, had been Gladstonian Liberal MPs and some in Radnorshire with long memories remembered him campaigning for Green Price in 1880 and advocating disestablishment. When he had been mentioned as a possible Conservative candidate in 1892 the *Hereford Journal* dismissed him out of hand on these grounds, while in the *Brecon and Radnor Express* of 10 March 1893 he was termed 'the renegade Liberal'.

Plate 28: Powlett Milbank

Though he was very much Ormathwaite's choice, Milbank was not a popular choice in some quarters. He failed to make a good impression initially amongst the Conservative rank and file for he stated right at the start that he did not expect to win back the seat at the first attempt, while his initial early campaigning in 1893 lacked urgency and gave some the impression that he was not a serious candidate. To others his stance against disestablishment seemed far from enthusiastic. Some in the Conservative ranks felt guilty that Bradney had been abandoned somewhat precipitately after his defeat in 1892 in favour of Milbank, a perception that gained widespread currency in the county to the degree that Bradney had to make a statement denying that this was the case.[15]

In the meantime Francis Edwards was maintaining a higher profile in the Commons than was the norm for Radnorshire MPs, with the exception of Cornewall Lewis. He made his maiden speech in the debate on the Second Reading of the Welsh Local Veto Bill and in 1893 inserted a clause in the Provisional Order giving control of Llandrindod's water supply to a private company that enabled the local board to purchase the water supply in the town if it so wished. In April-May 1894, he was one of the Welsh 'Revolters',

*Plate 29: Norton Manor, c.1920, the home of Richard Price,
Richard Green Price and Sir Powlett Milbank*

Lloyd George and two other Welsh MPs being the other three, who refused
the Liberal Whip so as to bring pressure on Lord Roseberry, who had
succeeded Gladstone as Prime Minister, to give a First Reading to the Welsh
Disestablishment Bill. In 1895 Edwards was the first Welsh MP to speak on
the Second Reading of that Bill.

During the parliamentary vacations Edwards nursed the constituency
assiduously, though he saw his task as that of advancing the Liberal cause
throughout Wales as a whole rather than in Radnorshire alone.

In the meantime Milbank began to win over Conservative opinion in the
county. In 1892 he had bought the Norton Manor estate from his brother-
in-law Sir Dansey Green Price, who was in financial difficulties, and made
Norton Manor the family home as his wife had found it difficult to settle
in Yorkshire. This gave him not only a residence in the county, but also a
large agricultural stake and a bond with the farming community. He had also
won over the admittedly partisan *Hereford Journal* which, at the beginning of
March 1894, was of the view that his frankness and his grasp of politics was
winning over the voters.

One of his first acts on taking over the Norton Manor estate was to
make his brother-in-law, Whitmore Green Price, the last remaining Liberal
in the Green Price family, his agent, and, in the summer of 1894, after he
had become a Conservative, his election agent. With the Green Price family
all in the Conservative fold, Milbank now had the still considerable Green
Price influence in the county behind him. He also had the full backing of

Ormathwaite who, in June 1894, ensured that he was appointed to the presentation committee of the wedding present from Wales to the duke and duchess of York. Such an appointment enhanced his status and may have influenced some of the more impressionable voters in the county.

The opening months of 1895 saw both parties preoccupied with local government elections including, for the first time, elections for the parish councils. As rumours of a dissolution of Parliament gathered pace in May, attention switched to the possibility of an imminent general election. Milbank could call upon the support of the great majority of the county establishment such as Robert Lewis Lloyd, General Sladen, Sir Herbert Lewis, Coltman Rogers and J.P. Severn, and also upon 'new blood', notably Dr Harding of New Radnor, a very effective, if abrasive, speaker, and James Hamer, the agent of the Severn estate, a nonconformist teetotaller. For the Liberals, the county establishment was conspicuous by its absence, for Evans Williams had sold Bryntirion and moved out of the country, while J. Williams Vaughan appears to have been inactive. Instead Francis Edwards had to rely upon farmers such as T.E. Duggan in the Radnor Valley, and J.R. Bache, who dominated Knighton politics, Richard Morgan the Rhayader tanner, Richard Rogers the Presteigne grocer, and Evan Bufton the Llandrindod Wells auctioneer.

The Radical *Brecon and Radnor Express* was, superficially at least, confident of success. In the issue of 14 June it reported that 'In Radnorshire the Tories are in a very despondent mood', while on 19 July it declared:

> The defeat of Mr Milbank seems absolutely certain; the only Question is by what majority he will be defeated.

Even so, the newspaper had some misgivings, for on 12 July it warned:

> Every non-conformist who at this crisis in our country votes for Milbank will be a traitor to his principles, and the sooner the better he leaves the non-conformist fold.

A week later it alleged that the landowners were putting 'the screw' on tenants 'with a vengeance'. For its part, the Conservative *Hereford Journal* of 13 July reported that Milbank 'had been reviled as an oppressor of his tenants and an oppressor of the poor', and denied the rumour that his decision to stand had been opposed by his wife and her family.

Though the campaign was relatively short, both sides worked hard. Meetings were held virtually every night and thorough canvasses carried out, particularly by the Conservatives who were assisted by volunteers from Ulster 'who paid house to house visits amongst the farmers and labourers.' On 22 July, 'Black Wednesday, when the sun did not shine' according to the

Radnorshire Liberals, Milbank polled 1,949 to Edwards' 1,847. The contest was expected to be close, but even so came as a surprise, and not only to the Liberals.

Some Liberals attributed their defeat to poor organisation, a failure fully to canvass voters, and non-resident voters, while others blamed it on the intimidation of tenants or bribery in the form of promises of blankets, drink or other gifts by canvassers, though such charges were always made in general terms without citing actual cases.[16] However, a number of other factors should be considered. In the first place the Liberals probably overestimated the appeal of disestablishment to the electorate, as the more immediate nonconformist grievances had been remedied by the Burial Act of 1880 which permitted nonconformists to be buried in the churchyard in accordance with their own rites, and by the Tithes Act of 1891 which transferred the liability for tithes from the tenant to the landlord. Again, given the conservative and hierarchical nature of much of Radnorshire society, the extensive Green Price and Ormathwaite influence carried great weight, without intimidation or bribes of blankets and puddings. Moreover, some who had voted Liberal in 1892 were disillusioned, for as Milbank and Dr Harding never tired of pointing out, the Liberal governments of 1892-95 had failed to implement most of the promises which had been made in 1892.

Francis Edwards' electoral prospects were also probably harmed indirectly by Monmouthshire's decision to abandon the scheme of sharing the United Counties Asylum with Breconshire and Radnorshire. This necessitated Monmouthshire compensating those counties for the costs they had incurred in building and running the asylum at Abergavenny. Since no agreement could be reached on the amounts payable, the Home Secretary sent the matter for arbitration, as a result of which Breconshire received an additional £3,000, but the sum payable to Radnorshire was reduced. Throughout the election campaign Dr Harding, a member of the County Council's asylum committee, maintained that Edwards should have intervened more forcefully once the matter had reached the Home Secretary and that his failure to do so had cost the ratepayers of the county the equivalent of a three penny rate. Given that received wisdom at the time was that the main objective of the County Council should be to keep its spending and the rates as low as possible, Harding's accusation, repeated on every possible occasion, almost certainly influenced some electors. Edwards' reply, that he had not been consulted early enough for him to have intervened effectively, seemed lame in comparison.[17]

Politics and local government
The establishment of county councils in 1889, district councils in 1892 and parish councils in 1894, together with the polarisation of public opinion on the major issues of the day, would seem to have provided the ideal circum-

stances for the politicisation of local government. However such a view needs some qualification, for in an informal sense party politics had always coloured local government. Prior to the establishment of such councils local government had been in the hands of the local gentry sitting as magistrates in Quarter Sessions, while those living near or in the boroughs of Knighton, New Radnor, Presteigne and Rhayader had considerable influence on the administration of the borough, if only in their capacity as magistrates sitting in Petty Sessions. The gentry's stance would inevitably be influenced by their political outlook which, after the eclipse of the Whigs in the 1880s was over-whelmingly Conservative. Thus it was claimed in 1893 that of Radnorshire's 101 JPs, 97 were Conservative.[18]

This built-in bias was ignored by the county establishment which tended to argue, as did the second Lord Ormathwaite in relation to the county council, that there was no place for party politics in local government since the councils were executive bodies overseeing the implementation of policies decided by the central government. However, in a rural, socially conservative and hierarchical society such as that of Radnorshire, particularly before the introduction of the secret ballot in local government in 1895, there was a tendency for representatives to be selected on the basis of social status. In such a situation most public bodies in the county tended to have a built-in and informal Conservative majority and it was to counter this that the Liberals began to organise on party lines.

Thus in 1882 with the Conservatives having been in the majority on the Knighton Local Government Board for some years, 'though not by open declaration of their views', the local Liberals ran as a party in the elections, and by April 1883 had six members on the Board as opposed to the Conservatives' three. Similarly Evans Williams believed that the failure of the Liberals to contest the initial county council elections of 1889 on strictly formal party lines played into the hands of Ormathwaite and the Radnorshire establishment. With no fewer that 13 of the 24 county councillors also serving as magistrates, it is not surprising to find that Ormathwaite, already Lord Lieutenant, chairman of the Radnorshire Bench and leader of the local Conservatives, was elected as chairman of the county council with seven Liberal county councillors voting for him. Not surprisingly, in 1893 the Liberals decided to contest the elections on party lines, though without success, for after the elections of March 1893, which the Conservatives also fought on formal party lines, they remained in the minority.[19]

By 1895 the elections for the county council, the rural and urban and district councils and the parish councils were all fought on party lines. In some parishes party feeling ran high and in the first election for the parish council at Llanyre in 1895 the chairman of the parish meeting, after accepting the nomination papers of nine Liberal candidates, rejected the papers of four Conservative candidates on the grounds that they had been completed incorrectly, including the nomination paper of Charles Dillwyn Venables Llewelyn. However party labels did not always count for much. Thus in 1895 the Llanbister voters, having returned the Conservative Lord Ormathwaite unopposed as their county councillor as usual, reversed their political allegiance to return only Liberals, ten in all, to serve on the parish council.[20]

Nor did party labels always explain the situation. Throughout the 1890s a significant proportion of county councillors were returned unopposed, which suggests that personality and local standing still counted for more than a party label (for apathy was not then an issue). In Llanyre in 1896 the parish council contest was not between Liberals and Conservatives, but between 'villagers' in favour of laying on a water supply to the village of Newbridge-on-Wye and their supporters on one side, and 'farmers' opposed to the scheme on the other. In some district councils, such as the Llandrindod Wells UDC, while candidates tended to stand under party labels, the business of the council was not conducted invariably on party lines. Within a few years the enthusiasm for party politics subsided, particularly as far as parish councils were concerned, while in 1896 the newly elected members of Rhayader RDC decided that it was in future to be non-political. However party politics revived in the bitter sectarian controversy following the Education Act of 1902 (see below) and again during the renewed campaign to secure the disestablishment of the Welsh Church.[21]

Francis Edwards and C.L. Dillwyn Venables Llewelyn 1900-1910
Powlett Milbank, who succeeded to his father's baronetcy in 1898, had been appointed Lord Lieutenant in 1895 in succession to Lord Ormathwaite as a reward, according to cynics, for winning the seat. He maintained a low profile in the Commons, though not always supporting the Conservative government; thus in 1897 he voted in favour of an Opposition motion to enable small freeholders to obtain loans using their land as security. Always the country landowner rather than the politician, he did little in the way of nursing the constituency. He always maintained that he had won the seat as a result of his opposition to the disestablishment of the Welsh Church and with the defeat of the Disestablishment Bill in 1895 and the subsequent Liberal downgrading of the issue, his political career may have lost direction.

Following the death of his father in 1898 Milbank's health began to deteriorate and by May 1899 he was talking of giving up the seat should his health break down. He may also have become rather disillusioned with political life, for at a meeting in Radnorshire in 1899 he described how Members on both sides of the House were giving up their seats because of the amounts they were expected to subscribe to good causes, £5,000 in one case, in their constituencies. Significantly he was told shortly afterwards by the chairman of a Conservative meeting at Rhayader that the only complaint they had was that they did not see enough of him. This was probably meant as a compliment, but suggests that his visits to that town were infrequent.

Milbank did not finally decide to retire until the end of March 1900, explaining to the Conservative Association at the end of April that his heart trouble had got worse and would not permit him to fight a contested election or face the long hours of the Commons. In his place the Association accepted the Executive Committee's recommendation that Charles Leyshon Dillwyn Venables Llewelyn should be the Conservative candidate, though, according

to the Liberal *Radnor Express*, some would have preferred the return of Bradney. The choice of Venables Llewelyn caused a measure of concern in neighbouring Breconshire, where he had been the prospective Conservative candidate for a time in 1896 and had been expected to have been the candidate in 1900.[22]

Venables Llewelyn was born in 1870, a younger son of Sir John Dillwyn Llewelyn of Penllergaer near Swansea, and was educated at Eton and New College, Oxford, returning to south Wales to study colliery management and mining engineering. In 1893 he married Katherine Minna, the daughter of the Revd Richard Lister Venables of Llysdinam, taking the additional surname of Venables by royal licence. With a 'Khaki' election expected in the late summer or early autumn in order that the government could exploit British victories in the Boer War, the young candidate had little time to establish himself. Moreover, with his militia

Plate 30: Captain Charles Leyshon Dillwyn Venables Llewelyn c.1900, in the dress uniform of the Carmarthenshire Royal Artillery Militia

Plate 31: Llysdinam Hall in 1904, the home of the Venables family

regiment, the Carmarthenshire RA Militia, on an active service footing in Pembrokeshire, he was unable to campaign for a further six weeks.

Edwards, on the other hand, had taken care to nurse the constituency. He had held regular meetings in the main towns of the counties and whenever possible 'read a chapter' in nonconformist chapels and presided at Chapel or Sunday School anniversary services. Even so, Edwards had his problems since the outbreak of the Boer War in 1899 had created divisions within the Liberal Party, for while the Liberal Imperialists, in keeping with public opinion at large, backed the war, others, the 'Little Englanders' or 'Pro-Boers', opposed it as unjust. Edwards may have had reservations about the war which he described as unnecessary in his electoral address, but with public opinion in the county firmly behind it, he could not afford to air them. The *Radnor Express* of 8 March took a firmly Liberal Imperialist stance after the relief of Ladysmith at the end of February 1900:

> The good news came as a 'bitter pill' to the pro-Boers of Presteigne ... Although there are a few Pro-Boers in he town, fortunately they keep very quiet, for Presteigne is loyal to the backbone and severe results would happen if any open demonstration of pro-Boer feeling were to be shown.

In the opening weeks of June, on leave from his regiment, Venables Llewelyn held a series of meetings throughout the county to make himself known to the electorate. At New Radnor he was supported by his father who stressed that his son wished to serve in the South African campaign but that his family responsibilities and his loyalty to his militia regiment prevented him from doing so. Throughout the summer, the central theme of Venables Llewelyn's speeches and of his election address, issued at the end of August, was the need to return the Conservative government to power in the general election, whenever it came, in order that the war could be brought to a successful conclusion, a firm and lasting peace achieved and the Empire strengthened. Such objectives would be placed at risk if the Liberals were returned, he argued, as they were divided in their attitude towards the war and towards the Empire. For the rest Venables Llewelyn wished to see the War Office reformed to eliminate the shortcomings uncovered by the war, the continuation of the Agricultural Rating Act of 1896 to assist agriculture and better provision for the aged poor. While he opposed disestablishment he was in favour of religious toleration and supported temperance rather than prohibition.[23]

The main contribution of the Radnorshire *Standard* to the Conservative campaign was to portray the Radnorshire Liberals, particularly those at Knighton, as overwhelmingly pro-Boer. In the issue of 12 September the *Standard* declared:

> If our soldiers return from the war in South African time for the election, the pro-Boers or Little Englander will barely be able to his face to the brave fellows who have been risking their lives in defence of their country.

However the newspaper, as yet, made no attempt to identify Francis Edwards with the pro-Boers.

Edwards opened his campaign a week or so before the dissolution of Parliament on 25 September with a public meeting at Knighton and the publication of his electoral address. He denounced the Conservative government for seeking to snatch a victory at the polls as a result of a war won by both Conservatives and Liberals, and on an expiring electoral register which disenfranchised thousands. As for 'the deplorable war', he felt the government had made insufficient preparations and seriously miscalculated Boer resistance. The programme offered by Edwards was much more detailed than that offered by Venables Llewelyn, envisaging land reform to give the tenant farmer greater security, disestablishment of the Welsh Church, reform of the Licensing and Electoral Registration Acts, better conditions for the aged poor and reform of the House of Lords. It was also hoped to halt the flight from the countryside by the provision of smallholdings and better housing for agricultural labourers. Finally Edwards condemned the Agricultural Rating Act of 1896 which benefited the landlord rather than the tenant farmer and the Voluntary Schools Act by which the taxpayers aided Church Schools over which they had no control.[24]

As election day, 10 October, approached, both sides redoubled their efforts, with Venables Llewelyn speaking at thirteen meetings in the constituency in the last ten days. Invariably relations between the two sides deteriorated, although the two candidates remained on the best of terms. Some Conservatives continued to portray the Liberals as pro-Boer and unpatriotic, while some Liberals dismissed Venables as an inexperienced youth and claimed that Sir Powlett Milbank and Whitmore Green Price did not support him, a charge which both immediately denied. Milbank found himself in another spat with the Liberals when he unwisely got together his tenants and dependents at Norton School and urged them to vote Conservative, only to be accused of attempting to intimidate them.[25]

When the poll was declared on 11 October, Edwards had regained the seat with a majority of 106, polling 2,052 votes to Venables Llewelyn's 1,916. As usual the victory was attributed by the losing party to the superior organisation on the part of their opponents. However in its analysis of the result, the *Radnorshire Standard* of 11 October displayed a degree of bitterness new to the Radnorshire political scene:

> The turncoats ... who converted Powlett Milbank's majority of 81 into a minority for Venables Llewelyn are the pro-Boers whose existence has been so often denied by the Radicals of this county. Their party should invite Kruger [the Boers' leader] and feast him.

Surprisingly, neither side attributed Edwards' victory, at least in part, to the votes of labourers only present in the county as a result of working on the Elan valley dams or on the pipeline to carry water to Birmingham.

Edwards was greeted with enthusiasm by his exultant supporters at Presteigne and Knighton but proceedings at Llandrindod Wells on Saturday, 13 October, ended in a near riot, possibly because feelings had been inflamed by the *Standard*, while the Liberals may have been a shade too triumphalist in a new town which was unused to political demonstrations. After a torch-lit procession through the main streets Edwards and his supporters returned to the Victoria Building to hear Edwards speak from the balcony. Some Conservatives tried to intervene and in the fracas that followed their Union flag was seized and burned. Uproar resulted and Edwards was pelted with apples, tomatoes and eggs, 'fists were freely used' and the Liberal banner was also burned.[26]

Unusually for Radnorshire the ill-feeling between the two parties continued long after the election. Defeated in conventional military campaigns, the Boers

Plate 32: Charles L.D. Venables Llewelyn from an election address of 1910

resorted to guerrilla warfare and to deprive them of supplies and shelter, the civilian population in some areas was 'concentrated' into camps where living conditions were initially at least, far from satisfactory. One of the Liberal MPs who voted for an inquiry into these conditions was Francis Edwards. Inevitably this produced its own criticism, particularly from the *Radnorshire Standard*. He was labelled a pro-Boer and it was said that if he had given a true statement of his views on the war before the election he would not have been elected. Others rushed to his defence saying that he 'had voted for the cause of humanity and against the ill-treatment of Boer women and children', and the Llandrindod Wells Free Church Council also rallied to his support.[27]

Shortly after a peace settlement had been reached and the Boers of the Orange Free State and the Transvaal were in the Empire once more, Edwards was successful in the House of Commons ballot for initiating a Private Member's Bill. He chose as a subject that of giving Welsh county councils wider powers. As the *Cambrian News* pointed out, the Local Government Act of 1888 had already given Wales a great deal more power in the direction of Home Rule than had yet been utilised by the county councils.[28] Edwards's Bill, which was not passed, nevertheless enabled him 'to cut a figure before his constituents and also, to some extent, before the whole Principality'.

Of more import was the great hostility engendered between the Anglicans, backed by the Conservatives, and the nonconformists, backed by the Liberals, as a result of the Education Act of 1902 which provided for Church schools to be supported from the rates. The Church met all building expenses, appointed the teachers, and controlled the religious education syllabus of the school, while the county council met all other costs, but appointed only two of the six school managers, thus giving the Church effective control. In effect nonconformist ratepayers were subsidising Anglican schools. This was a particular issue in Radnorshire, which had only 10 Board of Education schools (which now became known as council schools) which provided non-sectarian religious education, whereas there were 32 National schools providing an Anglican religious education and a further 9 parish schools, the great majority of which also provided an Anglican religious education.[29]

The nonconformist leaders in the county were ready to fight the Education Act 'to the death', but could expect no support from the county council where the Conservatives had been in the majority since its inception. Thus, when the county rate was being set in 1903 and the Liberal councillor Richard Morgan of Rhayader objected 'to the levying of any rate for sectarian schools not under popular control', the rate was approved by 17 votes to 5 without debate.

Nonconformists developed two strategies to demonstrate their opposition to the Act and to make life difficult for the county council, and the education committee. The first was 'passive resistance', the withholding of that part of the county rate to be spent on education. Thus in 1903, with the county rate fixed at 6½d (2.5p) in the pound, of which 2½d (1p) was in respect of elementary education, the passive resister withheld 2½d for each pound of rateable value. The refusal to pay would lead to a summons to appear at Petty Sessions at which the passive resister hoped to have the opportunity to state his views publicly (all the passive resisters were male; it is doubtful if action would have been taken against a female since this would have been considered ungallant). However most were not given a chance to make such a statement, the exception being at Rhayader under its chairman, General Sladen. Invariably, however, the magistrates gave an order for bailiffs to distrain upon the passive resister's goods which were then sold to meet the costs and the withheld rates. Twenty-one passive resisters at Knighton had goods distrained, 19 at Llandrindod Wells, 2 at New Radnor, 2 at Presteigne and 52 at Rhayader and St Harmon. Sales of the distrained goods attracted large crowds of sympathizers and were conducted with great good humour by sympathetic local auctioneers, the goods almost invariably ending back with the person from whom they had come.

Although Lloyd George had little time for the action, he featured in a song designed to encourage passive resistance in the county, to be sung to the tune 'Hold the Fort'. The last verse ran:

*Plate 33: The sale of goods of 21 'Passive Resisters' at Knighton
in March 1904. According to the* Radnor Express *of 17 March,
Philip Davies, the Presteigne auctioneer, conducted the sale
which was witnessed by 'some thousands'*

Fierce tho' the battle rages'
Victory is near;
Brave Lloyd George is our Commander,
Cheer, Radnorians, cheer![30]

The impact of the passive resisters on public opinion in the county is unknown and local Conservatives tended to dismiss them out of hand.[31]

Tension increased when the Builth and Knighton Poor Law Unions, responsible for collecting the county rate from the Radnorshire parishes within the Unions, withheld the education rate. The failure to pay the full county rate on time made the Unions liable to a discretionary surcharge of 10%, which the Conservative majority on the county council determined to impose. Before the sanction could be imposed the county council elections of March 1904 resulted in a sweeping victory for the Liberals, giving them 17 councillors to the Conservatives' 7. With four Liberals, including Frank Edwards, elected as aldermen by the county councillors and serving for six years, the Liberals took control of the county council and waived the surcharge. As both Poor Law Unions felt that they had made their point, they now paid the outstanding balances. Despite the close friendship between Frank Edwards and David Lloyd George, Radnorshire did not follow most Welsh county councils in refusing to administer the Act except on limited terms, thus avoiding sanctions imposed by the government, preferring instead to hope that a future Liberal government would amend the Act to make it acceptable to nonconformists. [32]

While the Liberals had put contentious issues as disestablishment and Irish Home Rule on the backburner, Joseph Chamberlain was urging the concept of Tariff Reform upon the Conservatives. He envisaged abandoning Britain's traditional policy of Free Trade in favour of uniting the Empire in a customs union and imposing import duties on foreign goods which would finance social reforms at home, colonial development and increased spending on the navy. However the proposal to abandon Free Trade did not go down well with all Conservatives, particularly with former Liberals such as Charles Coltman Rogers of Stanage. In December 1905, with his party in disarray, the prime minister, Arthur Balfour, resigned and the Liberal leader, Sir Henry Campbell-Bannerman, formed a minority government and immediately sought a dissolution of Parliament.

With the election scheduled for 23 January 1906 the campaign was short, but the bitter controversy over the 1902 Education Act had heightened political awareness on both sides, for while the Liberals voiced the concern many nonconformists felt over the perceived injustices of the Act, so the Conservatives backed the Anglicans in their stout defence of Church schools. The continued sniping of both sides over the application of the Act at the local level raised the political temperature and served as a recruiting sergeant for both political parties. Not surprisingly the local party agents, C.M. Nixson for the Liberals and E.P. and A.L. Careless for the Conservatives, had been particularly active at the revision courts of September 1905.

Frank Edwards' manifesto urged the amendment of the 1902 Education Act to give the people full control of the schools, and backed Free Trade, but otherwise it differed little from that of 1900, backing land reform in the interest of tenant farmers, temperance reform, reform of the electoral and registration law to eliminate plural votes and to reduce the period of qualification for inclusion on the electoral register, and legislation to improve the lot of the aged poor. Significantly there was no direct reference to disestablishment or Home Rule, nor any attack on Imperialism. For its part the Liberal *Radnor Express* contrasted the 'Big Loaf' of Free Trade and the 'Little Loaf' which it considered would result from import duties imposed on foreign foodstuffs. It also denounced the use of indentured Chinese labour, a policy tolerated by the Tory government, in very poor living conditions in South African goldmines.[33]

C.L. Dillwyn Venables Llewelyn was chosen as the Conservative candidate at the end of December 1905. His electoral address enthusiastically endorsed Tariff Reform, and backed support for farming, in particular the continuation of the Agricultural Rating Act, and better provision for the aged poor, along with religious toleration and improving educational opportunities. It also hinted darkly at the possibility of a Liberal government dependent upon the votes of Irish Nationalists who would insist on Home Rule as the price of their support.

Both candidates conducted busy campaigns, for example in the week 6-13 January, Edwards spoke at seven meetings in the county and Venables Llewelyn at nine. Even so, press coverage of the campaigns gives the impression that they were generally low key, with only one incident considered untoward, the organised booing of Venables Llewelyn at an election meeting in Knighton. In the main both candidates relied upon assistance from local speakers; Edwards upon Professor Rees of Brecon and the Revd T.E. Williams of Newtown, and Venables Llewelyn upon his father and local Conservatives such as Sir Herbert Frankland Lewis and Messrs Harding and Hamer.[34]

Even the Conservative *Radnorshire Standard*, not usually sparing in its denunciations of the 'Radicals' as they termed the Liberals, seemed subdued in its approach to the election. The issue of 17 January printed a race card for 'The Radnorshire Parliamentary Stakes', giving odds of evens on 'The Cottage' (Edwards) and 'Llysdinam' (Venables Llewelyn) at 6 to 4 on and gave a description of the horses' training runs. Thus 'Llysdinam', running over a six furlong course:

> ... cleared the Home Rule and Fiscal Reform jumps remarkably well, not jibbing at a single fence.

As far as 'The Cottage' was concerned:

> He went off at a good canter until he reached the Home Rule hurdle where he repeatedly jibbed. Having temporarily evaded this fence he galloped in rare style but fell badly at the Free Trade ditch and his jockey became disestablished ... In the preliminary canter his trainer wisely refrained from trying him at the big jump — the Agricultural Rates Hurdles — in fact the trainer remarked the other day, he wished they were absent. However 'The Cottage' had successfully evaded them in the past and although he was ageing considerably, he hoped with a final spring to clear them on Tuesday.

On the following Tuesday, the turnout, 76.8%, was almost identical with that in 1900 and Edwards was returned by 2,187 votes to Venables Llewelyn's 2,013, increasing his majority by a substantial margin. The Liberals were somewhat relieved as they had feared that the running down of the labour force at Elan Valley and on the water pipeline to Birmingham would have reduced their vote significantly. The *Radnor Express* was gracious in victory in its reference to Venables Llewelyn, claiming that, apart from his political views, he 'would have been welcomed with open arms virtually anywhere in the constituency'.[35]

The *Radnorshire Standard* of 24 January attributed the Conservative defeat to the 'Big Loaf' and Chinese Slavery issues, and claimed that although Venables Llewelyn had lost he had not been disgraced since the Liberals had been hoping for a majority of 250. For his part 'Fiscal Reform' of Presteigne in a letter to the *Hereford Times* of 27 January congratulated the Radnorshire Conservatives on what he saw as a moral victory as 'never was an election fought in such adverse and dispiriting circumstances'. In general the confidence of local Conservatives in Tariff Reform remained unimpaired, and the defeat was attributed to the fact that its time had not yet arrived.

For eighteen months or so after the election party politics was virtually suspended in Radnorshire as controversy raged as to whether it was necessary to build county buildings in Llandrindod Wells to house the county council, police headquarters and possibly quarter sessions and assizes. Conservatives such as Powlett Milbank and Richard Harding, along with Liberals such as Richard Rogers and John Bache from south-east Radnorshire united to urge the merits of the Shire Hall at Presteigne, on grounds of economy, whilst Conservatives and Liberals of the Radnorshire heartland saw county buildings at Llandrindod Wells as much more convenient.

By mid-1907, however, normal party politics had been resumed and over the next few years both parties sought to broaden the base of their popular support. Venables Llewelyn organised meetings throughout the county to explain Tariff Reform, and branches of the Tariff Reform League were set up at Llandrindod Wells, New Radnor, Presteigne and Rhayader. Mrs Venables Llewelyn set up the Radnorshire Women's Unionist Society to campaign against Irish Home Rule, with branches in the Radnorshire towns and some of the larger Radnorshire villages.

For their part the Liberals organised Free Trade meetings, noting the threat to British exports and employment as foreign countries reacted to Tariff Reform by raising duties on British goods. They also set up branches of the Young Liberal Association in Knighton, Llandrindod Wells, Presteigne and Rhayader, to build up their support amongst the younger generation, the moving spirit being Henry Tolson of Knighton, who had honed his political skills in local government in Yorkshire and Exeter. Liberalism in Radnorshire received a boost when Frank Edwards received a baronetcy in 1907, though the contrast between 'Frank Edwards' and 'Sir Francis Edwards, Bart' as he was now often styled, led to some not so gentle teasing over the next few years at the hands of the *Radnorshire Standard*. The paper termed Edwards 'the Caliph' and Bache as 'the Vizier', while some Knighton correspondents to the *Radnorshire Standard*, notably 'Clockface', took to referring to Edwards as 'Sir Bart' rather than by his name, while 'Clock' changed his own pseudonym to 'Sir Clock Bart'.[36]

By 1909 the hostility of nonconformists towards the 1902 Education Act had died away since it had not led to the dire consequences which they had feared. However two events of that year galvanised both parties into action; the introduction of a Disestablishment Bill in the Commons in April and the rejection of Lloyd George's Budget by the House of Lords and the ensuing constitutional crisis. Ever since the return of the Liberal government in 1906, Welsh churchmen had feared that sooner or later a bill to disestablish the Welsh Church would be introduced in the Commons, though in reality the Liberals gave such a measure a low priority. The introduction of the Bill in April 1909 was designed mainly to placate Welsh Liberal MPs and by July, after it had received a First Reading, it was dropped from the business for the session. Even so it caused widespread protests amongst Radnorshire clergy and churchmen who organised Church Defence meetings in most parishes over the next few years, with the Knighton incumbent, the Revd D.G. Macpherson, emerging as a formidable debater on behalf of the Church.

Even so, disestablishment was essentially a side issue in the period 1909-10, for the real clash came over Lloyd George's Budget which sought to finance the government's social reforms and increased spending on the Navy by increasing the rate of death duty on large estates, the introduction of super-tax in addition to income tax on incomes of more than £3,000 a year, and a new tax on unearned increases in land values which would involve valuing all the land and buildings in the country. The proposals provoked much hostility amongst Radnorshire landowners. Many small freeholders feared that the tax on unearned increments in land values would affect them, despite assurances that it would not apply to agricultural land unless it was sold for development. The refusal of the Lords to accept the Budget met with significant support in some quarters, with Budget protest meetings held throughout the county. The largest of these was that held at the Albert Hall, Llandrindod Wells, at the beginning of September, which was addressed by Venables Llewelyn and J.M. Gibson Watt and attended by 1,200 people with another 200-300 outside.[37]

For their part the Radnorshire Liberals rushed to champion 'The People's Budget'. Thus in the *Radnor Express* of 16 December there appeared *The Budget Song*:

We've got a splendid purser,	He be too tender hearted,
His name is D Lloyd George,	To tax our loaf of bread,
And by his 'Workmen's Budget',	Upon the wealthy nobles,
He'll make the Dukes disgorge.	He'll make the call instead.
He knows the lucky people,	He'll tax 'em while they're living,
Who's got a living fat,	He'll tax 'em when they're dead,
And to these landed gentry,	But our David ain't believing,
He's taken round his hat.	In taxing people's bread.

The rejection of the Budget by the Lords led to the dissolution of Parliament and a general election, the date of the election in Radnorshire being fixed by the sheriff, W.S. Bryan, for Wednesday, 19 January, one of the earliest of the possible dates. The choice of a Wednesday disadvantaged the Liberals as men working away from home during the week would find it difficult to travel back to vote, which would not have been the case if the election had been held on a Saturday or a Monday when they could vote early before leaving for work.

Edwards' election address centred on Free Trade and, more immediately, reform of the House of Lords in order to secure the budget and abolish the Lords' power of veto, and promised reform of the land law, the Poor Law, the educational system, electoral and registration law, together with temperance reform and progress towards the disestablishment of the Welsh Church. It also claimed that the Liberal Government had reformed and modernised the Army, strengthened the Navy and in South Africa had eliminated the use of indentured Chinese labour and had reconciled the Boers by the granting of self-government to the Orange Free State and the Transvaal coupled with the formation of the South African Federation.[38]

Venables Llewelyn's election address backed Tariff Reform, the continuation of the Agricultural Rates Act, the maintenance of the House of Lords, the expansion of the Navy and of the Territorial Army and opposed Irish Home Rule, disestablishment of the Welsh Church and reform of the 1902 Education Act. He also ran a much more effective campaign than Edwards who never got into his stride, despite the visit of Lloyd George to speak on his behalf at Llandrindod Wells towards the end of the campaign. Much of the groundwork had already been done for Venables Llewelyn by the Budget protest meetings and the meetings of the Church Defence League of the autumn of 1909. Thus, while the Revd D.G. Macpherson continued to harry Edwards on the issue of Disestablishment, in his election meetings Venables Llewelyn concentrated on what he maintained were the long term advantages of Tariff Reform: increased employment, better wages, a fall in the cost of living and increased food production in Britain and the Empire. In the meantime the *Radnorshire Standard* turned the 'dear food' argument against Edwards by pointing out that he had voted against reducing the duty on tea and sugar and had been absent from the Commons when a motion was introduced abolishing the duty on cocoa.[39]

Although the two candidates remained on good terms, the run up to the election and the election campaign itself saw a marked decline in the standard of conduct of political activists on both sides. Attempts were made to break up the Budget protest meeting at Llandrindod Wells in September 1909, while during the election campaign many Conservative posters were defaced or torn down. The two local newspapers dropped any attempt at objective reporting and concentrated on campaigning. In the *Radnor Express* the Conservatives were invariably referred to as 'the food-taxers' while the *Radnorshire Standard* termed its rival 'the Chinese Liars' and the Liberals as 'Radicals', on one occasion equating radicalism with socialism and socialism with atheism. Perhaps its greatest departure from good taste came in the issue of 30 October 1909 when the Lord Advocate of Scotland, Alexander Ure, was referred to as 'the Radical Socialist Man-Ure'.

Venables Llewelyn squeezed home by 14 votes on 19 January, with 2,222 votes to Edwards' 2,208, whilst nationally the Liberals remained in power, though with a greatly reduced majority. Conservatives were justifiably elated at the victory and at Felindre celebrations got out of hand as a crowd of 60 or so men and boys pelted houses of known Liberals with mud and stones, breaking the windows of the schoolmaster's house and shouting abuse outside the house of the Primitive Methodist minister. The Liberals blamed their defeat on organisational shortcomings for which Nixson, the Liberal agent, took the blame; the pressure of landowners on tenant farmers and farm labourers; and the votes of non-resident clergymen and out-voters 'who only pay a visit to the county at election time'. Sir Francis Edwards, looking forward to the abolition of plural votes, predicted that it was probably the last Conservative victory in Radnorshire.[40]

While these factors may well have had some bearing upon the Liberal defeat, they do not provide the full explanation. In the first place farmers were attracted by the higher prices Tariff Reform would bring for their produce and the *Hereford Times*, now backing the Conservatives, was to claim in November 1910 that the farmers in the Clyro and New Radnor areas were almost solidly Conservative, while the Knighton and Rhayader areas were no longer the Liberal strongholds they had been in days gone by. Again, Venables Llewelyn and his allies did not allow the Liberals to dictate the agenda and fight the campaign on their terms, namely the reform of the Lords and the 'People's Budget', and exploited landowners' fears over the valuation of land and the possibility of taxation on the unearned increments in land values. In particular Venables Llewelyn spelt out what he saw as the long term advantages of Tariff Reform, while his allies, the Anglican clergy, used the disestablishment issue to rally churchmen to the Conservative side.[41]

The Conservative resurgence in Radnorshire was confirmed by Conservative gains in the county council elections of March 1910, for the Liberals' control of the county council continued only because they held the majority of aldermanic seats. There were also rumours that Sir Francis Edwards would not contest the Parliamentary seat again; either because he was to be raised to the peerage as Lord Melenith and was to purchase Llwynbarried, Nantmel, as his seat, or because he was to contest the Mid Glamorgan seat of the former Liberal attorney general, Sir Sidney Thomas Evans, who had resigned in order to take up an appointment as President of a division of the High Court. The loss of Edwards, who had a large personal following in the county, would have been a serious blow to Liberal chances of regaining the seat, but fortunately for the local party, the rumours proved unfounded.[42]

While at the national level the major concern throughout 1910 was the role of the House of Lords, at local level the main issue was initially the composition of the Radnorshire Bench which, according to the *Radnor Express* of 5 May, was dominated by Conservatives and Anglicans. The newspaper claimed that of the 106 magistrates in the county, 70 were Conservative and 33 Liberal, while as far as religious affiliations were concerned, 69 were churchmen and 30 nonconformists. This heavy Conservative/Anglican bias had some political significance since Quarter Sessions elected half the members of the Standing Joint Committee, the senior local government committee which, amongst its functions, had supervised the police force since 1889. The Radnorshire Bench had consistently elected only Conservatives as its representatives on the Standing Committee, thus laying itself open to a charge of factionalism despite an awareness that the choice of magistrates on political grounds was by no means confined to Radnorshire, and was widely practised by both parties. In the autumn of 1910, in an attempt to curb this practice it was decided that the lord lieutenant of each county was to appoint a committee which, when a vacancy occurred, would make a recommendation to the Lord Chancellor.

Following the re-election of the Liberal government in January 1910, the House of Lords had reluctantly passed the Budget proposals. The Liberals then announced a Bill to curb the power of the House of Lords by which it would lose the ability to amend or reject a finance Bill, or to reject a Bill which had been passed by the Commons in three successive sessions. Such a measure was unacceptable to the Lords and after an all party conference failed to find a compromise, the new king, George V, undertook that if the electorate approved the measure in a general election, he would create sufficient peers to force the measure through the Lords.

Even before the dissolution of the Commons at the end of November, the local campaign was already under way with the *Radnorshire Standard* seeking to undermine Edwards' reputation as an efficient Member by calculating the number of divisions he had missed in the Commons, in particular those missed on the Agricultural Rating Act and on Old Age Pensions. Its headline 'For King and Country and Venables Llewelyn for Radnorshire' incurred the wrath of the local Liberals and a veiled rebuke from Lord Knollys, the King's private secretary. Venables Llewelyn began his campaign on 23 November and two days earlier the Revd D.G. Macpherson had held the first in a series of Church Defence meetings in Knighton.[43]

In his electoral address Venables Llewelyn opposed curbing the power of the Lords; opting for a strong House of Lords with a large proportion of elected peers, along with a proviso that if the two Houses could not agree on a measure it should be decided by the electorate in a referendum. He wanted to see the Budget amended to exempt agricultural land from the taxation on unearned increments in land values — the assurances given that the tax would not apply to agricultural land were not believed as all land had been valued — and to reduce the duty on licensed premises. He backed Tariff Reform and the maintenance of a strong army and navy but opposed Irish Home Rule, disestablishment of the Welsh Church, the payment of MPs and any reversal of the Osborne Judgment which had limited the ability of trade unions to use their funds for political purposes.[44]

Edwards' campaign seems, from the press coverage, to have been rather low key, apart from Lloyd George's visit to Llandrindod Wells on Saturday, 3 December, which merited a special edition of the *Radnor Express*. For his part Edwards stood on the record of the Liberal government and its programme of constitutional reform made necessary by the failure of the constitutional conference, which involved curbing the power of the Lords.

In the election, held again in mid-week, on 7 December, Edwards secured a majority of 42, gaining 2,224 votes to Venables Llewelyn's 2,182 on a slightly lower poll than that of January 1910. Reports from the polling stations suggested that Edwards polled well in the Radnorshire towns and their immediate neighbourhoods while Venables Llewelyn did best in rural areas, thanks to the farming interest. Both sides attributed the Liberal success to organisational factors, with the new Liberal agent E.J. Withington, who had shown his mettle in the revision courts of September, winning high praise from the *Radnor Express*, while in the now Conservative *Hereford Times* 'Arrowside' urged the Radnorshire Conservatives to appoint a full time agent to organise the county.[45]

The narrow margin of victory meant that there was no display of triumphalism on the part of the local Liberals, for as the *Radnor Express* of 15 December recognised:

> There is no doubt that Mr Venables Llewelyn has a very strong hold on the constituency and that he has become a very formidable candidate.

Certainly the two parties were now more evenly matched than they had been for much of the first decade of the century, the Conservative recovery having been based on winning over a significant proportion of tenant farmers from their traditional Liberal allegiance, and gaining the backing of those relatively few Liberal churchmen whose opposition to disestablishment of the Welsh Church counted for more than their loyalty to their party. At the local level the resurgence of Conservatism can be seen in the county council elections of 1913 which saw the party regain control for the first time since 1903.

Nationally, the Liberal victory in the general election of December 1910 meant that the government was in a position to push through its programme. The only measure to provoke a marked reaction in Radnorshire was the Act to disestablish and disendow the Welsh Church in 1912 which, as a result of the opposition of the Lords, was not to come into effect until 1914. While the Radnorshire parishes within the diocese of St David's seem to have accepted disestablishment as inevitable, those parishes within the diocese of Hereford, led by the Revd D.G. Macpherson of Knighton, put up a strong resistance to the 'Church Robbery Bill' throughout 1911 and 1912, ultimately winning the concession that the parishioners could decide whether they should remain with Hereford or join the disestablished Church of Wales. The strength of the Church in these parishes can be judged from the fact that two petitions against disestablishment in six parishes in the Lower Lugg and Teme valleys and in Radnor valley gained 1,673 signatures.[46]

For the Radnorshire Liberals the period between the election of December 1910 and the outbreak of war in 1914 was anticlimactic, for after Sir Francis Edwards had decided in April 1911 not to contest the next general election, considerable time was devoted to selecting a succession of prospective candidates to replace him; Sir Courtney Cecil Mansell of Coedgain, Cardiganshire in 1911, Dr Charles Hayward of Liverpool in 1912 and Mr William Lewis, a ship owner of London, in 1913. However Sir Francis Edwards was to be the last MP for Radnorshire, for the outbreak of war in 1914 led to the postponement of a general election for the duration and as a result of the Parliament Act of 1918, the county lost its separate parliamentary representation after nearly 380 years, being combined with Breconshire to form the Brecon and Radnor constituency.

Plate 34: David Lloyd George at the burial of Sir Francis Edwards at Knighton in May 1927

6 The Radnorshire Cottagers

The Radnorshire Cottagers issue, at its height in the later 1830s and early 1840s, obliged the Crown and the major landed gentry of the county to take into account the views of small farmers and cottagers in their deliberations upon enclosures and in the management of their estates.

There seems to have been little appetite for enclosure of the uncultivated commons and wastes in Radnorshire in the opening decades of the nineteenth century, for there were only eight enclosure Acts affecting parishes in the county between 1800 and 1840. Seven of these Acts were passed between 1810 and 1813, a belated response to the sharp rise in the price of agricultural products experienced during the French wars, while the eighth, the Rhayader Act of 1828, was a 'tidying up' measure.

While the post-war agricultural slump of 1815-18 and then, in the later 1820s and 1830s, doubts over the precise nature of the manorial rights which the purchasers of manors from the Crown had acquired, tended to discourage enclosure at those times, there was also a more general opposition to enclosure in the county prior to the 1840s. Thus, between 1810 and 1815 there were at least fifteen attempts at enclosure, affecting eighteen parishes, mainly in the northern half of the county, which came to nothing.[1]

The opposition of small farmers and cottagers to enclosure was understandable since the right to graze livestock on the commons and waste enabled them to farm more livestock than could be grazed upon their enclosed lands alone. The few acres they received on enclosure of commons and wastes did not compensate them for the loss of these grazing rights, let alone rights to peat, turf, deadwood and twigs for fuel, furze for fuel and fodder, bracken for litter, along with reeds and rushes for thatching.

However, notices giving notice of intention to oppose various enclosures in northern Radnorshire published in the *Hereford Journal* between 1812 and 1815 also included the names of members of the Radnorshire establishment, including Walter Wilkins MP, Hugh Powell Evans and his brother Evan, Frederick Jones and his brother Middleton, and John and David Oliver, along with substantial farmers such as Edward Meredith.[2] Wilkins' motives were no doubt political, but the opposition of the others to enclosure is surprising, since as major landowners they could be expected to gain substantially from such a measure. There is a strong possibility, however, that their opposition stemmed from the fact that their estates already included encroachments upon the commons and wastes which were thus allottable on enclosure, the loss of such encroachments and the construction of new fences and ditches perhaps outweighing the acres of former common gained through the enclosure.

Crown possessions in the county were to be found mainly, but not exclusively, in the manors and boroughs of Knighton, Knucklas, Rhayader and Presteigne and the manors of Cwmdeuddwr, Farrington and Cwmgilla, Gladestry, Rhyslin, Iscoed, South Neithon, South Rurallt, South Ugre and Uchoed. Although not all the manors were originally included in the lordship of Cantref Maelienydd, by the nineteenth century they were included in the lordship for administrative purposes. While the location of some of these manors is self evident, the location of others is more difficult to plot since the boundaries were not entirely clear, even in the nineteenth century, and their location is best indicated by identifying the parishes in which they lay:

Manor	Parishes in which located
Farrington	Knighton
Iscoed	Nantmel, Llanyre, Llanfihangel Helygen
Rhyslin	Nantmel
South Neithon	Llandegley, Llanddewi Ystradenni. Llanbadarn Fawr, Llandrindod, Cefnllys
South Rurallt	Llandegley, Llangunllo, Llanddewi Ystradenni, Llanfihangel Rhydithon, Pilleth, Whitton
South Ugre	Llanbister, Llanddewi Ystradenni, Llananno, Llanbadarn Fynydd, Llangunllo, Heyope, Beguildy
Uchoed	Nantmel, St Harmon

Figure 8: The location of the main Radnorshire Crown Manors

For the most part the value of the manors lay not so much in the lands owned by the Crown, which were for the most part sold in the 1820s, nor in the manorial fees, fines and market tolls, which yielded only a small revenue, but in the 'right of soil', a residual right in the commons and wastes which had a capital value which was realised when the commons and wastes were enclosed. In the opening decades of the nineteenth century the right of soil was calculated at one-twentieth of the value of the commons and wastes to be enclosed, rising to a greater proportion later in the century. Like any other lord of the manor, at enclosure the Crown was also entitled to one-twentieth of any encroachment made without consent on the common within the previous twenty years,

Figure 9: Sketch map showing the parishes in which the Crown manors were located

but, unlike other landlords, the Crown was further entitled to one-twentieth of the value of encroachments made on the common between the previous 20 and 60 years. The potential capital value of the 'right of soil' on Crown manors in Radnorshire was substantial, accounting, for example, for 78% of South Neithon's capital value of £1,714 12s 10d in 1821, the remaining 22% consisting of manorial fees and fines.[3]

Since 1761 the stewardship of the Crown lands had been vested in successive Earls of Oxford, a stewardship that became lax in its administration, particularly under the fifth Earl, who had succeeded to the title in 1790. Thus in 1824 it was discovered that manorial courts had not been held in the manors of South Ugre and Uchoed since 1795-97, whilst in Farrington and Rhyslin manorial courts had been held only in 1804. The failure to hold manorial courts regularly meant not only the loss of revenue but also a failure to halt encroachments by the cheapest and most acceptable means, namely presentation at the manorial court.[4] Not surprisingly, given such lax administration, the acreage accounted for by encroachments was considerable.

Following the survey of Crown lands and manors in the county in 1821, the Commissioners of Woods and Forests and Crown Lands, who administered

Manor	Commons (acres)	Encroachments under 20 years (acres)	Encroachments of 20 to 60 years (acres)
Cwmdeuddwr	1,100	31	0
Farrington and Cwmgilla	754	141	13
Gladestry	1,260	32	6
Iscoed	2,420	67	51
Rhyslin	2,261	68	54
South Neithon	2,669	78	77
South Rurallt	6,886	269	139
South Ugre	19,767	767	684
Uchoed	2,761	68	54

Figure 10: Common or waste lands and encroachments in the major Crown manors in Radnorshire, 1821 (TNA PRO CRES 49/4992, /5005 and /5050)

Crown lands and manors on behalf of the Crown, decided to dispose of them. In 1822 the Earl of Oxford was dismissed from the Stewardship and at the beginning of 1823 two Kington solicitors, James Davies and Richard Banks, were appointed in his place with the task of holding manorial courts to curb encroachments prior to the sale of the manors. On the advice of James Davies it was decided to sell the manors by private treaty rather than by auction or public tender, after they had been valued by Morris Sayce, a Kington surveyor.[5] Critics later argued that this arrangement favoured the county establishment and would lead to significantly lower prices, though Sayce's valuations gave a safeguard since they provided the Commissioners with a price guide, though his valuation of 20 years' purchase (i.e. 20 times the annual rent) was rather low by the late 1820s.

Manor	Date of sale	Purchaser	Valuation	Price
Cwmdeuddwr	1825	Robert Peel	£281	£270
Farrington	1826	Edward Rogers	£397	£397
Gladestry	1827	T. Frankland Lewis	£626	£450
Iscoed	1826	James Watt	£1,044	£1,200
Rhyslin	1826	James Watt	£697	£1,000
South Neithon	1827	James Watt	£1,346	£1,000
South Rurallt	1828	Richard Price	£2,656	£1,800
Uchoed	1826	James Watt	£838	£1,000

Figure 11: The sale of Crown manors in Radnorshire
(TNA PRO CRES49/4922, /5005, /5051)

As Figure 11 shows, most of the Crown manors in the county sold in the 1820s realised prices around Sayce's valuation, the two notable exceptions, Gladestry and South Rurallt, being the result of special circumstances.[6] The new owners needed to protect their investment by taking action to recover encroachments as these were included in the deed of sale, although not listed specifically and individually.

Occupants of encroachments of less than twenty years were proceeded against by presentation at the manorial court and legal action was only taken normally when a squatter ignored the findings of the court. With encroachments of between twenty and sixty years' standing the position was more complex, for the right to recover such encroachments was the exclusive right of the Crown and the only course open to the new lord of the manor, to whom this right had been transferred, was to take legal action to test his title and secure the ejection of the squatters, unless they were prepared to come to terms.

However, recourse to law was expensive and, given the tendency of Radnorshire juries to arrive at a perverse verdict, somewhat uncertain. Thus while Peel, Watt and Price were prepared to use the threat of legal action to pres-surise holders of encroachments into buying them or agreeing to hold them as tenants, in either case on very favourable terms, Edward Rogers took no such action and Frankland Lewis refused to include in his purchase of Gladestry manor the six acres of encroachments of more than twenty years' standing. Given the odium which both Richard Price and James Watt incurred in their efforts to assert their title to encroachments, this would seem to have been a small price to pay in order for Frankland Lewis to retain his local popularity.[7]

On the three manors which Watt had purchased, 246 encroachments were identified, some of them held by members of the county establishment such as the Revd Dr Richard Venables, Hugh Powell Evans, Henry Lingen of Penlanole and the Kington banker David Oliver. In all 232 encroachments were exchanged, purchased or became tenancies, with the humbler encroachers paying an annual rent of between sixpence (2½p) and five shillings (25p). In eleven cases Watt obtained judgments of ejectment but chose not to enforce them.[8] The remaining three encroachers, Thomas Weale, Richard Page and Thomas Watkins, all in the manor of Iscoed, were ejected. At first sight Watt's approach seems moderate enough, but in practice it was coercive, for few of the small encroachers had the means to go to law and had no choice but to become tenants. Whilst only paying a nominal rent initially, on renewal of the lease rents were likely to be set at commercial levels.

In 1828 Thomas Weale declined to agree to become a tenant to James Watt for an encroachment on Newbridge Common in the manor of Iscoed, made initially in 1816 and enlarged in 1826 to a holding of three acres, but when proceedings were begun against him he reluctantly changed his mind and agreed to pay a rent of three shillings (15p). However, at the beginning of 1830 he refused to pay and a writ of ejectment was secured against him. An initial attempt to eject him by officers acting on the instructions of the under-

Plate 35: Doldowlod Hall, c.1904, the home of the Watt and Gibson Watt families. The original house, built c.1827, was extended in 1878

sheriff, Richard Banks, was beaten off by the Weale family with the help of neighbouring cottagers. A second attempt made two days later succeeded and allegedly Weale, his wife who had recently given birth, and their six children were turned out onto the common in a snow storm and their cottage was razed to the ground, according to the account of the events given at the Cottagers' dinner at Presteigne on 28 December 1837.

Richard Banks' version of events was markedly different. According to him, after the first attempt at ejection had failed, Weale travelled to Kington to see Banks and offered to give the sheriff's officers peaceful possession of the encroachment if Banks would intercede with the authorities over the assault on the officers, which Weale attributed to his wife's 'ungovernable temper'. On the second attempt to enforce the warrant Weale was prepared to keep his word but his wife, fully clothed, jumped into bed and refused to move. The officers then picked up the bed with Mrs Weale in it, carried it to the neighbouring public house and deposited it on the floor of the bar next to the fire. Mrs Weale then 'sprang from her bed in perfect health' and walked off. Weale, according to Banks, had also asked if he could have the materials of his cottage and shed, to which Banks agreed, and Weale, a carpenter by trade, duly supervised the demolition and carried off the materials. The encroachment was subsequently added to the neighbouring farm, Merry Hall.[9]

Like Weale, Richard Page had accepted a tenancy for his three encroachments in Iscoed dating from 1804, but then refused to pay his rent in 1830 and was ejected from his holding. The third encroacher, Thomas Watkins, was also ejected. Watt, only too well aware that these ejections gave rise to considerable criticism in some quarters, justified them on the grounds that the three encroachers had 'acted in a most hostile manor and under objectionable advice', presumably from Cecil Parsons, the radical Presteigne attorney.

As a result of these cases tension was growing in the unsold Crown manors, particularly in South Ugre where substantial acreages of encroachments had been identified. Richard Banks had begun presenting known encroachers at manorial courts and it seemed likely that in the near future such manors would be sold, along with the rights to all encroachments of less than 60 years' standing which had been unrecovered. Thus in 1829, a memorial from the tenants of South Ugre was forwarded to the Commissioners of Woods and Forests querying the right of the Crown to sell the manors. They argued that when the tenants of Radnorshire's royal manors had repurchased them in 1634, after Charles I had sold them (to help fund his attempt to rule without Parliament and so also without its tax-raising powers) and returned them to the king, Charles had promised that he would never again alienate them. Although the argument was technically invalid in that a monarch could not be bound in law by the action of a predecessor, it did have sufficient moral force to make Richard Banks hesitate.[10]

In addition to those directly affected by the efforts to recover encroachments, the moves aroused widespread resentment across the county in general for it threatened the *status quo*. In the first place the moves were in direct opposition to the tradition of *tŷ un nos*, or the 'morning surprise' as it was termed in Radnorshire, whereby a squatter building a cottage overnight and having the chimney smoking by dawn, acquired a right to the cottage and half an acre or so of the adjacent common. The tradition was popularly believed to have a legal basis in Wales and the ejection of *tŷ un nos* squatters as a result of Parliamentary enclosures in Caernarvonshire had already excited considerable unrest.[11]

Though the majority of encroachments in Radnorshire were small in scale, most were not the work of *tŷ un nos* squatters but of landless labourers who fenced off a more fertile part of a common openly and in daylight. Other encroachments were created by smallholders and farmers straightening a boundary line or taking in a few acres of cultivable land from the common adjacent to their holdings. Some encroachments were the work of bolder spirits and consisted of plots of 5, 10 or even 50 acres. The failure of the Crown's officers to take action against encroachers in the two or three decades prior to 1824 seems to have created the impression that piecemeal encroachment upon the commons on Crown manors was considered acceptable by the authorities, and the sudden reversal of policy towards encroachments in 1824 left not only cottagers but also substantial members of the farming community vulnerable. As subsequent re-surveys of South Ugre were to show, a survey of 1821 did not uncover all the old encroachments and thus all landowners faced the possibility that at some point in the future that they might be required to become a tenant for some part of their holding which they were unaware was an encroachment of less than 60 years' standing.

Moreover, while the position of squatters on encroachments of less than 20 years was clearly untenable in common law, the Crown's claim to encroachments of between 20 and 60 years and its ability to convey this right to the purchasers of the manors seemed, at the very least, debatable.

In 1833 formal notice was served by James Watt on Mr Morris, a tenant farmer of Llanclewedog, Nantmel, in Iscoed in respect of an encroachment of half an acre made in 1808. The farm belonged to Cecil Parsons, a Presteigne lawyer of radical views, and following Parsons' refusal to attorn (accept a tenancy), an order of ejectment was sought by Watt. Parsons was a substantial landowner in the county with an estate of 1,453 acres (588 ha) in 1873, in addition to other estates in the counties of Brecon and Glamorgan. With his brother Guy, sheriff of Radnorshire in 1834, he was to found the Radnorshire Bank in Presteigne in 1834-35. Watt's case against Morris and Parsons was heard at the Summer Assizes in Hereford in August 1834, before a special jury who found for Watt, subject to the opinion of the superior court of Common Pleas.

The failure of Watt to obtain an unqualified verdict in his favour seems to have encouraged Parsons and his allies, and the verdict in favour of Parsons given by the court of Common Pleas in June 1835 seemed to justify such optimism. However the verdict was not as sweeping as was popularly believed, for it left intact the Crown's right to encroachments of between 20 and 60 years and found for Parsons solely on the ground that the conveyance of the manors to Watt was defective in that it did not specify precisely each of the encroachments the Crown had conveyed to Watt. Even so, the *Hereford Journal* of 24 June, after reporting the joyful reaction to the verdict in Presteigne, ignored this, commenting:

> The decision of this case, which has excited so much interest, will be received with joyful acclamation throughout the county of Radnor, as it will have the effect of restoring many hundreds of poor cottagers to the possession of their peaceful habitations.

Given that only three cottagers had been ejected in Iscoed and none in the other manors Watt had acquired from the Crown, this claim would seem somewhat extravagant.

Even so, popular opinion at large seems to have accepted that the verdict vindicated the encroachers. In South Ugre in July, Parsons and his ally Robert Lewis, the Presteigne timber merchant, held a series of rowdy meetings urging resistance to the Crown's claims on encroachments. At Llanbister the meeting lasted allegedly for six hours or more, 'with great noises, riot and disturbance', while at Felindre on 6 July effigies of Richard Banks, Richard Price and, according to one account, James Watt, were shot at and then burned.[12]

David Lewis, who had been surveying South Ugre since 1834 on behalf of the Crown to identify encroachments and persuade their holders to purchase them or attorn tenant, was also put under pressure. At Llanbister Lewis's assistant was told by one farmer not to enter his land as 'neither the King nor the Devil had any right to do so' and that he would shoot Lewis or the assistant if they did. At Beguildy Lewis' guides were told that if they accompanied Lewis again, their houses would be burned. Lewis himself was also warned not to come to Beguildy again

> as it was in the contemplation of several persons to darken their faces, so that my assistant may not know them when they shall come to kill me.

Not surprisingly, in 1836 Lewis decided to put some distance between himself and Radnorshire.[13]

Some in the remaining Crown manors were so convinced that they had been defrauded out of their encroachments that they decided it was no longer necessary to keep to agreements they had reached to rent or purchase the relevant land. By the end of 1835 purchase money amounting to £2,112 and rentals totalling more than £250 were outstanding in the Crown manors in the county. Richard Price was experiencing similar difficulties in his newly acquired manor of South Ruralt.[14]

Attempts by the Commissioners of Woods and Forests to take legal action to remedy the situation proved unsuccessful. At the Radnorshire Assizes of August 1835 attempts to indict Parsons, Robert Lewis and others for riot and disturbance at Llanbister and Felindre failed when the grand jury, chaired by Sir Harford Jones Brydges and including supporters of the Radnorshire Cottagers such as Walter Wilkins MP and Sir John Walsham, returned 'No true bill' in both cases. A charge on the part of Watt alleging that Weale had forcibly entered his old encroachment was ignored by the grand jury.[15]

Towards the end of 1835 a petition from the Cottagers of South Ugre stating their case and bearing 133 signatures was forwarded to the Prime Minister, Lord Melbourne, by Guy Parsons. Melbourne asked the Commissioners of Woods and Forests to comment and Richard Banks analysed the signatures on their behalf. He found that few of the signatures belonged to cottagers who had encroached on the commons — 'the Cottagers' as they became known. Fifty-seven of the signatories were from Presteigne, including Sir Harford Jones Brydges, the rector the Revd James Beebee, a solicitor Thomas Stephens, and two MDs, Jenkins and Davis. Another 34 of the signatories came from the Rhayader area and included substantial landowners such as Hugh Powell Evans of Noyadd, Thomas Prickard of Dderw and Thomas Evans of Llwynbarried. Of the signatories from South Ugre at least two, James Meredith and John Poole, were substantial farmers. Banks also believed that at least nine or ten of the signatures were in Parsons' handwriting. However, Banks' findings were not made public.[16]

Initially 1836 favoured the Cottagers for at the Radnorshire Spring Assizes when Watt sued Thomas Weale for trespass on his old encroachment — Weale had carried off a load of hay from it — the jury found in favour of Weale and awarded him £5 in damages. Richard Page was encouraged by this to seek to regain his old encroachment, while Weale felt free to renew his campaign against Watt. With a rumour circulating locally that all encroachments of less than 60 years were to be thrown open and the fences torn down, in April Weale tried, without success, to persuade the congregation at Llanyre parish church to meet with him to throw open all encroachments in Iscoed, promising them that they would be protected by Hugh Powell Evans. A few days later Weale made a similar appeal at Rhayader market and a group of about a hundred, consisting in the main of Hugh Powell Evans' tenants and their labourers, equipped with pickaxes, began to tear down fences of former encroachments now in Watt's hands and also fences surrounding some of his ornamental plantations. The attack was renewed a few days later and Watt was forced to obtain an injunction from the Court of Chancery to halt these activities.[17]

Watt then asked the Commissioners of Woods and Forests either to convey to him unambiguously all the encroachments of less than 60 years or to resume ownership of the manors and return the purchase money. In order to maintain the integrity of their sale of Crown manors, not only in the county but also in north Wales, the Commissioners were compelled to act, the Morris/Parsons' Llanclewedog encroachment, small as it was, being seen as a test case. In June the Court of Exchequer set aside as perverse the verdict in Weale's case reached at the Radnor Spring Assizes and the case was sent for retrial, while the chairman of the grand jury, Sir Harford Jones Brydges, was found by the Court of Exchequer to 'have treated the charge with great indecency and disrespect'. The Attorney General, on behalf of the Commissioners, also obtained a ruling to try a writ of intrusion against Parsons at Hereford Assizes rather than at Radnor Assizes.[18]

In August 1836 at Hereford Watt successfully sued Weale for trespass in returning to his encroachment, and also secured possession of Page's former encroachment. However the Commissioners had some difficulty in securing witnesses in the case against Parsons as feelings were running high, and judged it necessary to take out *subpoenas* to prevent witnesses 'having their minds poisoned by the artifices and statements of interested parties'. In fact, the special jury at Hereford on 5 August took only a few minutes to find against Parsons and in favour of the Crown, but, much to Watt's annoyance, the Commissioners made no immediate attempt to enforce the judgement. It was not until May 1837 that the writ of execution was delivered to the sheriff and Parsons surrendered possession of the encroachment to Watt, who later built a house on it. In 1838, in order to prevent any other actions against Watt, the Commissioners provided him with a deed of confirmation of his purchase and a schedule of the encroachments which were included in the transaction.[19]

Watt's victory over Parsons and the recovery of the Llanclewedog encroachment seems to have been regarded as irrelevant by the Cottagers. After a subscription had raised £162, Cecil Parsons was presented with a silver cup, salver and covered dishes as 'a testimony of admiration and esteem for his exertions in the cause of the cottagers' at a dinner in his honour at the Radnorshire Arms, Presteigne, on 28 December 1837. The speakers on this occasion studiously ignored the 1836 verdict, which was clearly regarded as no more than a lost battle, while the Court of Common Pleas verdict of 1835 in favour of Parsons was hailed as a triumph by all.[20]

After the verdict at Hereford in August 1836, the Cottagers' campaign became political rather than legal in character, concentrating upon the decision to sell the manors by private tender. The Cottagers alleged that through collusion with James Davies, one of the Crown's stewards, and the Revd Dr Richard Venables, Watt had obtained the manor of Iscoed at a lower price than might have been realised by competitive tender. Guy Parsons had already made this allegation in correspondence with the Commissioners, but in January 1837 the issue became public when a county meeting at Presteigne petitioned the Commons to investigate the 'private and fraudulent' method by which the manors had been sold and 'the slovenly manner' in which the manors had been conveyed to the purchasers, which had led to 'a series of most vexatious claims and grievous litigation'. Richard Banks did his best to play down the support for the petition: the meeting was thinly attended — he failed to mention the heavy snow storms which had disrupted travel in the county — with only one encroacher, Hugh Powell Evans, from the manors Watt had purchased, attending, and no more than six or eight encroachers from South Ugre being present.[21]

The petition had little effect. The Whig government had little sympathy with the Cottagers' cause, for Lord John Russell, the Home Secretary, had already blocked an attempt by William Ormsby Gore, MP for North Shropshire and previously MP for Caernarfon Boroughs, to establish a committee of inquiry into the matter, while Sir John Campbell, the Attorney General, clearly had little time for Cecil Parsons, whom he described as 'a pettifogging lawyer'. However after a deputation led by Walter Wilkins MP and Guy Parsons in July 1839 and a resolution of the Commons, the documents relating to the sale of Iscoed were published as a Parliamentary paper. It failed to substantiate the charges that Guy Parsons had made.

Following the resignation of the surveyor David Lewis in 1836, the policy of persuading squatters to purchase their encroachments or attorn tenant seems to have been abandoned in the unsold Crown manors. In the absence of any effective sanctions, the practice of encroaching on the commons continued unabated; between 1836 and 1852 8 further encroachments were identified in the manor of Knighton, 19 in Knucklas and 181 in South Ugre.[22]

In 1851 the Commissioners decided to re-survey South Ugre in order that encroachments could be identified with greater certainty, and when this was completed in 1854 it was decided to review the terms on which encroachments were offered to the squatters occupying them. Previously encroachments had been offered at seven years' purchase and their associated buildings at three and a half years' purchase but, aware of the need to conciliate public opinion, the Commissioners decided upon a scheme which discriminated between cottagers and large-scale encroachers. The seven years'/ three and a half years' term was to remain for encroachments of less than five acres, in addition to at least five years' rent, but for encroachments above five acres, where no improvements had been made, ten years' purchase with five years' rent for both land buildings was to be required.[23]

The proposal provoked concern in South Ugre and after public meetings had been held at Llanbadarn Fynydd and Llanbister, a petition bearing 115 signatures was presented to the Home Secretary by Lord Bateman (who was thought more sympathetic than Sir John Walsh) in February 1856. It claimed to be from those in possession of encroachments begun between 20 and 58 years previously, pointed out that only the Crown could claim after such long periods of adverse possession and that the Commissioners had encouraged such encroachments by remaining 'acquiescent or indifferent' to them for so long. The petitioners claimed that the valuations of the encroachments were excessive and then went on to warn, as they had in the 1830s, that 'poor people [would be] forcibly turned out of their dwellings', and reminding Parliament of Charles I's undertaking of 1634 and the verdict of the court of Common Pleas in 1835. Amongst the signatories were the incumbents of Beguildy, Cascob and Llanbadarn Fynydd, whilst 35 of the petitioners, unable to write, had made their marks.

Richard Banks informed the Commissioners that the petition had been drawn up by the Revd Christopher Blackburn, chaplain of the county gaol and headmaster of John Beddoes School, on the instructions of Cecil Parsons. He added that the public meetings in South Ugre had been attended by James Beavan, the clerk of another Presteigne attorney, Edward Lee James, and that Beavan had taken the petition around the county to obtain signatures. Banks went on to point out that Parsons and James were 'considerable encroachers', who also had an interest in some encroachments as mortgagors and potential purchasers.

Armed with this information, the Commissioners set out their own version of events in South Ugre since 1827, pointing out that amongst those holding encroachments were some of the greatest landowners in Radnorshire, including Sir John Walsh, MP and Lord Lieutenant of the county, the Earl of Powis, Lady Dunsany and Sir John Dundas. Richard Banks also maintained that Edward Lee James, one of the promoters of the petition, held 212 acres (86 ha) of encroachments, while another of the signatories held encroachments amounting to more than 150 acres (61 ha).[24]

The issue of encroachments of between 20 and 60 years in origin was to come to a head just months after the petition had been handed in when, in the second half of 1856, it was proposed to enclose the commons and wastes of South Ugre. In order to secure agreement to enclose the remaining open land, the Commissioners were prepared to sell such encroachments to the occupier at a price of £5 per acre. This proved not acceptable to those holding the encroachments and following meetings at the Burton Arms, Llanddewi Ystradenni and at Knighton Racecourse in August 1857, a memorial was drawn up asking that, in return for the freeholders consenting to an enclosure of the commons, those holding cottages and encroachments for between twenty and thirty years should have their possession confirmed and those holding encroachments for more than thirty years should, in addition, receive an allotment on enclosure.

Richard Green, the moving spirit behind the memorial, which bore 90 signatures, suggested that in return for the concession to the encroachers, the Crown should receive one-fourteenth rather than one-sixteenth of the commons in respect of the right of soil on the enclosure of South Ugre. The Commissioners declined this suggestion on the grounds that the proposed increase in respect of the right of soil was not a full equivalent to the rights the Crown would have surrendered to the encroachers. Moreover, as one of the Commissioners, James Howard pointed out, the concessions to the encroachers would have been at the expense of those in the manor with rights in the commons who had remained within the law by not encroaching.[25]

With no agreement reached, the Commissioners now began to move against the encroachers, with Cecil Parsons an early target. Early in 1858 notices were sent to sixty encroachers inviting them to purchase and in March 1859 a list of a further fifteen encroachers was prepared, of whom only three were archetypal 'cottagers'. Thus began an almost annual ritual which prevailed throughout the rest of the century whereby, as encroachments were identified, the holders were threatened with proceedings unless they purchased or accepted a tenancy.

Initially this policy provoked organised resistance, for prior to 1858 the Crown's rights had not been actively asserted for some time and as a result:

> Encroachers had acquired considerable confidence in the security of their possession and many still think that by remaining passive they would not be disturbed.

In 1860 the Commissioners became aware that an association, with a solicitor (Cecil Parsons?) at its head, had been formed to defend every action brought by the Crown against its members. Its headquarters was in Leominster and its members paid an annual subscription of ten shillings (50p). However nothing more was heard of this association, and thereafter resistance appears to have been passive but even so reasonably effective. Thus in 1876 the surveyor, J.M. Davies, complained to the Commissioners that he had been unable to insert the dates of the encroachments he had discovered on his survey of 1873 since everyone claimed not to know when they had been made:

> In Radnorshire the people are most unobservant and it is impossible to get information from them as to dates, not withstanding that they nearly all pay rents to the Crown for their encroachments.[26]

Although Cecil Parsons and his allies had lost both the legal and political battles of the 1830s, they won the propaganda battle, if largely by default for neither Watt, nor Price, the Commissioners and their local agents, James Davies and Richard Banks, made any real attempt to win over local opinion or to counter Cecil Parsons' highly selective version of the controversy. Parsons was thus able to claim that the law in the form of the laws of Hywel Dda, Charles I's undertaking of 1634 and the verdict of the court of Common Pleas, was firmly on the side of the Cottagers. He also portrayed the issue as a struggle between grasping and wealthy landlords, backed up by a distant and inefficient Commission of Woods and Forests on the one hand and, on the other a

> numerous class of men who for many years have been in quiet and peaceful possession of the little sheltered houses they have by their own labour secured from the wastelands.[27]

Parsons succeeded in modifying the popular view of the squatter, traditionally regarded as under-employed and scraping a living on the fringes of society, often by dubious means. Locally he was now portrayed as sturdy, independent and hardworking, earning a precarious living from his small plot won from the waste. Thus in the *Hereford Times* of 15 June 1839 the Radnorshire cottager was congratulated for not joining with the Chartists and was described as:

> content with the quiet possession of his humble house and an acre of ground and [who] envies not his richer neighbours, their extensive domains.

With popular opinion and the local press in the form of the *Hereford Times* and *Hereford Journal* firmly behind him, Parsons was able to isolate James Watt, Richard Price and the Commissioners, since the Conservatives in the county establishment such as the Revd Dr Richard Venables, the Severns and R.B. Mynors were not prepared to support them publicly, while in his election manifestoes of 1840 and 1841 Sir John Walsh maintained a studious silence on the issue.

In this situation Parsons was able to pressurise the Commissioners and the purchasers of Crown manors into coming to terms with the squatters rather than offering them the choice between commercial rents or ejection. The extent of Parsons' achievement is to be seen in Watt's attempt to enclose the manors' commons and wastes in the parishes of St Harmon, Nantmel, Llanyre and Llanfihangel Helygen in 1840 when, after intense campaigning, the Act authorised the enclosure of the wastes and commons in Llanyre only, while those holding encroachments in all four parishes were given the right to buy at a price of £5 per acre. The position of holders of encroachments of between twenty and sixty years in the Crown manors and those purchased from the Crown was further strengthened when they were recognised as free-holders by the barristers revising the electoral register in 1841. Holders of encroachments in the privately owned manor of Gollon also gained as a result of Parsons' efforts since the lords of that manor, anxious to conciliate local opinion, agreed in the enclosure Act of 1844 that encroachments of more than twenty years standing, and of less than five acres with a house occupied by the encroacher, could be purchased by the encroacher at a price not exceeding £5 an acre.[28]

While there was no serious attempt to enclose the whole of South Ugre after 1857, the opposition of those holding as yet undiscovered encroachments helps to explain why attempts to enclose single townships or parishes in the manor came to nothing and the great bulk of the manor, including most of Beguildy parish, the whole of Llanbister parish and those parts of the parishes of Llananno and Llanbadarn Fynydd parishes lying within the manor, remained unenclosed commons and moorland.

Public opinion in the manor was so firmly on the side of the encroachers that freeholders in favour of enclosure preferred to 'let sleeping dogs lie' rather than publicly endorse a proposal to enclose. As Richard Banks explained to the Commissioners at the beginning of December 1856 with regard to a proposal to enclose the manor:

> One of the largest proprietors in the manor is desirous of inclosure but did not subscribe [i.e. sign the petition for enclosure] because for country politics he is cautious of appearing as a promoter of the measure.[29]

Another large proprietor who had first supported the enclosure subsequently withdrew his consent as a result of pressure from its opponents. However it was not only the opposition of those with undiscovered encroachments which negated attempts at enclosure in South Ugre, for the Crown was demanding as much as one tenth or one twelfth in respect of its right of soil in return for its consent to enclosure, a proportion which the enclosure promoters judged to be excessive and which also coloured their decision to withdraw their proposal.

Nor was enclosure stopped in its tracks in the county by opposition from those with undiscovered encroachments. Watt faced no opposition in his enclosures of commons and waste in the manors of Uchoed, Iscoed, Rhyslin and South Neithon, and enclosure proceeded smoothly in the manors of South Ruralt and Farrington and Cwmgilla, as it did on the Crown manors of Heyope, Knighton and Presteigne and the township of Creigbyther and in Llanddewi Ystradenni.

One must also be careful not to take at face value all the claims of Parsons and his supporters that there were 'hundreds' of squatters at risk of ejection from their cottages and few acres. The 1851 census, which required the enumerators to give the acreage of land held by a householder, suggests that Parsons were exaggerating the number at risk. With only four known evictions by Watt on the manors which he had purchased, one would expect to find significant numbers of smallholdings in the parishes of St Harmon, Nantmel, Llanfihangel and Llanyre in which the manors were located. However, out of 242 holdings in these parishes in 1851, only 20 were in the 1-15 acres category, and not all of these were necessarily originally encroachments. This does not suggest that a significant number of cottagers had been driven to purchase or to accept a tenancy in the manors purchased by Watt from the Crown.

The situation in South Ugre is less clear cut, for the numerator did not always give the acreage of holdings in the parishes of Beguildy, Llananno, Llanbadarn Fynydd and Llanbister in which part of the manor lay. However a much larger proportion of the holdings were small in size. Thus of 282 holdings in these parishes, at least 90, nearly a third, lay in the 1-15 acres category, including half of the holdings in Llananno and a significant proportion of the holdings in the townships of Medallwedd in Beguildy and Cwmlewchwedd in Llanbister. Even so, these figures are far from the 'hundreds' claimed to be at risk of eviction.

Nevertheless, the Radnorshire Cottagers crisis may have resulted in the creation of a significant group of small owner occupiers in the northern half of the county as a result of the reasonable terms finally offered to encroachers to purchase the land. The 1895 abstract of parish returns of crops and livestock for Radnorshire, which also gives the number of owners and occupiers of holdings, gives some support to this hypothesis. In the 19 parishes spread across the north of the county, in which were located the Crown manors purchased by James Watt and Richard Price and the manor of South Ugre, 16.6% of the occupiers owned at least part of their holding, whereas in the 22 parishes in the hundreds of Colwyn and Painscastle in the south-west of the county the proportion of occupiers owning at least part of their holding was 8.3%.[31] However it remains unclear as to how many of these part owner-occupied holdings in the northern part of the county included former encroachments.

The Radnorshire Cottagers episode demonstrated that the county establishment could be successfully challenged and compelled to modify its stance by the 'lower orders', provided that the latter were effectively led and had local public opinion firmly on their side. Though they operated outside the formal structures of politics, the Cottagers certainly proved themselves to be an effective pressure group, even if they achieved only limited success.

7 The Rebecca Riots, 1843-44

Many in the rural Wales of the mid-nineteenth century owed allegiance to a communal code of rights and responsibilities and those who breached the accepted moral code were often subjected to the *ceffyl pren*, by which they were given a ritualised mock trial. They were then paraded either in person or in effigy through the locality, before suffering some humiliating form of punishment at the hands of vigilantes who had blackened their faces and wore some form of disguise, sometimes women's clothes, over their normal clothing.[1]

The attacks on tollgates by 'Rebecca and her daughters' in rural west and mid Wales in the early 1840s and the orchestrated salmon poaching raids in Radnorshire in the second half of the century were clearly influenced by this tradition. In both cases the participants blackened their faces and disguised their appearance, often wearing women's clothing, marched to and from their objective in a disciplined and military manner and went about their business with a degree of ceremony.

By the late 1830s many roads in Wales, as in England, were operated by turnpike trusts who charged road users tolls, the revenue from which was to be used to keep the road in good repair. In some areas such as south-west Wales, trusts had become deeply unpopular since they charged high tolls at their many gates, yet failed to keep the roads in repair. The attacks on tollgates in rural west Wales started in 1839 but did not become widespread in the region until 1842-43. In September 1843 attacks spread to Radnorshire where there were three turnpike trusts: the Radnorshire Trust, which covered most roads in the county; the Rhayader and Llangurig Trust, which operated ten miles or so of the Cheltenham to Aberystwyth road in the north-western Radnorshire; and the Presteigne and Mortimer's Cross Trust, which maintained a mile or so of road in the county in the vicinity of Presteigne. The gates were destroyed under the direction of a local leader termed 'Mother Rebecca', the name probably derived from a scriptural reference to Rebecca in Genesis 24:60:

> And they blessed Rebekah and said unto her, let thy seed possess the gates of those which hate them.[2]

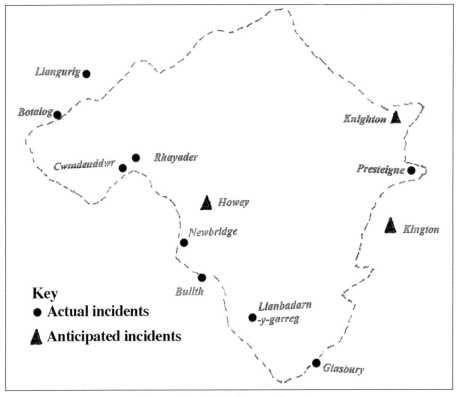

*Figure 12: Sketch map showing
the locations of Rebeccaite incidents in Radnorshire*

The first report of trouble in the county came in the *Hereford Journal* of 13 September which reported that an attack had been made on a turnpike gate 'leading from Builth to Rhayader' in the late evening of Monday 4 September. The tollhouse windows were broken and the gate taken away and damaged, the rioters making off when they were interrupted by a group of men on their way home after working late.

In the early hours of Friday 22 September a second attack took place, this time on the Pen-y-Pistyll Gate on the new Rhayader to Llangurig road. After breaking down part of the tollhouse, smashing the windows and partly destroying the gate, the Rebeccaites were disturbed and made off, after 'Rebecca' had promised the gatekeeper that she and her daughters would return again 'at a more convenient season'. This gate was particularly unpopular since its lessee charged the highest toll of either the Radnorshire Turnpike Trust or the Rhayader and Llangurig Trust for some categories of traffic.[3]

On the night of Monday 25 September the Felinfawr gate at the Llangurig end of the new Rhayader to Llangurig road was destroyed after the gate-keeper had been 'frightened almost out of his wits' when four shots had been fired close to his window.[4] Both the Pen-y-Pistyll and Felinfawr gates were repaired quickly and brought back into service as soon as possible.

Then, in the early hours of Friday 29 September, came the first attack on gates in Rhayader itself when a force of Rebeccaites, estimated to number between a hundred and two hundred strong, many of them armed, demolished the two Bridge Gates, sawing off the gateposts and throwing them in the Wye, along with the gates which they first broke into pieces. These gates targeted local travellers, the southern one the farmers of the Cwmdeuddwr area and the northern one the farmers approaching Rhayader along the old Aberystwyth road, each road in fact being kept in repair by the parishioners and not by the Radnorshire Trust. The rioters were helped by the fact that no magistrates were present in the town to organise resistance or to attempt to arrest the ringleaders. Gossip in the town suggested that the Rebeccaites were Cwmdeuddwr and Llanwrthwl men — it was said that all the tenants of Hugh Powell Evans were involved — while some thought that they knew the identity of the local Rebecca.[5] Again both of the gates were promptly repaired and quickly brought back into service.

At midnight or so on Monday 9 October the gate at Botalog, on the old Aberystwyth road from Rhayader, was attacked by a group of about 50 Rebeccaites after Eleanor Jones the gatekeeper, who had received prior warning of the attack, had been locked in the tollhouse. As she watched them

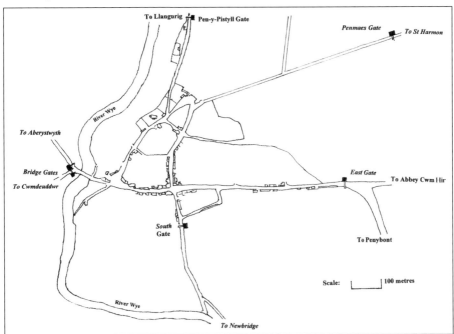

Figure 13: The location of the tollgates in Rhayader in 1843-44, based on a sketch map by Dr Colin Hughes

through a window, a gun loaded only with powder was fired towards her, the flash damaging her eyes. It may be significant that after this incident the Radnorshire Rebeccaites took care not to injure the keeper at any other tollgate they attacked, though invariably the gatekeepers were intimidated into agreeing not to continue to collect tolls. Certainly, although the authorities were convinced that she knew the identities of some of the Rebeccaites, Eleanor Jones refused to name them. Over the course of the next week it was decided to swear in special constables at Rhayader to be supervised by Sergeant Shaw of the Metropolitan Police, sent to Rhayader by the Home Secretary at the request of Sir John Walsh, while a troop of cavalry from the 4th Light Dragoons was to be stationed at Builth as a precautionary measure.[6]

The Newbridge Gate had been set up in 1829, when an undertaking had also been given that it would be removed in 1833 after sufficient revenue had been generated to put the road in good repair. The failure of the Radnorshire trustees to keep to this pledge had caused considerable local dissatisfaction. At 2 am on Friday 29 October a force of about 200 Rebeccaites, some of them mounted, destroyed the main gate, the adjoining gate for those on foot having been carried away and thrown into the Wye at the beginning of the month. Mr Parry, the gatekeeper, was intimidated into promising not to demand the toll in future; otherwise the gatehouse would be destroyed. Initially Parry kept his word, refusing to demand the toll, though if it was tendered voluntarily, he accepted it willingly enough. A detachment of six troopers from the 4th Light Dragoons was despatched from Builth to protect the gate while it was repaired and a week or so later they were replaced by ten men of the 7th Fusiliers, together with Sergeant Lupton, three constables of the Metropolitan Police and six special constables.[7] Parry was then constrained to demand the tolls.

The most serious incident occurred at 2 am on Friday 3 November, when, after warnings had been given, three contingents of 50 Rebeccaites from Cwmdeuddwr, Nantmel and St Harmon converged on the North or St Harmon Gate on the Llanidloes road. This gate was resented because the Radnorshire Trust made no attempt to maintain the road, despite the tolls collected, leaving the repairs to the parishioners. Mr Francis, the gatekeeper, was told 'Lie still or death will be your doom', and with Rebecca urging his men on with the words 'Work away little wenches' the gate posts were sawn down and the gate broken into pieces in ten minutes. After firing a volley of shots the rioters then moved on to the East Gate on the Penybont road kept by an old woman, Sarah Rees, who was warned 'Lie still in bed, we don't want to harm you or the house'. The gate was destroyed and a table of fees torn down and ripped into pieces. The East Gate was particularly disliked by farmers from Abbey Cwm Hir as it was located at a point where they had to pay the tolls, even though they had travelled from their parish on a track little more than six feet wide and almost impassable since the Trust failed to maintain it.

The Rebeccaites then marched into the centre of the town 'with a slow and measured step as regularly as drilled men' and with Sergeant Shaw and his six unarmed special constables powerless to intervene, destroyed one of the two recently replaced Bridge Gates together with the tollhouse, before dispersing. Mr James, the tollgate keeper, who had received prior notice of the attack, had removed his family to safety but lost his goods and chattels when the house was destroyed. In order to prevent further trouble a detachment of the 4th Light Dragoons led by Captain Arkwright was despatched to Rhayader from Builth on the following Saturday, while on Sunday thirteen constables from the Metropolitan Police led by Sergeant Lupton arrived from London. A week or so later the Light Dragoons were replaced by at first twenty and later forty men of the 7th Regiment of Foot, the Royal Fusiliers, commanded initially by a Lieutenant Hay and then Captain Stuart.[8]

By the end of the month both the North and East Gates in Rhayader had been replaced and were functioning again though guarded nightly by a detachment of armed police. The Bridge Gates however remained unrepaired, as did the gatehouse. The atmosphere in Rhayader and its vicinity remained tense and with rumours circulating of an impending attack on Howey Gate, two of the London police were despatched to guard it. On 25 November, practical jokers removed Rhayader's South Gate, which had not been attacked by the 'Beccas'; it was found later, undamaged, on the banks of the Wye.[9]

Events in the Rhayader area were imitated elsewhere in the county. On Monday 30 September, five young Presteigne men attacked Corton tollgate and house near Presteigne, 'battering the windows, doors and gate with stones' and having the satisfaction of seeing the keeper, 'a large athletic-looking man', hide under his bed, before they were disturbed by the arrival of a coach and ran off. They then tried the same tactics at Presteigne Lower Gate, only for the gatekeeper, 'Martha the Tollgate', to sally forth with her broom, knock one of them down and secure him while the others ran away, only to be quickly arrested. All of them were lodged in the county gaol for a few days. The whole incident smacks of a practical joke, although D.J.V. Jones, in his *Rebecca's Children*, considers it to have been a genuine Rebeccaite attack. Certainly, when a few days later James Davies, the Kington solicitor and Radnor clerk of the peace, received a letter, which may have been no more than mischievous, threatening the Kington tollgates, he took the matter seriously and began to enrol special constables to protect them.[10]

The nervousness of the county establishment is perhaps best illustrated by the panic induced by rumours which surfaced in the second week in November, of an impending attack upon Knighton workhouse. A prosperous farmer, Mr Evans of Treburvaugh, was told by an unreliable source that such an attack was planned, and immediately informed Richard Green. He in turn, without consulting the Knighton magistrates and, in particular, his uncle

Richard Price, contacted Sir John Walsh on 10 November, with the result that a detachment of troops from the 6th Regiment of Foot from Newtown was sent to Knighton. Special constables (i.e. unpaid and of local standing) were also sworn in, and other constables hired at 18 shillings (90p) a week to patrol the town at night. Richard Price did not like Walsh's interference in the affairs of Knighton which he seemed to regard as his personal fiefdom.[11]

In the second half of December, Rebeccaites were active in the south-west of the county. On 19 December the Maesllwch Gate at Glasbury was destroyed at 2 am by 40 or so protesters who gave three cheers and fired shots before marching off, leaving the gate on the road to Llowes and Clyro intact. Local people bitterly resented the Maesllwch Gate and a few months earlier had petitioned the Trust to have it removed, but had received no answer. The gate was quickly replaced by a chain, and four special constables were then employed at 18 shillings a week to keep watch at night.

The last incident of 1843 occurred on the nights of 26 and 27 December at Llanbadarn-y-garreg when Rebeccaites attacked two bailiffs sent by the Kington banker James Davies to distrain on a tenant farmer, during which the tenant's stock and furniture were recovered and restored to him.

The Felinfawr Gate at Llangurig was attacked for a second time on 23 January 1844 when between fifteen and thirty shots were fired at the walls and door of the tollgate house, while the keeper remained inside.[12]

Judging from press reports and the testimony of witnesses at the sittings of the Commission of Inquiry, which had been set up by the Home Secretary to investigate the disturbances in south Wales, at Rhayader and Presteigne, there were considerable concerns regarding the administrative and financial competence of the Radnorshire Trust. The tolls were not only considered to be too high, but were also levied upon some categories of goods which the Act setting up the Trust had exempted, notably manure, potatoes and brush-wood for fencing. It was also felt that the tollgates on local roads were too frequent and unjustified since the Trust rarely spent money on repairing them; the users of local roads were in effect subsidising the users of the Gloucester to Aberystwyth road on which tollgates were to be found every ten miles or so, since they not only paid much more frequent tolls on the local roads (see below) but also maintained them through their own labour. It was also alleged that the Trust had lost money by not taking security from lessees of gates and surveyors, who had subsequently defaulted on their payments. However, the Trust's finances were far from transparent since their accounts were presented in such general terms that a detailed picture of the Trust's income and expend-iture could not be obtained.

The criticisms of the Trust were perhaps more keenly felt in the Rhayader area than elsewhere in the county. Sparsely populated, with a density of less than eight persons to the square mile, it bore a disproportionate burden of tolls, for it contained eight of the Trust's 33 tollgates and contributed one-third of its revenue of nearly £2,000.[13] Surrounded by six tollgates, the people of Rhayader were only too aware of the frequent tolls on the local roads which served the market town. On the Rhayader to Llanidloes road there were three gates over 14 miles, on the Rhayader-Ty Llewyd section of the old Aberystwyth road there were four gates over a similar distance, while on the road between Rhayader and Builth, a distance of 13 miles, there were three gates.[14] Many believed that the interests of the Rhayader area received scant consideration from the Trust since most trustees came from the Knighton/Radnor/Presteigne area, while meetings were invariably held in Presteigne, not easily accessible to the few trustees from the north-west of the county. Certainly most suspected that of the one-third of the Trust's income not expended in paying interest on the Trust's loans or on maintaining the Aberystwyth road, most was spent on roads in the southern half of the county.[15]

Even so, the shortcomings of the Radnorshire Turnpike Trust represented only one of the many grievances of the hard pressed small farmers of the Radnorshire uplands, and this was recognised at the outset by Sir James Graham, the Home Secretary, and by Thomas Frankland Lewis, the chairman of the Commission of Inquiry. Most possessed little in the way of cash reserves and when the wet harvests of 1842 and 1843 were accompanied by a slump in the industrial areas, an increase in unemployment and a sharp fall in livestock prices, their situation became precarious.[16] Nor was there much chance for them to cut overheads since the county rate, poor rates and tithe payments were rising. To some extent, the attack on the tollgates was therefore a product of their frustration that the government at both the national and local level, far from coming to their aid, was making their situation worse.

Since the 1820s the magistrates meeting in Quarter Sessions had embarked upon a number of expensive capital projects, first the building of a new county gaol, shire hall and judge's lodgings in Presteigne at a cost of more than £10,000; and then in the later 1830s and early 1840s, in conjunction with the Radnorshire Trust, in an extensive programme of bridge repair and construction, some of the new bridges being 'chain' or suspension bridges, an expensive innovation for Radnorshire, that built at Penybont in 1835 costing nearly £1,200. While the magistrates may have considered that such capital projects were necessary to maintain the county's standing, the cost was borne by the ratepayers, including the struggling small farmers. Not only was the rate burden considered far too high, many believed that the cost of building the new bridges might have been lower had Benjamin Wishlade, the county surveyor, not been permitted to be 'contractor at his own price and surveyor of his own work'.[17]

If there were reservations concerning the competence of the gentry in their capacities as turnpike trustees and as administrators of the county, there was also grave concern as to their fitness to act in a judicial capacity at petty sessions. In the first place there were doubts as to their impartiality since it was feared that they might favour the cause of their fellow magistrates, their dependants, friends and tenants. Even if they did not, their decisions remained suspect in some quarters. Secondly, questions were asked as to their legal expertise, though the claim made by the *Times* reporter, Thomas Campbell Foster, that there was 'a total want of legal knowledge' on the part of the magistrates in general is inaccurate, given that some had had at least a grounding in the law and others had more experience; for example the Revd Dr Richard Venables had been an active JP for more than 20 years and chairman of the Radnorshire Bench for most of that time.[18]

As for the rise on the poor rate, the implementation of the Poor Law Amendment Act of 1834 had been bitterly opposed in the Rhayader area from the outset, to the point that the area covered by the Rhayader Poor Law Union had been deliberately kept as small as possible by the Poor Law Commission in order to reduce its influence in the county. The Rhayader Poor Law Union Guardians, 13 of the 18 Guardians being small farmers, had refused to build a workhouse for those requiring poor relief in order to keep the poor rate low, but in spite of all their efforts the cost of poor relief rose. Part of the problem were the 'bastardy clauses' of the New Poor Law which transferred the cost of maintaining illegitimate children from the putative fathers to the parishes in which the mothers lived. The impact of this can be seen in Foster's claim that of £800 spent on poor relief in Nantmel in 1842-43, the maintenance of illegitimate children accounted for no less than £200. It was also popularly believed that the salaries of the Poor Law officials such as the relieving officers and the medical officer were to blame for the increasing poor rates, and the Rhayader guardians found it necessary to publish a notice denying this and pointing out that the increase in expenditure was a result of the trade depression and the increase in the number requiring relief.[19]

The sense of grievance on the part of the small farmer of the Radnorshire uplands in the early 1840s was further increased by the Tithe Commutation Act of 1836 which determined tithe payments by reference to a moving seven year average cereal price. As a result of the high grain prices of the later 1830s, the seven year average price in the early 1840s was significantly higher than the market price the farmer was receiving for his grain. Even if this anomalous situation had not arisen, many of the farmers were unhappy with the arrangement since the average cereal price had little relevance in determining the level of tithes in what was essentially 'a grazing county' where the prices of cattle, wool and sheep should have been the determinants. In the view of Cecil Parsons, the farmers viewed tithes as more oppressive than the tolls.[20] No doubt since many farmers were nonconformists, views on the payment of tithes were coloured in part by religious affiliations.

The relatively large numbers involved in the attacks on gates and toll-houses in the thinly populated Rhayader area suggests that 'Rebecca' enjoyed significant support in the locality and was well organised. When Richard Banks, the under sheriff, had posted copies of the Queen's Proclamation offering rewards of up to £500 for information leading to conviction of those involved in the disturbances he found that 'Considerable industry had been exhibited in pulling down or defacing them' and he had to ask the Home Office for a further hundred copies in order to replace them. The failure of the authorities to arrest and bring to trial any of the reputed Rebeccaites in the locality, in spite of the fact that the identities of some seem to have been well known, also suggests that they enjoyed a measure of sympathy from the public at large. However it should not be forgotten that elsewhere 'Rebecca' had used coercion and intimidation to compel some to join them and to secure the silence of potential witnesses, and she may well have had recourse to such methods in Radnorshire. Certainly the authorities were convinced that Eleanor Jones, the keeper of the Botalog Gate, had recognised some who had attacked the gate, though she denied this. Other gatekeepers in the county, along with carpenters repairing tollgates and some magistrates, were threatened, usually in anonymous letters.[21]

Sir John Walsh, the Lord Lieutenant, was responsible for the maintenance of law and order in the county and favoured taking a firm line, insisting that while those with grievances were at liberty to seek redress by due process, they were not entitled to break the law with impunity. In this he was broadly supported by the local gentry and at the end of September a declaration was drawn up at Rhayader deploring the acts of violence perpetrated in the area and offering a reward of £50 for information leading to the arrest of the ring-

leaders. The declaration was signed by 25 of the leading landowners of the district including Walsh, the Revd Dr Richard Venables, Hugh Powell Evans and his brother Roger, James Watt, David Oliver, and Horatio James and John Jones of Cefnfaes. At this Rhayader meeting, as a gesture of goodwill, Walsh and Venables undertook to propose at the next Quarter Sessions that the Newbridge Gate, regarded as the most objectionable in the district, should be removed.[22]

However the county establishment was not as unanimous as the declaration might suggest, for while Walsh

Plate 36: Revd Dr Richard Venables

could rely upon the support of David Oliver, James Davies, the clerk of the peace and J.A. Whittaker of Newcastle Court, who was 'as fiery and energetic against these Rebeccaites as the others are timid', the stance of many of the other gentry was more ambiguous. Revd Dr Richard Venables, for one, was clearly influenced by the widespread popular support for the rioters in the locality. Thus Walsh noted of Venables in his diary entry for 30 September that he 'was not deficient in firmness and his evident disposition to succumb is a sign that there is great apprehension'.[23] Other local gentry such as Horatio James, John Jones, Henry Lingen and Hugh Powell Evans had a degree of sympathy for the rioters.

Despite the September declaration, affairs at Rhayader seemed to be drifting out of control, even though the tollgates were rebuilt and brought back into use as quickly as possible, since some, emboldened by the Rebeccaites' success, were refusing to pay tolls. On 6 October J.A. Whittaker volunteered to go to assist the authorities. Within a few days he, David Oliver, and later Hugh Powell Evans were fining those who were refusing to pay the toll. Gradually the Rhayader magistrates took a firm line and by the beginning of December 25 people had been fined for attempting to evade paying tolls, including two commercial travellers journeying from Aberystwyth who refused to pay at the East Gate. Whittaker had ordered a police constable to pursue them and when he caught up with them at Kington they were brought back to Rhayader where they were fined £5 and £2 3s 8d in costs, including their transport back to Rhayader.[24]

In the meantime the county magistrates, meeting at Penybont on 11 October, agreed to appoint special constables at Rhayader to keep order, requesting the Home Secretary, Sir James Graham, to send a sergeant from the Metropolitan Police to take charge of them. In the nearly three weeks free of trouble between the attack on the Botalog Gate on 9 October and the attack on Newbridge Gate on 28 October, Walsh attempted to conciliate the Rebeccaites by securing the removal of the Newbridge Gate at the Quarter Sessions meeting, but this was rejected by the magistrates on 19 October. Their failure to back Venables and Walsh was never made public and it thus seemed to many in the area that Walsh and Venables had gone back on their promise.[25]

The attacks on the Newbridge Gate and a few days later on the North, East and Bridge Gates in Rhayader may well have been an attempt to ratchet up the pressure on the authorities to make concessions. If this was the case, the attempt failed, for after wisely rejecting a proposal that Sergeant Shaw and the special constables should be armed, Walsh, backed by James Davies and Whittaker, sought assistance from the Metropolitan Police and the military. At Rhayader Petty Sessions on 15 November the Bench agreed to three resolutions which recognised the existence of 'a confederacy systematically

organised for the purposes of resistance and obtaining its objectives by force';
that the presence of the police and troops was essential 'until the inhabitants
of the Hundred have given the clearest evidence of their ability and their
determination to resist [the rioters]'; and acknowledging that Petty Sessions
did not have the power to abolish tolls, gates or tollhouses. Although Foster,
in his *Times* article of 2 December, criticised this stance, which he typified as
'the law must be vindicated' irrespective of the circumstances, it remained at
the centre of Walsh's policy. It was reiterated at a meeting at the Severn Arms,
Penybont, on 5 December, when the magistrates stressed that they were determined to avoid the violence which had occurred elsewhere after the attacks
on the tollgates, despite the cost to the ratepayers in employing constables
and troops.[26]

However the division of opinion in the Radnorshire establishment remained
deep. Thus at a meeting of magistrates on 22 November, convened to consider
when the troops and police might be dispensed with, broke up without a decision having been reached, with Hugh Powell Evans, the senior magistrate in
the county, making the withdrawal of the London police a precondition for
the swearing in of more special constables. Again, when the farmers of the
Rhayader area, most of them sympathisers with the Rebeccaites, held a series
of weekly meetings at the Lion and Castle Inn in Rhayader, beginning on
8 November, to formulate their grievances to be put to the magistrates, the
lead was taken by Henry Lingen of Penlanole, a former London barrister and
high sheriff of Radnorshire in 1839, and John Jones of Cefnfaes, a former
clerk of the Bank of England and chairman of the Rhayader Poor Law Union.
Amongst those attending the meetings was Cecil Parsons, who may have been
'fishing in troubled waters', though neither enclosure nor cottagers' rights
were discussed at the meetings.[27]

Lingen and Jones, both members of the local establishment, may well
have been seeking to maintain ties with local people, and Jones often spoke
in favour of moderation. Thus at the meeting of 8 November he urged 'that
more ought not be asked for than could be granted'; and at a meeting on 15
November he stressed that tolls could not be swept away completely as income
was needed to pay interest on loans and to repay loans. Initially, however, the
farmers were truculent and Walsh was taken aback by the tone in which they
made their demands. On 20 December they were refusing to agree to act as
special constables until the turnpike trustees had made clear their intentions
as to the 'objectionable gates around Rhayader'.[28]

However, pressures were building up on both sides to reach an understanding. The county authorities were coming round to the view that the
Rebeccaites, though not averse to intimidation, enjoyed the tacit support of
many of the local population and could not be dismissed as unrepresentative
extremists. Walsh was only too well aware that Sir James Graham, the Home

Secretary, was reluctant to provide as many Metropolitan policemen and troops as he requested, when the county was unwilling to form a rural police force to maintain law and order in its locality.[29] Finally, many of the magistrates were very uneasy that it had been necessary to bring in Metropolitan police and troops since this reflected badly upon their ability to govern the county, and they were prepared to compromise. Their view is best expressed in a letter of A.H. Wall published in the *Hereford Times* of 20 January 1844:

> Let the gentlemen of the county show the farmers and ratepayers that they are willing and anxious to extend the olive branch of peace — that their chief aim is their country's good and that the prayers of the oppressed shall not poured forth in vain. The disgrace of being ruled by a Military and Civil Force will be removed.

For their part the Rebeccaites and their sympathisers were also under pressure to find a settlement, for it was rumoured that the presence of troops and the London police was costing £40 a day, a bill which would have to be met by the ratepayers of Rhayader Hundred.[30] Their grievances had been made known to the Special Commission of Inquiry at sittings in Rhayader and Presteigne and although the hearings were private, local public opinion must soon have been aware that much of the evidence heard was an accurate reflection of their views.

By the close of 1843 the crisis was easing. At a meeting of the Radnorshire Trust on 8 December a resolution, proposed by Venables and seconded by Richard Price, that the Newbridge Gate be removed, was carried by 21 votes to 9. At Knighton the detachment of the 6th Regiment of Foot was sent back to Newtown, though the expensive constables were retained for the time being, much to the annoyance of the people of Knighton, the *Hereford Times* of 16 December commenting:

> These uncalled for and (to the inhabitants) annoying so-called protective measures will not soon be effaced from their memories.

The special constables employed at Knighton were finally stood down in early January 1844, while the Radnorshire Trust decided that the destroyed Glasbury Gate would be removed completely and the constables employed there dismissed.[31]

In the meantime Sir James Graham had given instructions for the Metropolitan Police detachment to be withdrawn from the county during the course of January, the Radnorshire magistrates having declined to establish a rural police force. Instead they decided to build lock-ups in Knighton, Presteigne and Rhayader, where experienced police officers were to be appointed as superintendent officers to supervise the parish constables of the localities. However Walsh was able to prevail upon Graham to keep two officers at Newbridge, where he hoped to find sufficient evidence to arrest some of the ringleaders of the Rebeccaites who had destroyed the tollgate, and also to retain four constables at Rhayader until the lock-up had been built and a superintendent constable appointed.[32]

By the spring of 1844 the Radnorshire Rebeccaites had succeeded in reducing the number of tollgates in the west of the county, for neither the Newbridge or the Maesllwch Gate at Glasbury was replaced, and the Bridge Gates in Rhayader had not been rebuilt. In addition the tone of the Report of the Special Commission of Inquiry on South Wales, published in March 1844, seemed largely sympathetic to their cause. Even so tension remained high as the notorious North Gate continued to function, guarded by troops and local police, while also in March the Radnorshire Trust invited bids to rent their tollgates, with the exception of the Newbridge Gate and presumably the Maesllwch Gate at Glasbury. For their part, the authorities kept a detachment of 40 men from the 7th Regiment of Foot stationed at Rhayader until at least the beginning of October, with a further detachment stationed at Builth. Fraternisation between the troops and the local population was kept to a minimum and any soldier forming a romantic attachment to a young lady of Rhayader found himself immediately transferred back to Builth.[33] The wary stance of the authorities was undoubtedly the result of continuing isolated Rebeccaite attacks on tollgates, such as those at Cardigan towards the end of March, at Longtown, Herefordshire, towards the end of June and at Builth and Rhayader on 12 and 13 September respectively, both of the latter being relatively minor incidents, which were not reported in the local press.[34]

The Commission of Inquiry had recommended that the turnpike trusts in each county in south Wales should be consolidated and placed under the management of a single county body, and this was enforced through the South Wales Turnpike Trust Amendment Act of August 1844. Henceforth the management of turnpike roads was placed in the hands of county and district road boards and a uniform system of tolls was to apply over the whole of the region. The debts of the trusts in each county were paid off by monies advanced by the Public Loans Commissioners, to be repaid, with interest, over thirty years. The liabilities of the two Radnorshire trusts amounted to £14, 866 and the county's annual repayment of loan and interest amounted to £791.[35] (The third trust, the Presteigne and Mortimers Cross Trust, was essentially based in Herefordshire and lay outside the remit of the Commission.)

At first Radnorshire declined to set up district boards and the County Board managed all the county's roads, but eventually the Rhayader, Radnor, Knighton, Colwyn and Painscastle Highways Boards were set up to maintain minor roads. The County Board decided that 130 miles of road in the county should continue as turnpike roads with tolls charged at 17 tollgates, with the payment of a toll at one gate freeing the payer from further tolls at specified gates for at least seven miles within the county and for two miles over the border into any other Welsh county. The revenue from the tollgates paid the salaries of the board's officers and the cost of maintaining and repairing the roads, the county road rate being used for the annual payment to the Loans Commissioners. The areas covered by the district highways boards varied considerably, with the Colwyn District Board managing 63 miles of local roads and the Knighton Board no less than 231 miles. The county and district boards published detailed annual accounts showing sources of revenue and, in the case of District Boards, how this was raised and spent on road mainte-nance at parish and township level, thus providing a transparency which had been lacking in the Radnorshire Trust accounts.

The Rebecca Riots had pressurised the authorities into transforming the pattern of road management in Radnorshire and the other counties of south Wales. However the quality of both the parish and turnpike roads remained poor, since the main priority of many ratepayers was to keep the rates as low as possible rather than to improve the roads. Thus a Knighton correspondent complained in the *Hereford Times* of 24 November 1849 of the high tolls and the poor road between Knighton and Newtown, 'whenever, at the risk of horses, men and carriages, we dare venture there'. In the south-east of the county travellers crossing into Herefordshire or Shropshire from Presteigne and Knighton found themselves facing frequent tolls once they had crossed the border. Thus travelling the seven miles between Presteigne and Kington involved paying tolls at the gates of no fewer than three turnpike trusts. As far as the parish roads were concerned, there was a considerable variation in terms of expenditure per mile of road between the various districts. Thus expenditure per road mile in the very large and sparsely populated Knighton district tended to be rather less than half of that spent in the Painscastle district.

The Rebecca Riots probably contributed to other changes in the law too. For example, the 'bastardy clauses' of the New Poor Law were amended in 1844, enabling the mother of an illegitimate child to take action against the putative father to secure maintenance for the child. However, relations between the Rhayader and Builth Poor Law guardians, most of them small farmers, and the central Poor Law authorities remained strained as both Unions waged a war of attrition against London as they sought to retain some discretionary powers and to block any unnecessary capital expenditure on labour yards or workhouses. The Unions met with a measure of success, for not until 1873 did both Rhayader and Builth Unions agree to build work-houses, and only then as a result of threats to dissolve them and to include their parishes in neighbouring Unions. Once the workhouses were opened, in

Rhayader in 1876 and in Builth in 1879, the central authorities were quick to stifle any local departures from current accepted practice.

However the Rebeccaites' complaints concerning the shortcomings of the local magistracy received short shrift. During the lieutenancies of Sir John Walsh and his son, the Hon. Arthur Walsh, the Radnorshire Bench became even more socially exclusive as practising lawyers and clergymen were excluded, apart from 'squarsons' such as the Revd Dr Richard Venables and those of a gentry background such as the well connected, but chronically financially embarrassed, Revd Oliver Ormerod, the rector of Presteigne. Thus, in response to a suggestion from Sir James Graham, the Home Secretary, that additional magistrates should be appointed in the Rhayader area, Sir John Walsh replied:

> I fear that there are one or two remote districts in the county where it would be difficult to appoint resident magistrates without descending to a grade of person who has not usually been added to the commission, and could scarcely be qualified by their intelligence and acquirements to fulfil the duties of the office.

Arthur Walsh's views on the magistracy were even more exalted than those of his father since he believed that only those who were potential future high sheriffs should be admitted to the Bench.[36] Not surprisingly the gulf between the small farmers of the Radnorshire uplands and the magistracy, largely English in background and education, widened considerably.

The complaint over the high level of local taxation which helped to fuel support for Rebecca in Radnorshire was the stock response of the small farmer in difficulties. However the trend was for local taxation to rise, partly from rising expectations concerning the level of provision of services and partly because the county establishment was anxious to maintain the county's standing and prestige. Thus the need to make better provision for the insane led to the county sharing in the cost of building and maintaining an asylum first at Abergavenny and then at Bronllys, while the establishment of a county police force in 1857, partly financed by the Home Office, created another call upon the county rates. The county establishment in the form of the Bench and later the county council was anxious to maintain the dignity and standing of the county and was quite prepared to spend in order to do so. Thus in 1868-70 the Bench spent more than £2,000 remodelling the county gaol in Presteigne rather than pay 10 shillings a week per prisoner to keep its few prisoners in Hereford County Gaol.

The success achieved by Rebecca in pressurising the authorities into changing the methods of road management and maintenance and modifying some aspects of the New Poor Law stemmed from the fact the views expressed reflected a wide section of public opinion in south Wales, including many who, despite the 1832 Reform Act, had no say in the formal political process. Certainly not all their objectives had been achieved, but even so one can see why Thomas Frankland Lewis could consider the Rebecca Riots 'a very creditable portion of Welsh history' since, unlike his more illustrious son Cornewall, he had an intuitive understanding of the small farmer of the Radnorshire uplands.

8 The Salmon Rebeccas

The protests in upper Radnorshire against the strict enforcement of the regulations concerning salmon fishing, which started in 1856 and carried on intermittently through the 1860s and 1870s into the 1880s and beyond, saw a revival of the traditions of Rebecca. Orchestrated poaching raids carried on by groups of men with blackened faces and disguised in women's clothing, or more frequently with a shirt over their normal clothes, were well publicised beforehand and sometimes attracted hundreds of spectators. The main disturbances occurred during 1856-58, 1866-68 and 1875-81 and affected the upper Wye and its tributaries, the Ithon, Elan, Marteg and Edw with their feeder streams in west-central Radnorshire and other tributaries such as the Eifon, Llyfni and Cammarch in the adjacent area of Breconshire, with the triangle lying between Rhayader, Llanbister and Llandrindod Wells being the area most affected by the disturbances.[1]

During the opening decades of the century the upper Wye and its tributaries had been freely fished by the people of the area, sometimes with the tacit consent of farmers whose lands lay on the riverbanks or from the extensive commons through which the rivers flowed. No regard was paid to the 'fence months' or close season of the autumn and winter intended to protect the spawning salmon, for this was the time when the fish were most plentiful and accessible. Salmon were both a valuable source of food, some of the fish being salted or smoke-dried for use later in the year, as well as an additional source of income. Nets were employed in the deeper waters, but at the weirs and shallows gaffs and spears were used, usually at night, with the aid of torches and lanterns.

While some gentry employed a 'river watcher' or water bailiff on their estate to safeguard their riparian interests, there was initially no real effort at collective action on their part, partly because sporting rights tended to be undervalued.[2] In the early 1840s concern was expressed as the upper Wye and its tributaries became 'the scene of wasteful destruction', and in response Rhayader Petty Sessions appointed river watchers. Several people were charged with killing or being in possession of 'unseasonable' salmon and fined 10 shillings and costs. Such steps may have been the result of pressure from the Wye Fishing Association, set up in 1842 with the aims of checking the use of nets of illegally small mesh and increasing the protection for spawning salmon in the close months. Though primarily a Herefordshire body, the Association included amongst its members many of the Radnorshire establishment and by 1844 had set up branch committees at Glasbury, Builth and Rhayader, though attempts to check poaching during the close months seem to have been ineffectual.[3]

By the mid-1850s there was growing concern over widespread poaching on the upper Wye, and some anxiety that lead-mining above Rhayader would 'convert the crystal Wye into a pea-soup coloured poison'. Between 1855 and 1858 the Society for the Preservation of the Upper Wye was formed to protect the salmon population, with sufficient resources to employ a large number of river watchers.[4] This more determined attempt to curb poaching during the close months cut across fishing rights as popularly perceived and inevitably provoked opposition — and the re-appearance of Rebecca.

During the course of Saturday 29 November 1856, an unusually large number of men were seen on the streets of Rhayader and as the evening approached rumours began to circulate that Rebecca and her daughters were to parade the streets that evening. At 9.30 pm Rebeccaites were observed blackening their faces at Cwmdeuddwr and at 9.45 Rebecca herself appeared with a gun, accompanied by two sword bearers and followed by 80 men with blackened faces, white shirts over their normal clothes and handkerchiefs covering their heads, marching in ranks of four, the outside men armed with cutlasses and the inside men with spears or pitchforks. They were followed by four men carrying a stretcher laden with straw tied in bundles, to be used as torches, and then another group of disguised men with blackened faces and bearing arms.

After marching to the Lion Hotel and then around the market square and firing three volleys of shots, they then marched to Cwmdeuddwr bridge where they were joined by another group of 40 or 50 Rebeccaites. They then marched to two nearby fords where they caught only half a dozen small salmon rather than the twenty or so that they had expected. The chief river watcher, Samuel Owen, the superintendent constable, Mr Jones, and his sons, who had anticipated the Rebeccaites, disturbed the river and frightened away the fish. The Rebeccaites then fished several other fords, allegedly with equally disappointing results. The proceedings inevitably attracted many spectators, but these were kept at a distance by the Rebeccaites themselves. Mr Talra, the steward of Prickard of Ddrew, headed towards the river and was fired upon and wounded in the elbow, whilst a Rhayader sawyer, getting too near, had three spears pointed at his chest and was ordered to move away.[5] At the end of the evening the Rebeccaites dispersed amidst rumours, which proved to be false, that they would appear again the following Saturday.

Plate 37: Rhayader Bridge, a line drawing from the Saturday Magazine,
22 June 1838

The county establishment were taken aback at the scale of the demonstration and the following week the local magistrates, Thomas Lewis Lloyd, David
Oliver and John Jones, met at the Lion Hotel, appointed special constables and
offered a reward of £10 for information leading to the apprehension of the
ringleaders. A few of the 'usual suspects' were arrested, but denied involve-
ment and, lacking witnesses or evidence, the authorities had to release them.[6]

During 1857 the official stance towards illegal fishing hardened. In
December, four Nantmel men were fined £5 each for illegal fishing while
at Quarter Sessions in January 1858, according to the *Hereford Journal* of
13 January, Edward Middleton Evans reported that, after a large Rebeccaite
disturbance at Nantgwyllt in December 1857 similar to that at Rhayader the
previous year, the local magistrates and farmers had resolved to put an end
to such proceedings in the area by unofficial action since they suspected that
they knew the identities of the ringleaders.

However trouble flared again in 1858, and between 7 and 12 December
there were a number of Rebeccaite disturbances along the Wye and its tributaries watched by hundreds of spectators. Following incidents on the Wye
and the Elan on 11 December, three Rebeccaites were arrested and bailed to
appear at Quarter Sessions in January 1859, and a fourth ordered to appear as

a witness. However the prosecution was unable to prove the charge of riot, thanks to the lack of independent witnesses, while the defence was able to find witnesses willing to provide an alibi.[7]

To discourage any further Rebeccaite poaching raids, Captain J.D. Telfer RN, Chief Constable of the Radnorshire Constabulary formed in July 1857, who also served as Chief Constable for Herefordshire, drafted a strong force of Radnorshire and Hereford police into Rhayader each weekend and they, in conjunction with an increased number of river watchers, ensured that there were no further disturbances over the next few months. [8] Though their presence was to maintain law and order rather than to ensure that the close season was strictly observed, public opinion in the Rhayader area tended to see them as additional water bailiffs acting on behalf of the riparian interests of the gentry who sat as magistrates at Petty and Quarter Sessions. The cards seemed stacked against anyone in breach of the salmon regulations and this explains the undoubted public sympathy towards those accused which led to a reluctance to give hostile evidence, a willingness to 'gild the lily' as to character on the part of witnesses and an inclination for juries to reach perverse verdicts. For some Rebeccaites it also provided a degree of justification for the intimidation of witnesses and magistrates, and the use of violence against both police and river watchers.

By 1859 the Society for the Preservation of the Upper Wye was short of funds and was pressing for new legislation to replace the ineffective Salmon Act of 1843. The evidence given to the Inquiry into Salmon Fishing set up by the government in 1859 by Radnorshire witnesses in 1860 was mixed however, with Henry Venables of Llysdinam and Charles Thomas of Pencerrig painting a depressing picture as to the extent of poaching during the close season, while Samuel Owen, the superintendent of the watchers at Rhayader, opined that even if the law was strengthened such poaching would continue in the Rhayader area since it was a significant element in the local economy. Only Thomas Lewis Lloyd took a more optimistic view, though he argued that the police should be used to enforce the fishing regulations.[9]

The Salmon Fisheries Act of 1861 strengthened the position of the boards of conservators which managed the salmon rivers, but poaching in the close season continued, albeit on a small scale, in the Rhayader area throughout the early 1860s. The only two incidents of note in the autumn of 1863 occurred, firstly, above Penybont where a group of railway navvies with blackened faces poached the Ithon after dispersing the river watchers with a hail of stones and, secondly, at Llanbister where police and river watchers caught one of a gang of poachers in disguise, only to hear that Knighton Petty Sessions subsequently discharged him on payment of costs.[10]

The Act of 1861 also tackled the perceived bias of allowing alleged breaches of the fishing regulations to be heard by magistrates with a vested

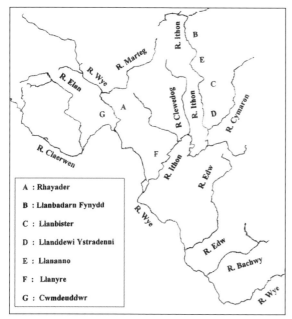

A : Rhayader

B : Llanbadarn Fynydd

C : Llanbister

D : Llanddewi Ystradenni

E : Llananno

F : Llanyre

G : Cwmdeuddwr

*Figure 14: The upper Wye
and its Radnorshire tributaries*

interest in the matter. Thus a special petty sessions was convened at Newbridge in January 1865 to hear cases of poaching in the close season in the Rhayader district, brought by the Wye Preservation Society. Since the magistrates who usually acted in the Rhayader Division were either riparian owners or subscribers to the Society, they were disqualified from acting and two magistrates from outside the Division, James Vaughan and the Revd Thomas Thomas, were brought in to hear the cases.[11]

In the later 1860s a series of violent confrontations occurred between the Rebeccaites and the police and river watchers. On 22 December 1866, 10 watchers, including Samuel Owen, confronted a party of 20 or 30 Rebeccaites at a ford on the Ithon. As usual the Rebeccaites had blackened faces and wore a variety of disguises such as petticoats, long shirts or all enveloping mackintoshes, although in a departure from the norm one had an artificial hump on his back and another had a large quantity of straw around his hat with a cock's head at the front. Since they were not heavily outnumbered, the watchers attempted to effect arrests and, after a violent struggle, seized three of the poachers who were placed in Penybont lockup and charged with assault and resisting arrest.

At Penybont Petty Sessions in January 1867 the case was heard by J.P. Severn who, like some of the other

Plate 38: John Percy Chesment Severn

153

local gentry, believed that the Wye Board of Conservators were managing the river in the interests of the commercial fisheries and other proprietors of the middle and lower Wye, and Edward Middleton Evans. As soon as the prosecution had begun to present their case Severn intervened, pointed out that, as the watchers had worn no badges of office and failed to show their warrants, the defendants had no case to answer and refused to accept the charge. Counsel for the Wye Preservation Society and Middleton Evans pointed out that Samuel Owen was well known to the poachers, and the latter were therefore fully aware of the identity of the watchers. But as the two magistrates disagreed, the case was dismissed.[12]

In the *Hereford Times* of 19 January, 'W' argued that the intimidation and defiance of the law on the part of the Rebeccaites 'should be put down by the arm of authority'. He went on to suggest that the dismissal of the case implied that there was either no law to punish poachers or that the magistrates were afraid to enforce it, and that in either case more rioting, and on a larger scale, could be expected. Matters were not helped by the arrogance and high-handed manner of some of the watchers, whose behaviour towards those who lived near the Ithon was described as 'obnoxious' in the *Hereford Times* of 9 February 1867. Other watchers were deemed highly officious since they failed to seek the permission of the farmers before patrolling the river banks.

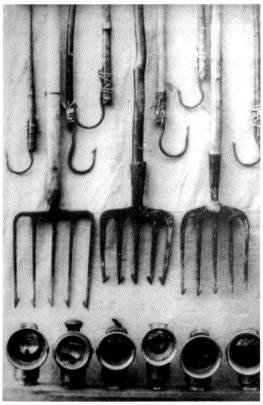

While Severn and Middleton Evans refused to issue a summons for the assault charge to be retried, they offered to issue a summons for illegal fishing as a way out of the impasse. The Home Secretary believed that a summons should be re-issued to hear the charge of assault, but for their part the Wye Board of Conservators sought counsel's opinion before deciding upon their course of action. In mid-March the summons was eventually reissued, but on a charge of illegal fishing. The case was

Plate 39: Poaching equipment of the 1930s: gaffs, salmon spears and lights seized at Abbey Cwm Hir, 1932

heard before Thomas Prickard, his son Major Prickard, Henry Lingen and Thomas Lewis Lloyd. The men pleaded guilty, but instead of inflicting the maximum penalty, a fine of £5, the magistrates decided that, since they were farmers' sons and men of good character, they should each be fined £1 with costs of 12s 6d (62½p). The men were not impressed by this leniency, for they had been severely beaten in the fight and had spent five days over Christmas in confinement, and for a time there was talk of an action for wrongful imprisonment. Later, counsel advised the Wye Preservation Society that a writ could be sought to compel the magistrate to rehear the assault charge, but wisely the Society decided to waive further proceedings in order to avoid appearing vindictive.[13]

However, the situation between the authorities and the Rebeccaites and their sympathisers remained tense, and the prosecution of a few young men for poaching in the early autumn of 1867 provoked a flurry of activity along the Wye and its tributaries on the part of Rebeccaites. Samuel Owen and his watchers tried to stem the raids, but to no avail. Five poachers were brought to court in November, but only two who pleaded guilty were fined, the case against the others failing since no witnesses could identify them. One of the magistrates, Charles Lingen, recognising one of the watchers giving evidence as someone who had been before him on several occasions on charges of poaching salmon, wondered aloud about the class of people from whom the Wye Fishery Board chose its water bailiffs.[14]

The deteriorating situation in the district can be seen in the attack on one of the river watchers, Edward Marston, on 26 December. Marston and a companion had met with a gang of 20 Rebeccaites on the upper Wye, but as they were so outnumbered, had decided simply to observe. Marston lost contact with his companion when moving from one ford to another and decided to give up for the night. However, on his journey back to Rhayader he was confronted by three men and, in an altercation, was stabbed in the thigh by a fishing spear. At Rhayader Petty Sessions in January 1868 a young man, Philip Jones, was fined £5 for the assault on Marston.[15] Thereafter, possibly with both sides adopting a less confrontational stance, tension died down — for a few years.

By 1875 the situation began to deteriorate once more and it was estimated that Rebeccaites had killed as many as 500 salmon on a stretch of just a few miles of the Ithon. The Wye Fishery Board was anxious to tighten up the regulation of the river, but the proprietors of the upper Wye felt that their interests were overridden by those of the commercial fisheries of the middle and lower Wye. As Arthur Walsh warned the Home Secretary, Richard Cross, it was essential to keep the upper Wye proprietors on side so that they would keep the Rebeccaites in check, as Walsh considered it most dangerous to give a very wild excited population like that of the Upper Wye a taste for the lawless proceedings they indulge in when spearing the fish.[16]

A few weeks earlier, on Wednesday 12 January 1876, 50 Rebeccaites, with blackened faces, most with white shirts over their normal clothing, some with their faces disguised by long white beards, others wearing tall hats secured by handkerchiefs tied under the chin and all armed, assembled at Rhdgwair ford near Morgan's tannery at Rhayader. Cheered on by a large crowd of spectators, the Rebeccaites fished the Wye as far as the town mill, before crossing the bridge and continued, unchecked, along the Elan and then the Wye back to Rhayader.[17]

The Wye Board of Conservators, under their new chairman, the Duke of Beaufort, the son-in-law of Lord Ormathwaite, decided in 1877 to make a determined attempt to check the destruction of fish during the close season. Inevitably this produced a reaction on the part of the Rebeccaites and, according to Penry Lloyd, the former Radnorshire Chief Constable, the countryside in the vicinity of Llandrindod Wells, Penybont and Rhayader had, in November and December 1877, been plagued by Rebeccaites. Armed men, with blackened faces and in disguise, had marched through the country unhindered and after a successful poaching raid paraded in triumph, beating kettles and frying pans and discharging their guns. Since the entire Radnorshire police force amounted to no more than fourteen officers and there were only seven river watchers in the upper Wye area, the Rebeccaites went unchallenged.[18]

In the *Hereford Times* of 29 December, 'A Welsh Magistrate' painted a threatening picture of Rhayader at that time:

> The moment I left the hotel I was stopping at ... I found pickets of men watching and dogging my movements. When they found out which road I took, they assembled together, some standing in my way, others running to and fro past me and all making threatening noises.

In the *Times* of 16 January 1878, 'A Welsh Magistrate', probably the writer of the letter to the *Hereford Times* cited above, hinted that the situation in the Rhayader area was drifting out of control. Describing the 'lawless pranks' practised by the inhabitants, he noted:

> Sometimes they destroy the ornamental trees of a neighbouring squire, at other times they sack a church and smash the harmonium to pieces. Not long since the throat of an inoffensive donkey was found cut in the morning in a vicar's field. The police, too, are roughly handled, and in a midnight affray with a party of eight or ten disguised natives recently, had some difficulty in maintaining their own. The chief

delight however, of the inhabitants is now and then on winter nights to assemble together to the number of 200. They then march along the turnpike roads for miles near the river and brooks where the salmon are breeding. Some of the party beat improvised drums and let off guns, while others are spearing fish in the fords by torchlight. The greater part are fantastically dressed and disguised. According to individual fancy, they turn their coats inside out, wear shirts outside, and muffle their heads; the ringleaders generally blacken their faces. These large gangs are called Rebeccaites, and on more than one occasion this winter have marched unmolested along the chief roads of the county. In the face of such numbers the police and river watchers prudently retire to a safe distance.

In his report to the Epiphany Quarter Sessions, the Chief Constable, J.T. Wheeldon, made no reference to the disturbances. In exchanges which followed with Penry Lloyd, the former chief constable, now a magistrate and on the Wye Board of Conservators, Wheeldon even denied knowledge of the disturbances. Penry Lloyd then asked the Bench, on behalf of the Wye Board of Conservators, to appoint six additional constables, not to protect the salmon, but to deal with the salmon riots. Lloyd was backed by Dansey Green Price — in spite of opposition from Sir Richard Green Price, Percy Severn and Stephen Evans Williams — and the Bench agreed to the request but only for a period of six weeks. However, given the strength of feeling in the upper Wye district, it is not surprising that Wheeldon failed to recruit more than three additional constables.[19]

During the winter of 1878-79 the Rebeccaite poaching raids were renewed. A raid on 11 November in the Rhayader area attracted about 150 specta-tors who cheered each catch. Another on 24 November attracted more than 300, including, it was alleged, most of the men of the Rhayader Company of Radnorshire Volunteers. On neither occasion did the police intervene since the Rebeccaites were upon private property and there was no riot or any disorder. River watchers, however, were given short shrift: on 22 November two watchers were attacked by a gang of men whose clothes were turned inside out and their faces covered. A few days later the windows of a cottage in which a watcher lodged was broken by a hail of stones. Two men were charged with the assault on the two watchers — one was fined £1 and the other discharged — while one was prosecuted after the stone throwing inci-dent, but acquitted.[20] At the other end of the county popular opinion also had little time for the water bailiffs; the *Kington Gazette* of 17 December regarded the stone throwing incident as 'a good joke' designed 'to waken the water bailiffs thought to be dozing in front of the fire'. The report went on to describe Rhayader as 'very lively' and to conclude that 'the spirits of the inhabitants know no bounds.' Towards the end of December the rising level of the Wye and scarcity of salmon led to a lull in Rebecca activity, but even so at the Christmas Market at Rhayader a large headless salmon was displayed with a ticket which read 'Bred and fed by Mr John Lloyd of Hereford [a leading Conservator],[21] butchered by the Rebeccaites of Rhayader.'

At the Epiphany Quarter Sessions it was agreed to appoint an additional six constables for the next six weeks until the end of the close season, to be stationed at Penybont, Rhayader and Llanbadarn Fynydd. A letter was read from the Duke of Beaufort urging the magistrates to resist 'the notorious and riotous proceedings' occurring on the upper Wye and stressing the determination of the Wye Conservators to put down 'the systematic destruction of fish and the intimidation of their servants'. Dansey Green Price backed the action of the Wye Board of Conservators, but not all the magistrates were so supportive: Percy Severn was sceptical that events along the upper Wye were the work of a widespread Rebeccaite conspiracy, while S.C. Evans Williams regarded the situation to be a result of the legislation on salmon fishing, which enabled the Conservators to ride roughshod over the wishes of the majority of the inhabitants of the upper Wye. As John Jones Hope of Rhayader commented in a letter to the *Hereford Times:*

> ... considering the great quantity of fish reared in these waters, they have a perfect right to a few fish in season, but from this they are debarred by the avarice of the owners of the lower waters, who take particular care to get the lion's share and not leave the Radnorshire men a dozen clean fish in their rivers, therefore, being debarred from taking fish in season they take them out of season, not for the value of the fish, but just to show that they will not be trodden on with impunity.[22]

The issue was discussed at length in the letters columns of the *Hereford Times* throughout January and February with much criticism levelled at the Conservators and the watchers whom one correspondent described as 'the most useless and most idle fellows of the district', and justifying the Rebeccaites. Richard Dansey Green Price, however, warned the Rebeccaites that though they had got rid of the turnpike trusts, they were not going to get rid of the Salmon laws, while John Lloyd suggested that the proprietors of the upper Wye were permitting the Rebeccaites to operate in order to wring concessions from the conservators. The stance of the *Hereford Journal* was uncompromising, equating the Rebeccaites with rick burners and the Luddites.[23]

The winter of 1879-80 saw a renewal of Rebeccaite activity with most of the raids taking place in the New Year. On 4 January the Rhayader police saw a group of 24 disguised men fishing with spears and lights in the Wye, but they escaped before the police could intercept them. The police expected another raid the following night and brought in additional constables, but the

Plate 40: Rebeccaite salmon poachers on the River Edw, at Aberedw, 1932

Rebeccaites did not appear, although a large salmon was attached to the town hall with the following note:

> Where were the river watchers when I was killed?
> Where were the police when I was hung here?

Though 10 or 12 police constables were now stationed at Rhayader, along with a large group of watchers, on 6 January the poachers were out again, wearing a variety of disguises, including masks of black crepe paper, and fishing a number of fords near Rhayader. On Sunday 11 January another salmon was attached to the town hall with the note: 'To Superintendent Arthur Williams,[24] with Rebecca's compliments'. A few nights later, on 14 January, a group of Rebeccaites said to number 80 strong fished the Elan, watched at a distance by the police and watchers, while on 21 January another large salmon was affixed to the end of the town hall by a fishing spear.[25]

Though these incidents were reported in the *Hereford Times*, with no attempt made to minimise the embarrassment of the police and watchers, one can detect a change of mood on the part of some in the locality in the letters column. Thus in the *Hereford Times* of 10 January a correspondent commented:

> It is to be hoped that the Rebeccaites will, for the future, desist from making any public display of their proceedings, and not bring our little town into any worse repute than it is at present.

In the issue of 31 January another correspondent talking of the Rebeccaites wrote: 'Amongst that lawless rabble were more than one Rhayader tradesman, men who claim to be respectable.'

Date	Location	River	Numbers involved
4 November	Llanddewi Ytsradenni	Ithon	40-50
13 November	Llananno	Clewedog	50-60
20 November	Llanddewi Ystradenni	Ithon	20
22 November	Cwmdeuddwr	Wye	60-80
29 November	Llandewi Ystradenni	Clewedog	40
1 December	Llanbister	Ithon	40
1 December	Llanyre	Wye	40
2 December	Llanddewi Ystradenni	Cymaron	20-30
3 December	Llanbadarn Fynydd	Ithon	Not known
4 December	Llanddewi Ystradenni	Ithon	Not known
6 December	Llanddewi Ystradenni	Cymaron	40
6 December	Llanbadarn Fynydd	Ithon	40

Figure 15: Rebeccaite Salmon Poaching Raids in Radnorshire Nov-Dec. 1880 (Hereford Times, 11 June 1881)

The Rebeccaites made their first appearances in the close season of 1880-81 early in November at Llanddewi Ystradenni and Llananno with two poaching raids on the Ithon and Clewedog, but although as many as 60 poachers were involved, no reports of such raids appeared in the local press. However, the raid of 22 November, which began in Rhayader, attracted considerable press attention, not least because it attracted a crowd of about 400 spectators as it was known about a few days beforehand. The Rebeccaites assembled with torches at the Groe and fished up the Wye and then the Elan, followed by a crowd of spectators and, at a distance, by 12 watchers stationed in the town. The watchers made no attempt to interfere with the poachers but clashed with the spectators whom they ordered back when they attempted to cross a railway bridge. The spectators replied with hoots, yells and a volley of stones which injured some of the watchers. After finishing their work the Rebeccaites mingled with the crowd and got away as it dispersed. Three watchers followed on the outskirts of the crowd but were spotted and chased. Two got away but the third stood his ground, was seized, beaten with clubs and kicked and but for the intervention of six or so spectators would probably have been killed. Sixteen men were later charged at Rhayader Petty Sessions with aiding and abetting salmon poaching, but the magistrates decided that they were only unoffending spectators and dismissed the cases.[26]

Additional police were sent to Rhayader bringing the number to 12 (of the county's 15 police) now stationed there. On 29 November it was rumoured that the Rebeccaites would gather in the town, but this proved to be false. Even so a printed notice appeared on the town hall from 'the children at Llanidloes' saying that they would send down 200 to help Rebecca if they were required.[27]

On 1 December the Rebeccaites were out on the Wye again, when 40 disguised men marched through Newbridge after firing two shots and fished down to Penybont Ford and then up through the village towards Rhayader, followed by up to 300 spectators. The police constable on duty in Newbridge recognised two of them, intercepted them on their way home and found them to have bonnets and sticks. At the police station they were further found to have wet waistcoats and slime and fish blood on their clothes, while one of them had a blackened face and the other's face had been recently washed. At Rhayader Petty Sessions on 7 December the chairman, Edward Middleton Evans, viewed the evidence as 'circumstantial but irresistible as far as the charge of catching salmon was concerned' and the defendants were fined £5 and costs each, but on the charge of using lights and spears, he gave them the benefit of the doubt.[28]

There seem to have been no further organised poaching raids in the Rhayader district for the remainder of the close season, though such raids continued in the Ithon district in December. Here the worst incident occurred at Llanbadarn Fynydd on 5 December. Patrolling the road near the village the police officer intercepted three armed men and in the ensuing struggle had his arm fractured and his nose cut. The men then initially made off, but returned with others and followed the officer back to his house, which also served as the police station, where they fired at the door and through the window. Two men were subsequently charged at Penybont Petty Sessions, but produced alibis which were accepted by the magistrates and left the crowded court room to cheers from the crowd. Guns were also used in a poaching raid at Llanbister and a watcher was shot in the thigh. Two men were subsequently arrested and fined £5 each with costs for illegal fishing at Knighton Petty Sessions, but there was insufficient evidence to charge a particular individual with causing wounding.[29]

Though popular opinion was firmly behind the Rebeccaites, the authorities were becoming concerned about the increasing violence, though some attributed this to provocation by the watchers. Amidst rumours that the military were to be brought in to bring the situation under control, the magistrates of the Cefnllys Division requested the Lord Lieutenant to call a magistrates meeting to approve the appointment of additional police. The meeting was held at Presteigne on 9 December and authorised the Chief Constable to employ 20 additional police officers until the end of February 1881, and suggesting the number of police permanently stationed in the upper division of the county should be increased by three. The cost of the additional police was estimated at £200 and it was decided that this should be borne by the 16 parishes of upper Radnorshire It was also decided that the constables were to be permitted to carry cutlasses in the disturbed areas.[30]

The decision to employ additional police did not meet with support in upper Radnorshire. In the *Hereford Times* of 18 December 'Scrutator' of Llandrindod protested that this only added to the expense of an already unnecessarily large police force and was the result of the inability of the Wye conservators to protect the river with their watchers. The decision that the 16 parishes should pay additional rates to cover the cost of the additional police met with vigorous protests, being seen as essentially a fine imposed upon the inhabitants of those parishes for failing to assist the authorities in suppressing the riots. Memorials were soon circulating for signature, for presentation at Quarter Sessions, claiming that the additional police were unnecessary and that the preservation of fish should not be an appropriate function for a police force, while the Llanbister memorial specifically pronounced the salmon laws 'dishonourable, disgraceful and distasteful'.[31]

Although a resolution confirming the employment of the extra police was agreed upon at the Epiphany Quarter Sessions, the Home Office, whose authority for the move was required, only reluctantly gave its approval and insisted that the cost was chargeable to the county as a whole, not just the 16 parishes in upper Radnorshire. Quarter Sessions acknowledged that the employment of additional police officers provided no long term solution and Dansey Green Price pressed for a government inquiry, while Sir Richard Green Price suggested a county meeting to discuss the grievances of the upper district, to be followed by a deputation to the Home Office with a view to remedial legislation.[32]

This view was accepted by Arthur Walsh, the Lord Lieutenant, and a meeting was held at Rhayader on 8 February with the chairman of the County Bench, the Revd Richard Lister Venables, in the chair as neither Walsh nor Sir Richard Green Price was able to attend. The meeting suggested that the salmon laws should be amended to abolish night netting on the lower and middle Wye and to allow fishing by spear at certain times and fishing for samlets (young salmon) by line. It also proposed to send a deputation to the Home Secretary to press for these amendments to the salmon legislation.[33]

Within a few weeks the Home Office set up a commission of inquiry to investigate the disturbances in the upper Wye district, with hearings arranged at Penybont, Builth, Hereford and Welshpool in order that witnesses could present evidence to the two commissioners. In the meantime, under pressure from the upper Wye proprietors, the Wye Board of Conservators agreed to abolish night netting and to permit 'reasonable use' of the fishing spear

Plate 41: Revd Richard Lister Venables

and angling for samlet, the two latter decisions by very narrow majorities.[34]

All three concessions were bitterly opposed by the Carmarthen, Severn and Usk Boards of Conservators and this may have encouraged dissident Wye conservators to seek to overturn the decision. Thus at the Hereford sitting of the commission of inquiry on 31 March it was alleged that the upper Wye proprietors were using the disturbances to push the middle and lower Wye proprietors into strictly limiting the use of nets in their fisheries, while in mid-April the *Times* and the *South Wales Daily News* also attacked the concessions. In the *Hereford Times* of 23 March, John Lloyd, a former chairman of the Wye Board of conservators, citing Lord Aberdare's report of 1876 on salmon fishing on the Wye, argued that it was not excessive use of nets in the lower and middle Wye which had reduced salmon stocks in the upper Wye, but rather the poaching of salmon in waters in the spawning grounds and 'the almost annual poisoning' of the upper 20 miles of the Wye as a result of pollution from the Plynlimon lead mine.[35]

The commission of inquiry's report was published in early June. It found the riots to be the work of poachers and of 'a better class of person' excluded from their ancient fishing rights by the enclosure of the commons, and resentful of the restrictive regulations of the Salmon Fishing Acts and of the by-laws of the Wye Board of Conservators. The situation was made worse by the failure of the upper Wye proprietors to enforce these regulations and by-laws. The commission recognised the very strong hostility felt by the general public in the district towards the river watchers and suggested that they should be placed under the supervision of the police, thus tacitly accepting that the watchers were not entirely blameless. Finally the commissioners found themselves unable to agree to the Wye Board's decision to ban night netting and to allow the use of the spear and fishing for samlet.[36]

There then seem to have been negotiations between the upper Wye proprietors, the Wye Board of Conservators and the Home Office for, on 13 July 1881, by-laws came into force banning night netting before 15 May, extending the open season for rod and line until 1 November and introducing a significantly lower priced fishing licence on the Wye above Builth bridge. These by-laws were clearly a compromise which served the interests of the upper Wye proprietors, and there would appear to have been little in them to satisfy the Rebeccaites. However they did open the way for further negotiations and in the early autumn a further agreement was reached whereby, in return for the Wye Board withdrawing their river watchers, the magistrates and riparian owners of the Rhayader district and most of the Ithon district undertook to protect the salmon.[37]

Some along the lower and middle Wye bitterly opposed the concessions made to the upper Wye district by the Wye Conservators and looked to continuing Rebeccaite activity to show that magistrates and riparian owners were not fulfilling their duties of protecting the salmon. The malcontents seized upon a report from Llanidloes in the *Times* of 29 December to the effect that the Rebeccaites intended to kill all the spawning salmon in the county, a Rebeccaite raid at Boughrood ford by poachers from both Breconshire and Radnorshire, and rumours of poaching on the Edw, as proof that the upper Wye proprietors were unable to control the Rebeccaites, but their claims were refuted by no less a person the Duke of Beaufort, the chairman of the Wye Board, in a letter to the *Times* of 9 January 1882. The sniping at the upper proprietors continued with a letter in the *Hereford Times* of 28 January, claiming that they used the disturbances to gain their own ends.

Although small scale poaching continued, there was no Rebeccaite activity on the upper Wye for the remainder of the close season and in a letter to the *Hereford Times* of 18 February, 'Rebeccaite' of Rhayader suggested that this was because they had achieved two of the major objectives for which they had fought, namely the reduction of netting on the lower waters and the complete removal of the watchers from the upper district. He went on to admit that some objectives, namely the use of spears in the season and the right to fish for samlet with rod and line, had not been achieved and expressed the wish that agitation to obtain these would continue, although not in 'such a turbulent manner'. His letter concluded with the assertions that the upper Wye proprietors could not claim any credit for the cessation of Rebeccaite activity since they were powerless to quell the disturbances.

Initially at least there had been some ambiguity in the response of the gentry to the disturbances, with some, such as Percy Severn and Robert Mynors, regarding the raids of the 1850s and 1860s as extreme manifestations of the poaching they had come to expect as normal during the winter months, and the fines normally imposed at petty sessions tended to reflect this, being well below the maximum possible. There was also a measure of sympathy for the Rebeccaites since many of the upper Wye proprietors believed that the Wye was being managed in the interests of the commercial fisheries of the lower and middle Wye with a ban on spearing after 1861 and the prohibition of angling for samlet. This sympathy was still present in the 1870s and 1880s when most had come to share the view of Dansey Green Price that the Rebeccaites were members of a secret society with its own rules, subscriptions, secret names for its members, a central committee and a network of local leaders.[38] The sympathy towards the Rebeccaites occasionally manifested itself in unusually lenient treatment of those convicted of illegal fishing and the dismissal of supplementary charges such as being in possession of a spear and lights or a gaff.

However such lenient treatment may have come about as a result of intimidation, as the Rebeccaites made no secret of how they regarded the magistrates. Thus at the Epiphany Quarter Sessions of 1879 Dansey Green Price reported that certain magistrates had been serenaded, presumably with 'rough music', another, on his sick bed, had been told that he would be 'put down the river', while another had been told that he would be 'hurrahed all over the county'. Even the chairman of the County Bench, the Revd Richard Lister Venables, was susceptible to such pressure. Thus in a letter to his brother, George, he explained that he had been present at Rhayader Petty Sessions, though not sitting as a magistrate, when two young men were fined £5 each for catching unseasonable salmon, and at the conclusion of the proceedings had talked to them. After going to bed that night he thought he had heard people shouting 'Rebecca for ever!' but was told the following day, to his obvious pleasure and surprise, that they had been shouting 'Venables for ever!'[39]

The belief that the Rebeccaites were a secret society with their own funds may explain a switch in the magistrates' tactics in the 1880s whereby those convicted of illegal fishing were usually fined the maximum of £5 in the hope that once the Rebeccaites' resources were exhausted their activities would wind down. Thus in another letter to his brother in December 1880, Lister Venables explained that the two young men found guilty at Rhayader Petty Sessions were each fined £5 but that if the Rebeccaites funded the payment of their fines, costs and legal expenses, the two cases would cost them a total of £20. Lister Venables clearly believed that the Rebeccaites' financial resources were not inexhaustible and that ultimately they would have to at least scale down their activities in the face of sustained financial attrition in this form.[40]

The measured response towards the Rebeccaites whereby the Bench sought to enforce law and order rather than simply protect the salmon, owed much to the Chief Constable J.T. Wheeldon. Thus towards the end of 1880 he informed Lister Venables that he was satisfied that the Rebeccaites' sole objective was to break the salmon laws in order to force their amendment and that they were not waging a general vendetta against the gentry, pointing out that in all their rioting they had not done the least damage to private property.[41] However as violence began to escalate the magistrates began to take a firmer line, not least because, with reports of events in Radnorshire in national newspapers such as the *Times* and *Daily Telegraph* and magazines such as *The Field*, some began to compare the disorders in the county with those in Ireland, while others began to doubt the competence of the Radnorshire gentry to maintain law and order in the county. However the Radnorshire Bench also looked beyond the immediate problem of disorder in the upper Wye district and showed some skill in brokering a settlement with the Wye Board of Conservators which not only enhanced the value of their riparian interests, but also secured sufficient concessions to the Rebeccaites as to induce them to abandon their campaign of large scale breaches of the salmon laws. The settlement certainly represented a success for the Rebeccaites, for once again the authorities, in the form of the Wye Board of Conservators, had been pressurised into modifying their policy by a group which lacked any formal political influence.

Rebecca did not disappear immediately, for isolated Rebeccaite incidents were reported in the late 1880s and in the 1890s, while small scale salmon poaching remained a lively feature of life in the upper Wye district. However sustained Rebeccaite activity did not reappear until the mid-1900s after navvies working on the dams revived the tradition, and again in the crisis years of the early 1930s. Rebecca's reappearance on both occasions seems to have been provoked by over-enthusiastic activity on the part of the water bailiffs.

Conclusion

Given the deeply conservative and hierarchical nature of Radnorshire society, it is perhaps not surprising that its formal political life was dominated in the nineteenth century by the local landed gentry, despite the gradual extension of the franchise. Nor was their dominance limited to the parliamentary sphere, for the early days of the county council the local squire was almost certain to be elected to it, irrespective of his politics. Only rarely was he defeated at a county council election poll by a social inferior, one instance of such an upset occurring in 1889 at Presteigne when Francis Evelyn of Kinsham Court was defeated by Richard Rogers, a grocer in the town. The local administration of justice was also dominated by the gentry since the Radnorshire Bench throughout the period was very much their preserve.

As far as Parliamentary elections were concerned, for the first three-quarters of the nineteenth century it was local influence rather than party affiliation that determined the outcome in both Radnorshire parliamentary seats where contested elections were an exception rather than the norm. Too strong an identification with any political party was regarded by some as a disadvantage, at least in theory, since it was thought that a Member should seek to represent effectively all interest groups within the constituency. Until the re-election of Richard Green Price as Member for the Boroughs in 1868, the members for both Radnorshire seats had worn their party allegiance relatively lightly and had cherished their reputation for independence, while even in the 1880s and 1890s some, such as first George Stovin Venables and later Penry Lloyd, could move so easily between the Whigs and Conservatives that it was sometimes difficult to decide where precisely their allegiance lay.

An opportunity for the middle classes in Radnorshire to secure a measure of political influence came initially with the split in the Liberal party over the issue of Irish Home Rule in the middle 1880s when the great majority of Radnorshire Whigs deserted the Gladstonian Liberals for the Liberal Unionists or the Conservatives. The power vacuum in the Liberal Party was filled mainly by the emergence of tradesmen and businessmen from the Radnorshire towns along with a few farmers. Only later in the day did local businessmen and professionals begin to broaden the appeal of the Conservatives in the county and to energise the local party organisation. Even so, one should not overstate middle class influence on either party, for candidates of both parties in the closing decades of our period were drawn from the social elite, while in the local Conservative party real power still lay with the gentry.

Given that the majority of Radnorians were nonconformists whose cause was championed by the Liberals, one would have assumed that, after the Third Reform Act, the Liberals would have gained an easy dominance in the county. However, political allegiance within Radnorshire was more evenly divided than one might have expected and in the elections of 1885, 1895 and January and December 1910 the majority was no more than 2% or less of the votes cast, while between 1885 and 1892 and 1895-1900 the county was represented by a Conservative in the Commons. Nonconformist concerns issues such as Disestablishment counted for less in Radnorshire than might have been expected, for Anglicanism was strong in the south-east of the county and in the lower Wye valley, while some nonconformists gave a higher priority to such issues as the unity of the Empire, Protection or Imperialism. The failure to recognise this may have contributed to the Liberal defeats of 1885, 1886 and 1895 and January 1910. Again, given the hierarchical and deferential nature of much of Radnorshire society, one could expect many still to follow the gentry's lead in politics, and the Radnorshire gentry were overwhelming Conservative in their politics. Nor did the popular press, which might have exercised a countervailing influence, have any great impact outside the Radnorshire towns, given the very scattered nature of the rural population, while in the towns the working men's clubs and reading rooms tended to be the preserve of the shopkeeper and skilled craftsman, rather than of the labourer.

If politics in Radnorshire at the parliamentary level lacked a Welsh dimension until the arrival on the scene of Francis Edwards, the same could not be said of the more informal politics behind the Radnorshire Cottagers crisis, the Rebecca riots of 1843-44 and the salmon Rebeccaite troubles of the second half of the nineteenth century. All three disturbances were highly localised and occurred in small, isolated and largely self-sufficient communities so characteristic of the Welsh uplands. In such communities local traditions and custom had evolved, over the years, into an elaborate network of mutual rights and obligations which were regulated by informal means, and which had little or no basis in formal law. Any innovation or restriction imposed by an external authority gained acceptance slowly and only then if it was modified to fit in with local needs, as was the case with the Old Poor Law.

While this hypothesis appears to fit the Radnorshire Cottagers crisis, in that it stemmed from an attempt of the Commissioners of Woods and Forests to impose a 60 years rule in regard to encroachments on the commons in the Crown manors, and the salmon disturbances, which stemmed from the attempts of the Wye Preservation Society and then the Wye Board of Conservators to ride roughshod over what were regarded as traditional fishing rights, it would seem to be irrelevant in relation to the Rebecca riots of 1843-44 in the county. The Rebecca disturbances of this period in Radnorshire were, after all, in the main part of a wider regional response to the shortcomings of the turnpike system and the general hostility in rural south Wales to the New Poor Law, the impact of tithe commutation and the general depression in trade. However it is significant that the disturbances of 1843-44 occurred in the main in the Radnorshire uplands and in particular in the Rhayader area and were a response to the mismanagement of the Radnorshire Turnpike Trust which was dominated by the gentry of the anglicised lower Wye valley and the south-east margins.

Since all three outbreaks of disturbances occurred in those areas which were more Welsh in outlook, it may well be that cultural as well as sociological factors were at work. In his evidence to the commission of inquiry at Hereford towards the end of March 1881, Dansey Green Price attributed part of the problem to what he termed 'the clannish feeling' of the people of Radnorshire. This suggests that he had sensed that the people of the Radnorshire uplands felt that they were different in outlook, traditions and interests from their neighbours in the Radnorshire lowlands to the south and south-east.

Politics in nineteenth-century Radnorshire were far more complex than an initial impression might suggest. In terms of formal politics the county, ostensibly placid and socially conservative in outlook, was dominated by the gentry and in many ways appeared more English than Welsh. However at a popular level Radnorshire politics could be much more turbulent and potentially violent. The establishment could find itself in difficulties when the isolated communities of the Radnorshire heartland felt that their interests were being ignored and their customary rights threatened, and harmony was restored only when these were acknowledged and a compromise reached.

Bibliography

Abbreviations used

BRE	*Brecon and Radnor Express*
DWB	*Dictionary of Welsh Biography*
HCRO	Herefordshire County Record Office
HJ	*Hereford Journal*
HT	*Hereford Times*
KG	*Kington Gazette, Radnorshire Chronicle and General Advertiser*
NLW	National Library of Wales
NLS	National Library of Scotland
PAO	Powys Archives Office
RE	*Radnorshire Express*
RS	*Radnorshire Standard*
REch	*Radnorshire Echo*
TNA	The National Archives
TRS	*Transactions of the Radnorshire Society*

The National Archives
Crown Estate Papers
CRES 49/4902-4913 South Ugre General Correspondence
CRES 49/4919-4929 Cantre Melenith General Correspondence
CRES 49/5005-5007 Sale of certain Crown manors to J. Watt
CRES 49/5051-5052 Sale of the manor of Gladestry
CRES 5/27 Manor of South Ugre Court Roll, 1852

Home Office Correspondence HO 45/454 and HO 45/462

National Library of Scotland
MS 2843 Major General Sir George Brown's Correspondence

National Library of Wales
Harpton Court Collection
Llysdinam Collection
Ormathwaite Papers

Herefordshire County Record Office
Brampton Bryan Estate Papers

Powys Archives Office
R/D/PEN/1-3 Penithon Estate Papers: Letter books 1872-74, 1874
R/QS/DE/7 Llanfihangel Rhydithon Enclosure Award
R/QS/DE/2?3 The manor of Gollon enclosure Act
R/QS/OB7 Radnor Quarter Sessions Order Book 1813-24
R/QS/S?1542-43 Summaries of County expenditure 1797-98

The Banks Archives
MISC 5/2 and 5/3, Radnorshire election addresses and songs
RB 8/1, RWB 6/24-37, RWB 19/1/14-15, Letters to and from Richard and R.W. Banks

Contemporary Printed Sources
Parliamentary Papers 1839
Report of the Commission of Inquiry for South Wales, 1844
Report of the Select Committee of Inclosure of the Commons, 1844
Revd Sir G.F. Lewis (ed), *Letters of Sir George Cornewall Lewis to Various Friends*, London, 1870
C.J. Robinson, *The Mansions and Manors of Herefordshire*, Hereford, 1872
Jonathan Williams, *History of Radnorshire*, Brecon, 1905
W.R. Williams, *The Parliamentary History of the Principality of Wales*, Brecon, 1895

Contemporary newspapers
Brecon and Radnor Express
Hereford Journal
Hereford Times
Kington Gazette
Radnorshire Echo
Radnorshire Express
Radnorshire Standard
The Times

Thesis
D. Roy Ll. Adams : The Parliamentary Representation of Radnorshire, 1536-1832, MA thesis, University of Wales, 1970

Secondary Sources
Burke's Peerage, Baronage and Knightage, London, 1928 edition
Burke's Landed Gentry, London, 1969
Dictionary of Welsh Biography, Cardiff, 1959
R.W.D. Fenn, *The Life and Times of Sir George Cornewall Lewis Bart*, Logaston Press, 2006
W. Hatfield, *Knighton*, Hereford, 1947
W.H. Howse, *Radnorshire*, Hereford, 1949
Colin Hughes, 'A Very Creditable Portion of Welsh History', *TRS*, lxvii, 1997
D.J.V. Jones, 'The second Rebecca Riots: A Study of Poaching on the River Wye' in *Llafur*, Vol 2, No1, Spring 1976
Rebecca's Children, Oxford, 1989
C.W. Newman (ed) 'Report on the Abbey Cwm-Hir Estate', *TRS*, xxxv, 1965
RCB Oliver, 'The Lewis Family of Downton Hall', *TRS*, lxi, 1991
 'The 'Gwardole' Letters of 1843', *TRS*, lxii, 1992
Roy Palmer, *The Folklore of Radnorshire*, Logaston Press, 2001
Keith Parker, 'Parliamentary Enclosure in Radnorshire', *TRS*, lxxiii, 2003
                'The Sale of Crown Lands in Radnorshire, *TRS*, lxxxv, 2005
                'The Radnorshire Cottagers Controversy', *TRS*, lxxvi, 2006
P.D.G. Thomas, *Politics in Eighteenth-Century Wales*, Cardiff, 1998
R.G. Thorne (ed), *The House of Commons, 1790-1820*, London, 1886
Ion Trant, *The Pen Ithon Estate in the Late Nineteenth Century*, typescript, 1987
David Williams, *The Rebecca Riots*, Cardiff, 1955

References

Chapter 1

1. Peter D.G. Thomas, *Politics in Eighteenth-Century Wales*, Cardiff, 1998, p.47
2. D. Roy Ll. Adams, *The Parliamentary Representation of Radnorshire, 1636- 1832*, MA thesis, University of Wales, 1970, p.490
3. Adams, p.492, *HT* 27.2 1869
4. W.R. Williams, *The Parliamentary History the Principality of Wales*, Brecon, 1895, p.182; R.G. Thorne (ed), *The House of Commons, 1790-1820*, London, 1986, Volume V, p.888; HCRO Brampton Bryan Collection, Bundle 59, Norton Manorial Roll, 6.9.1766
5. R.G. Thorne, Volume 1, p.512; NLW Harpton Court Collection c/626
6. R.C.B. Oliver, 'The Lewis Family of Downton Hall', *TRS* lxi, 1991, p.24-33'; *HJ* 6.5.1807, 13.5.1807
7. For the circumstances leading to the building of the town hall in Knighton, see *HT* 2.12.1882
8. NLW Ormathwaite Papers FG1/8, Sir John Walsh's diary 1834-36, p.27-28; Harpton Court Collection c/534, c/539, c/740; *HT* 3.1.1835
9. Thorne, Volume V, p.558
10. *HJ* 14.1.1835
11. TNA PRO CRES 49/4925
12. Ormathwaite Papers FG 1/7, Sir John Walsh's diary 1833-34, p.204,271
13. W.R. Williams, p.176
14. Harpton Court Collection c/1757
15. *Burke's Peerage, Baronage and Knightage*, 1928 edition, p.1048; C.J. Robinson, *A History of the Mansions and Manors of Herefordshire*, 1872, p.158; K. Parker, 'The Sale of Crown lands in Radnorshire', *TRS* lxxv, 2005, p.160
16. *HJ* 16.10.1844, 30.7.1845, 5.11.1845, 20.5.1846, 16.9.1846
17. Banks Archives MISC 5/3/20, John Whittaker's election address
18. Harpton Court Collection c/1757, c/1765. See also c/740
19. Ormathwaite Papers FG 1/18, Sir John Walsh's diary 1849-50, p.9; Harpton Court Collection c/3192; *HJ* 13.8.1851, 21.4.1852
20. Ormathwaite Papers FG 1/19, Sir John Walsh's diary 1850-52, p.117-18; *HJ* 21.4.1852
21. Ormathwaite Papers FG1/19, p.215; Harpton Court Collection c/939
22. W.R. Williams p.183
23. Revd Sir GF Lewis (ed), *Letters of Sir George Cornewall Lewis to Various Friends*, London 1870, p.290; NLW Llysdinam Collection B1278; Harpton Court Collection 3922, p.21, 24
24. *Letters of Sir George Cornewall Lewis*, p.290-91; Banks Archives MISC 2/1/22, Cornewall Lewis's election address; *HJ* 3.2.1855
25. R.W.D. Fenn, *The Life and Times of Sir George Cornewall Lewis Bart*, Logaston Press, 2005, p.147; Banks Archives RB 8/1/10-14, 8/1/18; Harpton Court Collection c/1267
26. Harpton Court Collection c/770, c/1968, c/2607, c/2701; *Letters of Sir George Cornewall Lewis* p.291; Fenn p.152-52; Banks Archives RB 8/1/20, 8/1/24
27. Banks Archives RB 8/1/31, 8/1/35, RWB 6/24, 6/27, 6/37-38
28. *HJ* 4.5.1859; Ormathwaite Papers FG 1/26, Sir John Walsh's diary 1858-59, p.118-19
29. Ormathwaite Papers FG 1/25, Sir John Walsh's diary 1857-58, p.25-26; Harpton Court Collection 3922, p.28
30. Harpton Court Collection c/1273
31. Harpton Court Collection c/3255-56, 3258
32. *HJ* 25.4.1863, 2.5.1863
33. Ormathwaite Papers, FG 1/32, Sir John Walsh's diary 1864-65, p.217, *HT* and *HJ* 15.7.1865
34. *HT* 21.11.1865, Ion Trant, *The Pen Ithon Estate in the later 19th Century*, 1987, typescript, p.1-3. I am grateful to Mrs Jennifer Lewis for sight of this source
35. *HT* 5.9.1868
36. *HJ* 7.11.1868, *HT* 26.7.1868, 31.10.1868, 21.11.1868

Chapter 2

1. Adams p.493
2. Adams p.414, W.R. Williams p.176
3. Thorne Volume V p.578; NLW Harpton Court Collection c/454, c/623-24
4. NLW Glansevern MSS 2198, cited by Adams
5. Harpton Court Collection c/281, c/493, c/627
6. Harpton Court Collection 2161, c/281
7. PAO R/QS/S/1542-43 and Radnor Quarter Sessions Order Book 1813-24, 12.1.1820
8. *HJ* 3.6.1818, 16.2.1820
9. The election campaign is described in detail in *HJ* 2.4.1828, 9.4.1828 and 16.4.1828
10. *HJ* 10.2.1830, 17,2.1830, 24.2.1830, 3.3.1830, 10.3.1830
11. *HJ* 17.3.830, 18.6.1830, 21.7.1830
12. *HJ* 18.5.31
13. *HJ* 30.3.1831, 13.4.1831; Adams p.468
14. *HJ* 18.5.1831
15. *HJ* 16.11.1831
16. *HJ* 28.8.1832
17. Banks Archives MISC 5/3/4, 5/3/11; *HJ* 27.8. 1834, 3.9.1834; *HT* 23.8.1834, 30.8.1834, 6.9.1834
18. W.R. Williams p.176; Ormathwaite Papers FG 1/7 p.207, 209, FG 1/36 p.46, 80
19. NLW Ormathwaite Papers FG 1/7, p.206-07; *HT* 6.99.34; *HJ* 3.9.34
20. Ormathwaite Papers FG 1/7 p.266
21. Ormathwaite Papers FG 1/8 p.6-7
22. Ormathwaite Papers FG 1/8, p.19-26
23. TNA PRO CRES 49/5005, 29.12.1834 D. Lewis to J. Wilkin; *HT* 30.5.34, 6.9.1834, 20.12.1834, 27.12.1834; *HJ* 17.12.1834
24. *HJ* 17.12.1834, 24.12.1834, 31.12.1834; *HT* 30.8.1834, 6.9.1834,13.12.1834, 27.12.1834, 3.1.1835
25. Banks Archives MISC 5/3/16, MISC 5/3/17b, MISC 5/3/18. Though all three pamphlets are undated, internal evidence shows them all to refer to the campaign of 1834-35
26. Ormathwaite Papers FG 1/8 p.32 and p.60; WH Howse, *Radnorshire*, Hereford, 1949, p.101

27. Banks Archives MISC 5/3/10; Ormathwaite Papers FG 1/7 p.272, FG 1/8 pp.1-2, 34, 160-61
28. *HJ* 24.12.1834; *HT* 24.1.1835; Ormathwaite Papers FG 1/8, pp.16, 34
29. *HJ* 12.8.1835, 28.10.1835; *HT* 1.7.1837; Ormathwaite Papers p.126-27, 152-53, 157
30. *HT* 15.7.1837, 5.8.1837; Banks Archives MISC 5/3/5 Parker's election address; Ormathwaite Papers FG 1/10, pp.1349-42
31. *HT* 16.6.1838, 30.6.1838
32. Harpton Court Collection c/632
33. Ormathwaite Papers FG 1/10 p.149-50, 152
34. Ormathwaite Papers FG 1/14 p.214-20, FG 1/12 pp.13-15; *HT* 6.6.1840
35. *HT* 6.6.1840; Ormathwaite Papers FG 1/12 pp.14-15, 22, 32
36. Ormathwaite Papers FG 1/12 p.215, 219-20; Banks Archives MISC 5/3/19 Harley's election address
37. *HT* 11.7.1840, 18.7.1840; *HJ* 7.7.1840
38. *HJ* 30.6.1841, 7.7.1841; Ormathwaite Papers FG 1/12 p.223, FG 1/30 p.262, FG 1/36 p.85. T.B.M. Baskerville, Mynors' brother, had assumed the additional name of Baskerville in 1818 in order to inherit his cousin's estate
39. TNA PRO CRES 49/4927 29.5.1841, 23.7.1841, 18.8.1841 Harley to Woods and Forests, 5.8.1841 Banks to Woods and Forests; Ormathwaite Papers FG 1/12 pp.225, 229-31
40. Ormathwaite Papers FG 1/13 p.1, FG 1/18 pp.79-80, FG 1/15 p.103, FG 1/16 p.13-15, 38; *HT* 22.3.1851
41. *HT* 22.5.1875
42. Harpton Court Collection c/633, c/634-35; Ormathwaite Papers FG 1/13 pp.121-23, 130
43. Ormathwaite Papers FG 1/21 pp.30, 57
44. Ormathwaite Papers FG 1/25 pp.55, FG 1/26 p.52

Chapter 3

1. NLW Harpton Court Collection 3843-45, 3850, 3857
2. Harpton Court Collection 3850: *HT* 30.1.1869
3. *HT* 23.1.1869; *HJ* 23.1.1869; CW Newman (ed), 'Report on the Abbey Cwm-Hir Estate, *TRS* xxxv, 1965, p.44
4. NLW Ormathwaite Papers FM 1/10 Arthur Walsh's diary 1868-70 (unpaginated)
5. *HT* 30.1.1869; *HJ* 30.1.1869
6. *HT* 27.2.1869
7. *HT* 27.2.1869
8. *RE* 4.5.1899
9. Harpton Court Collection 3857; *HJ* 31.5.73
10. *Burke's Peerage, Baronetage and Knightage*, 1928 edition, p.574; *HT* 7.6.1873, 31.1.1874, 7.2.1874; *HJ* 31.5.1873, 7.2.1874, 14.2.1874
11. *HJ* 31.1.1874
12. *HT* 14.2.1874
13. *HT* 5.7.1879; *HJ* 30.8.1879
14. *KG* 6.4.1880
15. *HT* 17.4.1880
16. NLW Llysdinam Collection B2524-25, B2527, B3007; *KG* 16.9.1879
17. W.R. Williams p183-84; *HT* 9.8.1879
18. *HT* 12.7.1879, 29.11.1879, 24.4.1980

19. *HJ* 18.10.1879, 22.11.1879; *HT* 22.11.1879, 27.3.1880
20. *HJ* 9.8.1879, 22.5.1880
21. *HT* 15.5.1880, 22.5.1880; W. Hatfield, *Knighton*, Hereford, 1947, p.47
22. *HT* 22.5.1880; *HJ* 22.5.1880
23. *KG* 28.6.1880
24. *KG* 3.6.1884, 17.6.1884
25. *HT* 15.5.1880, 18.10.1884; *HJ* 8.5.1880
26. W.R. Williams p.184
27. *HJ* 11.10.1884; *HT* 11.10.1884,18.10.1884
28. *HT* 1.11.1885, 30.4.1887

Chapter 4

1. *RE* 31.10.1918
2. W.R. Williams p.177; *HJ* 1.4.1865; *HT* 15.8.1865
3. NLW Ormathwaite Papers FG 1/35 p.199
4. Ormathwaite Papers FG 1/35 p.203-04, 207
5. *HT* 2.5.1868
6. *HJ* 7.11.1868, 21.11.1868
7. NLW Harpton Court Collection 3857,3860
8. *HT* 10.5.1873; *HT* 17.5.1873
9. *HT* 7.6.1873, 22.7.1873, 2.8.1873
10. *HT* 19.7.1873
11. PAO Pen Ithon Estate Papers R/D/PEN/2, letter-book 1872-79, p.199,211,217-18, 233
12. *HT* 20.9.1873
13. Pen Ithon Estate Papers R/D/PEN/2 p.199, R/D/PEN/3 p.8; *HT* 2.9.1873, 31.1.1874, 7.2.1874
14. Pen Ithon Estate Papers R/D/PEN/3 p.8,14; *HJ* 14.2.1874
15. *HT* 14.2.1874; Banks Archives RWB 19/1/14
16. Pen Ithon Estate Papers R/D/PEN?2 p.18
17. Ormathwaite Papers, Introduction p.12, FH 2/2 f92
18. Ormathwaite Papers FH 2/2 f93; FH2/1 f117-18
19. Llysdinam Collection B3005; Ormathwaite Collection FH 2/2 f92-94
20. J. Williams, *History of Radnorshire*, 1905 edition, p.381; Llysdinam Collection B3005
21. *HT* 27.3.80, 3.4.1880
22. *HT* 10.4.1880
23. *KG* 6.4.1880
24. *HT* 8.3.1882; *HJ* 3.7.1886; *RE* 4.5.1899
25. *HT* 14.6.1884, 21.6.1884, 28.6.1884
26. Ormathwaite Papers FH 2/3 f45-46
27. Ormathwaite Papers FH 2/3 f45
28. *HJ* 23.5.85,30.5.1885
29. *HJ* 11.7.1885
30. *HT* 3.10.1885, 21.11.1885, 12.12.1885, 19.12.1885
31. *HT* 28.11.1885
32. *HT* 14.11.1885, 5.12.1885
33. *HT* 8.5.86
34. Llysdinam Collection B1747, B1748
35. *HJ* 31.10.1885
36. *HJ* 16.1.1886, 15.5.1886; *HT* 8.5.1886
37. *HT* 8.5.1886
38. *HT* 19.6.1886
39. *HT* 19.6.1886, 26.6.1886 *HJ* 12.6.1886; Llysdinam Collection B1808
40. *HJ* 26.6.1886, 3.7.1886
41. *HT* 26.6.1886, 3.7.1886, 10.3.1886
42. *HT* 19.7.1886

Chapter 5
1. *DWB* p.186; W.R. Williams p.177; *RE* 4.7.1907
2. The *Times* 14.8.1890; *BRE* 4.7.1890
3. *REch* 4.3.1887
4. *BRE* 9.10.1891; The *Times* 2.9.1892
5. *BRE* 23.10.1891,13.11.1891; *HT* 9.1.1892
6. NLW Llysdinam Collection B3940; *BRE* 30.10.1891
7. *BRE* 4.12.1891, 5.1.1892, 21.3.1892, 8.4.1892, 15.4.1892; *HT* 2.4.1891, 9.4.1891, 16.4.1891, 20.2.1892, 21.5.1892; *HJ* 8.1.1892
8. *DWB* p.48; *Burke's Landed Gentry*, 1969 edition, Vol ii, p.61
9. *BRE* 10.6.1892; *HJ* 9.7.1892
10. *BRE* 20.5.1892, 8.7.1892
11. *HJ* 28.5.1892
12. *HT* 11.6.1892
13. The *Times* 2.9.1892; *HJ* 2.7.1892, 10.9.1892
14. *BRE* 29.7.1892, 12.1.1894
15. *HJ* 9.1.1892; *BRE* 25.9.1892, 13.10.1893
16. *BRE* 2.8.1895, 8.10.1896
17. *BRE* 6.9.1895, 13.3.1896
18. *BRE* 11.8.1893
19. *HT* 25.3.1882, 17.3.83, 7.4.1883, 23.2.1889, 6.2.1892; *HJ* 23.1.1892
20. *BRE* 11.1.1895, 22.3.1895
21. *BRE* 4.4.1896; *HT* 4.4.1896
22. *RE* 5.4.1900, 26.4.1900; *HT* 5.5.00, 9.6.1900
23. *RS* 5.9.1900
24. *RS* 29.9.1900; *RE* 4.10.1900
25. *HJ* 11.8.1900, 6.10.1900; *RE* 11.10.1900
26. *HT* 20.10.1900; *RS* 17.10.1900
27. *RS* 26.4.1901, 26.6.1901, 3.7.1901, 20.11.1901; *RE* 4.7.1901
28. *RE* 23.1.1902; *RS* 5.3.1902
29. *RE* 29.1.1903
30. *RS* 11.2.1904, 16.3.1904; *RE* 30.7.1903, 23.12.1903, 10.3.1904, 17.3.1904, 24.3.1904, 31.3.1904, 14.4.1904, 12.5.1904
31. *RE* 18.2.1904, 14.4.1904
32. *RE* 16.7.1903, 24.3.1904
33. *RE* 18.1.1906
34. *HT* 6.1.1906
35. *RE* 25.1.1906, 1.2.1906
36. *RS* 24.10.08
37. *RE* 9.9.1909; *RS* 4.9.1909, 11.9.1909
38. *RE* 6.1.1910. 13.1.1910
39. *RS* 1.1.1910, 8.1.1910, 15.1.1910
40. *RE* 27.1.1910; *RS* 5.2.1910
41. *RE* 27.1.1910
42. *RS* 5.3.1910, 9.4 1910
43. *RE* 1.12.1910; *RE* 24.9.1910, 15.10.1910, 19.11.1910, 26.1.10
44. *RE* 3.12.1910
45. *RS* 15.12.1910; *HT* 24.12.1910
46. *RS* 13.7.1912

Chapter 6
1. K. Parker 'Parliamentary Enclosure in Radnorshire', *TRS* lxxiii, 2003, p.127-28
2. *HJ* 23.9.1812, 6.10.1813, 19.10.1814, 2.11.1814, 18.10.1815
3. TNA PRO CRES 49/5005
4. CRES 49/4923, Schedule of presentments
5. CRES 49/4923, 31 May 1824, Davies to Woods and Forests
6. In his survey of the Crown manors Sayce was found to have included 400 acres or so of another manor in the Gladestry acreage and the price of the manor was adjusted accordingly. There was no plan of South Ruallt and since the boundaries of the manor were not clearly defined, the valuation was considered to be unreliable and the price was reduced substantially
7. *Report of the Select Committee on Commons Inclosure*, London, 1844, Question 1236
8. CRES 49/5006 'A statement of Mr Watt's case'
9. The Cottagers' version of events is to be found in *HT* 6.1.1838. Banks' version is to be found in his letter to Woods and Forests of 5.1.1830, CRES 49/5007
10. The Memorial is included in TNA PRO CRES 49/4924
11. *HJ* 24.6.1827
12. NLW Ormathwaite Papers FG 1/8, pp.126-27; *HJ* 19.8.1835; CRES 49/5005, 17.8.1835 Pemberton to Woods and Forests
13. CRES 49/4926 25.7.1838 and 27.7.1835 Lewis to Woods and Forests
14. CRES 49/4926 28.12.1835 Lewis to Woods and Forests
15. *HJ* 19.8.1835
16. CRES 49/5006 16.1.1836 Banks to Woods and Forests
17. CRES 49/5006 26.4.1836 Watt to Woods and Forests
18. *HJ* 15.6.1836
19. CRES 49/5006 8.8.1836 Pemberton to Woods and Forests, 10.1.1837 Watts to Woods and Forests; CRES 49/5007 13.6.1838 nd 15.9.1838 Banks to Woods and Forests
20. *HT* 6.1.1838
21. *Parliamentary Papers, 1839, xxx* p.416-19; *HT* 21.1.1837; CRES 49/5007, 12.1.1837 and 26.1.1837, Banks to Woods and Forests
22. TNA PRO CRES 5/27 South Ugre Manorial Roll, 1853
23. CRES 49/4902 16.3.1854 Woods and Forests to J. Wilkin (copy)
24. CRES 49/4903 2.4.1856 Banks to Woods and Forests and an undated draft reply from Woods and Forests to the Home Office
25. *HT* 8.8.1857, 22.8.1857; CRES 49/4906 22.8.1857 Banks to Woods and Forests, 28.8.1857 Green to Woods and Forests, 9.11.1857 undated draft letter from Woods and Forests to Green
26. CRES 49/4907 23.8.1858 Howard to the Treasury; CRES 49/4911 Davies to Woods and Forests
27. *HJ* 24.6 1835
28. PAO R/QS/DE/7 The Llanfihangel Helygen Enclosure Award; R/QS/DE/2/32 The Manor of Gollon Enclosure Act
29. CRES 49/4904 2.12.1856 2.12.1856 Banks to Woods and Forests
30. TNA PRO MAF 68/1593

Chapter 7

1. Roy Palmer, *The Folklore of Radnorshire*, Logaston Press, 2001 p.217-19
2. An alternative explanation is noted by David Williams in his *Rebecca Riots*, Cardiff, 1955 p.188-89: an early leader of the rioters in west Wales, Tom Rees, was so large that the only women's clothes that he could use as a disguise were those of 'Big Rebecca' of Llangolman, Pembrokeshire.
3. *HT* 30.9.1843, 11.11.1843; *Report of the Commission of Inquiry for South Wales*, London, 1844, p.13
4. R.C.B. Oliver, 'The "Gwardole" Letters of 1843' *TRS* lxxii, 1992, p.20
5. *HT* 30.9.1843; 'The "Gwardole" Letters' p.23-24; NLW Ormathwaite Papers FG 1/14 p.43; *Times* 3.10.1843
6. TNA PRO HO 45/454 f800, 18.10.1843 Chief Constable of Newtown to the Home Office
7. *HT* 4.11.1843, 11.11.43; *Times* 7.11.1843, 13.11.1843; NLS MS 2843, f156 14.10.1843 Major General Sir George Brown to Sir John Walsh
8. *Times* 13.11.1843; *HT* 11.11.1843
9. *HT* 25.11.1843, 2.12.1843
10. D.J.V. Jones, *Rebecca's Children*, Oxford, 1989, p.241; *HT* 11.11.1843
11. *HJ* 15.11.1843, 6.12.1843; *Report of the Commission of Inquiry* : Minutes of Evidence, Question 7243, 7246, 7248-50
12. *HT* 23.11.43; HO 45/454, f959 11.12.1843 Walsh to Home Office, HO45/ 642 26.1.1844 Chief Constable of Montgomeryshire to Home Office
13. *HJ* 10.4.1844; *Report of the Commission of Inquiry* p.14
14. *Times* 2.12.1843
15. *Report of the Commission of Inquiry* Minutes of Evidence, Questions 6781-82
16. *Report of the Commission of Inquiry* Minutes of Evidence, Questions 7195-96, 7198, 7308
17. *Report of the Commission of Inquiry* Minutes of Evidence Question 6788
18. *Times* 2.12.1843
19. TNA PRO MAF12 631 Rhayader Union 631 16715 27.12.1843 Board of Guardians public notice; *Times* 2.12.1843
20. *Report of the Commission of Inquiry* Minutes of Evidence, Questions 7215, 7219
21. HO 45/454 f798 11.10.1843 Walsh to Home Office, f806 9.11.1843 Banks to Home Office
22. *HJ* 4.10.1843, 11.11.1843
23. NLW Ormathwaite Papers FG 1/14 p.45-46, 48, 51
24. Ormathwaite Papers FG 1/14 p.51-52; *HT* 14.10.1843, 2.12.1843
25. *HT* 11.11.1843; *HJ* 15.11.1843
26. HO 45/454 865-67 1.11.1843 Walsh to Home Office; Ormathwaite Papers FG 1/14 p.53; *HT* 11.1.1843, 18.11.1843
27. *HT* 25.11.1843, 21.12.1843
28. Ormathwaite Papers FG 1/14 p.62; *HT* 23.12.1845; Reports of the farmers' meetings are to be found in *HT* 11.11.1843, 18.11.1843, 2.12.1843 and 23.12.1843
29. Ormathwaite Papers FG 1/14 p.60
30. *HJ* 15.11.1843
31. *HT* 16.12.1843; *HJ* 17.1.1844
32. TNA PRO HO 45/642 5.1.1844, 6.1.1844, 2.2.1844 Walsh to Home Office
33. *HT* 12.6.1844; *HJ* 31.1.1844, 28.2.1844, 30.3.1844
34. D. Williams, p.270; *HJ* 3.4.1844; *HT* 6.7.1844
35. HO 45/454B p.1049
36. HC 45/454 f763 8.10.1843 Walsh to Home Office; Ormathwaite Papers FH 2/2 f112 14.7.1880 Walsh to R. Green Price

Chapter 8

1. D.J.V. Jones 'The Second Rebecca Riots: A Study of Poaching on the River Wye, *Llafur*, Volume 2, No 1 Spring 1976, p.34
2. Significantly, Sayce's valuation of the Radnorshire Crown Manors in 1821 makes no mention of sporting rights: TNA PRO CRES 49/4922 'Memorial relative to the property of the Crown in the Lordship of Cantremelenith'
3. *HT* 7.1.1843, 1.4.1843, 8.4.1843, 3.6.1843; *HJ* 20.3.1843
4. *HJ* 20.2.1856
5. *HJ* 3.12.1856
6. *HT* 13.12.1856
7. *HJ* 22.12.1858; *HT* 5.1.1859
8. *HT* 15.1.1859
9. *HT* 6.10.1860
10. *HT* 16.5.1863, 30.1.1864
11. *HT* 4.2.1865
12. *HT* 8.1.1867
13. *HT* 16.3.1867, 30.3.1867
14. *HT* 30.11.1867, 7.12.1867, 21.12.1867, 28 12.1867
15. *HT* 5.1.1867
16. NLW Ormathwaite Papers, FH 2/2 f43 15.1.1876 Walsh to Home Office, f45 30.1.1876 Walsh to Home Office
17. *HT* 15. 1 1876; *KG* 18.1.1876
18. *HT* 5.1.1878
19. *HT* 14.1.1878
20. *HT* 4.1.1879
21. *HT* 31.12.1878
22. *HT* 4.1.1879
23. *HT* 18.1.1879, 25.1.1879, 15.2.1879; *HJ* 25.1.1879
24. *KG* 13.1.1880, 20.1.1880; *HT* 10.1.1880, 17.1.1880
25. *KG* 20.1.1880, 27.1.1880
26. *HT* 27.11.1880, 4.10.1880, 18.18.1880; *KG* 30.11.1880, 4.1.1881
27. *HT* 4.12. 1880
28. *KG* 14.12.1880
29. *KG* 14.12.1880; *HT* 15.1.1881
30. *HT* 18.12.1880
31. *HT* 8.1.1881
32. *HT* 8.1.1881, 9.4.1881
33. *HT* 12.2 1881
34. *HT* 12.3.1881
35. *HT* 19.3.1881, 2.4.1881, 23.4.1881
36. *HT* 11.6.1881
37. *HT* 14.1.1882
38. *HT* 2.4.1881
39. *HT* 4.1.1879; NLW Llysdinam Collection B1557
40. Llysdinam Collection B1559
41. Llysdinam Collection B1557

Index

Also from Logaston Press

The Celtic Christian Sites of the central and southern Marches

by Sarah & John Zaluckyj

Paperback, 448 pages with some 250 photographs, £12.95

Introductory chapters detail the arrival of Christianity in Britain and its early nature and style. The philosophy behind what became the Celtic brand of Christianity is discussed and biographical details given of saints who had contact with the area covered. The nature of a *llan* is described, as are the features often considered to indicate early Christian sites: holy wells, yew trees, circular and/or raised churchyard enclosures, and the Christianisation of pagan sites denoted by barrows or yews. This sets the scene for looking in detail at the 168 sites covered in the gazetteer, 21 in Montgomeryshire, 28 in Radnorshire, 42 in Breconshire, 30 in Herefordshire (that part which was the kingdom of Ergyng) and 47 in Gwent.

Artisan Art: Vernacular wall paintings in the Welsh Marches, 1550-1650

by Kathryn Davies

240 pages with 312 mainly colour plates; Hardback £24, Paperback £17.50

Many ordinary people in the late sixteenth and early seventeenth centuries had art in their homes – not the high art of easel paintings but a form of rough and ready art painted on their walls. This book looks at what this decoration was, how it was done and its significance. Kathryn Davies has researched vernacular buildings throughout the Welsh Marches and discovered extensive painted decoration in houses surviving from this period. They reveal the ways in which people hoped to impress their friends and neighbours. A gazetteer includes photographs of almost all the paintings.

The Fitzalans, Earls of Arundel and Surrey, Lords of the Welsh Marches (1267-1415)

by Michael Burtscher

Paperback, 192 pages with 52 illustrations, £12.95

The Fitzalans ruled over estates in Sussex, Surrey, and Norfolk and were also powerful lords in the Welsh Marches where in their time they tangled with the Mortimers and Owain Glyn Dŵr. Two of them were beheaded for treason: Earl Edmund, a staunch supporter of King Edward II, was executed at the hands of Queen Isabella and Roger Mortimer, while Earl Richard III, who became embroiled with King Richard II for his role as one of the Lords Appellant in the 1380s, was similarly condemned. The Fitzalans also supported Henry Bolingbroke in the coup d'état against King Richard II. The careers of the five earls are considered here, along with the management of their estates and their financial dealings – for it was on this wealth that the power of the Fitzalans rested. Many of the castles they built can still be seen, not least Arundel Castle and its gothic Fitzalan Chapel, but also many of their Marcher castles: Chirk, Oswestry, Clun and the ruins of Holt and Shrawardine. The family is also associated with Haughmond Abbey near Shrewsbury.

Radnorshire from Civil War to Restoration
by Keith Parker
Paperback, 288 pages, illustrated, £12.95

Whilst this book is a record of the social, political, religious and military state of affairs in Radnorshire from before the Civil War to the Restoration, by its nature much reference is made to events in neighbouring counties and further afield. This is a story of Radnorshire gentry, farmers and clergymen caught up in an age of danger and vibrant political and religious debate, when many had a rare chance to shape the future.

The Pubs of Radnorshire
by Tony Hobbs
Paperback, 368 pages, over 450 photographs and illustrations, £12.95

This books deals with all the pubs that have existed in Radnorshire about which there is some information. The county is covered by town and groups of villages, looking at the stories of the pubs and of local characters and events. There is the wayward lioness that temporarily cured one guest's rheumatism; the pub described as the scruffiest in Britain; the two pints that cost £350 apiece; the mynah bird that squawked 'Whoa there' to passing horses and then ordered a drink for the bemused rider; duelling; cock-fighting; visiting royalty and celebrities ...

The Folklore of Radnorshire
by Roy Palmer
Paperback, 272 pages, over 100 illustrations, £12.95

Roy Palmer weaves the folklore of the old county into a seamless whole, where ancient spirits, half-remembered tales, traditions handed down over the centuries, acts of pranksters, inexplicable events, and stories that leave one wondering at the truth, are brought together to create a vibrant view of Radnorshire and its beliefs and customs. Illustrated with a mixture of old and current photographs, drawings, ballad sheets and music samples, this is a book you can choose either to dip into or settle down to read from cover to cover.

Early Photographs of Radnor
Photographs by W.H. McKaig, text by Laurence Smith
Paperback, 98 pages, 80 illustrations, £9.95

This is a collection of McKaig's photographs along the English/Welsh border, along with a brief introduction to McKaig and the making of photographic postcards in the early 1900s.

Photographs of Radnorshire
by P.B. Abery
Paperback, 72 pages, 60 b&w photograph, £4.95

Abery captured a way of life, recording events and activities throughout Mid-Wales and the Border Counties during the first half of the twentieth century. This book is a collection of his photographs of Radnorshire and illustrates the towns, villages, social life, people and landscape of the county.